Paul C. Dahm

PARADISE LOST

The Bush Legacy

Paul C. Dahm

Preface by John Milton

Nearly all men can stand adversity,
But if you want to test a man's
Character, give him power.
Abraham Lincoln
1809-1865

Running Tide Press

Running Tide Press
55 SW Brook Street Apt 4
Newport, OR 97365
Phone: (541) 574-2940

2nd Printing 2006

First published by AuthorHouse 7/20/2006

ISBN: 1-4259-2183-3 (sc)

Printed in the United States of America
Bloomington, Indiana

This book is printed on acid-free paper.

To my sister Mary Janet Dahm,
the most spiritual and gentle person I know.

I know not with what weapons
World War III will be fought,
But World War IV will be
Fought with sticks and stones.
Albert Einstein
1879-1955

PREFACE

And out of good still to find means of evil.

A mind not to be chang'd by place or time.
The mind is its own place, and in itself
Can make a heaven of hell, a hell of heaven.

Awake, arise, or be forever fallen!
Paradise Lost, Book 1

MY NAME IS JOHN MILTON. My apologies for intruding into the lives of the living. Many of us who have passed away are extremely worried about the future of Western civilization. The Renaissance is coming "to life". Shakespeare is writing plays and sonnets again. There is moaning and groaning from the graves of those longer dead. Plato is beside himself.

I was chosen by my colleagues to inspire one of the living to give warning that the fate of civilization itself may ride on the outcome of the 2004 and 2008 American presidential elections. The title of my most famous work is Paradise Lost. My colleagues were of one mind that Paradise Lost: The Legacy of George W. Bush most aptly describes the wretched state in which we now find ourselves.

Al Gore was elected in the year 2000 by a significant majority of voters, yet through bizarre machinations, the man that came to power now threatens all that we stand for. The name of that man is George W. Bush.

Much has already been lost in the first four years of George Bush's presidency.

- All of the nations of the world came together at Kyoto to sign a treaty to save the planet from environmental disaster. Bush stood against the world and now the preventable disaster of global warming looms ahead in the shrouds of time as an iceberg ready to scuttle the "unsinkable" vessel of civilization.

- The world unified behind America after the tragedy of September 11, 2001 to fight the scourge of global terrorism. Almost single-handedly, George W. Bush destroyed this unity of purpose. The nations of the world are now disunited. Terrorism is on the march. William Butler Yeats spoke of this in his poem, "The Second Coming".

A sign was sent to George Bush to change course. Shortly before his planned invasion of Iraq, extremely minor flaws in the structure of the space shuttle Columbia led to its breakup almost precisely over Bush's ranch in Crawford, Texas. We thought the message was clear. Even the best-laid plans of men can come to ruin. The civilized world opposed the invasion of Iraq because it was wrong. In the words of Kofi Annan, the secretary general of the United Nations, the invasion was a violation of the UN Charter.

The world was on course for increasing unity, lifting mankind to a higher plane, a paradise. Bush has already done terrible things already into his second term in office. It is difficult to imaging what terrors he will achieve in the remainder of his present term.

My warning is clear. If you are among the living, heed my warning.

John Milton
1608-1674

FOREWORD

PAUL C. DAHM IS EVERY man. He speaks from the vantage of senior citizenship. He is not famous or rich, but he writes this book from his heart as one who has seen his beloved country change right before his eyes, and not for the better.

So who is Paul Dahm? His father was a salesman, who sold metal tiles. His mother was a homemaker. Paul was the eldest of four children, including Jerry, Bill, and Janet. They grew up during the Depression.

School was very important to young Paul. After graduating from high school, he went to college and earned Master's degrees in history and education and a Bachelor of Science degree in English and social studies from Miami University in Oxford, Ohio.

Paul is a lifetime advocate of social causes. He supported Dr. King's march in Selma, Alabama, and the protests of the 1968 Democratic Convention in Chicago. His social advocacy began with the integration of baseball by Jackie Robinson in 1948; Paul is a lifetime Dodger fan. He was instrumental in passing the Bottle Bill in Maine.

In the early 1970s, he was the only male member of NOW. He planned to "pie" Phyllis Schlafly when she appeared to protest the Equal Rights Amendment, but NOW leadership vetoed the idea. In retrospect, he wishes he had done it anyway. In 1983-84, he formed the West's Coastal Alliance and, known as "the Tree Man", he dressed as a tree to protest against clear cutting.

In 1997, Paul published The Rainbow Bridge, a must-read book for anyone who has ever lost a beloved pet. It is a compilation of stories and poems about animals and the place they have in our lives and hearts. It is about how we grieve for them, the same as we do humans, when they are gone.

An earlier book, Riel and Tillie, is a poignant love story of two Maxima Canada geese and is considered by many to be a classic protest against hunting.

Paul C. Dahm wrote this book as another protest against what is happening to our nation's capitol and especially in the current Bush administration with all the "advisors" and "nominations" that have Bush's ear.

Before getting into the meat of this book, Paul would like to share two of his poems from the Rainbow Bridge with you.

A PLEDGE TO THE ANIMALS

CONSCIOUSNESS IS FOUND IN ALL living things – plants, animals, and man. In Genesis, God said, "I have breathed the spirit of life into all living things." Chief Seattle told us, "If all the beasts were gone, man would die of a great loneliness of spirit, for what befalls the beasts, befalls man."

Rachel Carson, mother of the Earth's Environmental Movement, stated, "We can never be civilized as long as we kill another living being."

Animals are the celestial beings God has placed in our care. They are totally innocent, for God, in His infinite wisdom, had made them so. Animals create the songs in our hearts which the birds sing in the meadows and are the nurturing angels God has sent to solace man in his troubles. It is their nature to give to us perpetrating love, companionship, and caring, and they ask nothing in return.

Birds are God's messengers, for they alone may fly back to Him. Their songs are the murmuring of innumerable bees gathering nectar, never bruising the flower. Birds soft-sigh us home. They are the White Goddesses of Love, the Mother of all things.

The animals are self-contained, so placid, so at ease with their ordained place on Earth. We can but marvel at the spider's touch, so exquisitely fine, and in imaginations we seek to take flight on the eagle's wings.

Man is enchanted by the small, spider-less eternity of the fly. He feels the gentle tautness of the greyhound, revels in their love of life.

The Indians saw God in the clouds, heard him whisper in the wind, and were brothers to all the beasts. They believed in the connectedness of all living things. The beasts were a sacred trust from the One Above and the Indian was moved to look after and care for them.

Man must emulate the Indian's care, for all life is sacred, even unto the lowly gnat. Animals are the true hearts. Observe the calmness of the cat, the ancient Egyptian god. Cats are so wise, so all knowing.

We are awed by our pets' unmatchable fidelity. Who is not humbled by the look in a dog's eyes, afire with love and devotion? Who cannot but see and be aware of the spirit dwelling within? We know that we are totally and completely loved by another living creature.

We feel sorry for the Curate who states that our pets have no souls. In his mind's impermeability he has failed to grasp and see the wondrous spiritual beings therein.

We may love our animals in a way, which surpasses the love we feel for our fellow humans. They are most special to us, for they have become our friends, beings to whom we confide our innermost feelings and thoughts. They are our beloved companions, and we love them without reservation.

The poet William Blake wrote, "Each man is haunted until his humanity is awakened." Mahatma Gandhi concluded, "The greatness of a nation can be judge by the way it treats its animals."

THE RAINBOW BRIDGE

FAR BEYOND THE SKY IN another dimension lies a beautiful enchanted land. It is the resting-place for all the animals that have served man, many of whom sacrificed their lives to save mankind. To enter this land, the animals cross over Rainbow Bridge. The bridge was called so by the angels for its profusion of brilliant colors, which glow and fade in welcome to the new arrivals.

It is a land of lush green meadows, flowing streams, and an endless variety of trees. Ponds are scattered about for the new arrivals to bathe and wash away all traces of their previous existence. They emerge refreshed after their long journey across the Rainbow Bridge.

There are myriad flowers, many growing in vines, which crisscross the branches in the trees. The air is fragrant with their sweet perfumes. Bones and catnip rain intermittently from the air above.

In this magic land, all become young again. The old and infirm run about as they did in their youth. The crippled and maimed are made whole again. Their days are spent cavorting across the many fields and enjoying the company of the many varieties of animals here. Most happy, if this can be so, are the dogs and otters that are even more playful here than on Earth.

There is but one note of sadness here. It is reflected in the eyes of the animals that were pets of humans who loved them on Earth. If one looks deeply into their eyes, this sadness is evident. They miss that unique love, care, and devotion they received from their own special companions. Many had received more love from their owners than their owners had given to their fellow human beings.

And then one day, one special, magical day, your own pet looks up. A familiar sound has reached its ears. Its nose begins to twitch, its ears go up, and its tail wag uncontrollably. It stares, then begins to run to you.

He knows you have come for him. He takes on great leap and once again is in your arms. Your face is kissed and kissed and kissed again. You look once more into the trusting, loving eyes of your beloved pet.

Together, you walk across Rainbow Bridge, never again to be separated.

These poems, printed on parchment
And suitable for framing,
May be purchased by writing:
PO Box 2402
Newport, OR 97365

The cost for both poems is $10.00,
plus $2.00 S&H,
or $8.00 for one poem, postage paid

Iraq Painting is $8.50
plus $1.50 S & H

TABLE OF CONTENTS

BUSH FAMILY VALUES

The Patriarchs

If you cannot get rid of the family skeleton,
You may as well make it dance.
George Bernard Shaw
1856-1950

SKELETONS OR SKULLS ANYWAY HAVE played a big part in Bush family history. Most of it started at Yale and one of its secret societies, Skull and Bones. Both presidents 41 (Bush, Sr.) and 43 (Bush, Jr.) were members, as were Bush, Jr.'s grandfather and great grandfather. For more than half a century, members of the Bush family have been setting policy and making decisions for all Americans, i.e., making those skeletons dance.

Let's look at the family that has had such an impact on the lives of human beings worldwide. The two Bush presidents are so closely linked, especially over Iraq, that the 43rd can't be understood apart from the 41st. Beyond that, for a full portrait of what the Bushes are, we must return to the family's emergence on the national scene in the early 20th Century.

Many people say that it started with Prescott Bush, George W's grandfather, but actually it started much earlier. When Prescott Bush married Dorothy Walker, it was more than just a marriage; it was a melding of two old and prosperous families. The first Bush to attend Yale was James Smith Bush, W's great-great grandfather. He went on to become an Episcopalian minister. His son, Samuel Prescott

Bush, learned engineering at Stevens Institute of Technology in New Jersey. He went on to become wealthy as president of Buckeye Steel Castings, a railroad equipment manufacturing firm. The Walkers were the wealthier, though.

Kevin Phillips, author of *American Dynasty*, says that W's other great-great grandfather, David Walker, made his fortune by building the largest dry goods import firm west of the Mississippi. Much of his business was with England, and he sent his son, George Herbert Walker, to school there in the 1880s. Walker's connections and the new ones he made during WWI would become important to the life and career of Prescott Bush later on.

In 1904, Walker and his father build a summerhouse on Walker's Point in Kennebunkport, Maine. Phillips' book tells the early story of the Bush-Walker connections quite succinctly and sets up the connections between money, power, and the rites of passage. He says, [their connections at prep school, Yale, and Skull and Bones) "fit well, thereby unfolding a kind of red carpet on which they would later walk comfortably through the upper echelons of American life."

Prescott Bush was the epitome of that convergence, which impressed his wealthy father-in-law, thereby aiding his unfolding career. Prescott was a managing partner at Brown Brothers Harriman, the Wall Street firm, and sat on several prestigious boards, where his business, social, and government connections were valued. But Cyril Connolly, an Englishman, who attended Eton, made this observation. "These institutions and their secret organizations tended to instill a state of permanent adolescence in their alumni, arresting aspects of personal development and extending a taste for wine, song, pranks, initiations, oaths of secrecy, inner sanctums, and other rites of loyalty far into middle age."

Some of the more "bone-headed pranks" that Prescott indulged in seemed to set up the Bush family practice of lying about things or distorting them so that they didn't happen the way that they said. For example, when Prescott was a 23-year-old new army captain in 1918, he sent a letter to his hometown newspaper. He announced that he had been awarded the Distinguished Service Cross, the Victoria Cross, and the Legion of Honor on WW1's western front for saving the lives of Generals Pershing, Foch, and Haig by using his bolo knife to bring down an almost fatal artillery shell. His parents had a lot of explaining to do.

Earlier that year, along with four other Bonesmen, he was said to have plundered Geronimo's grave to take the Apache chief's skull back to the Skull and Bones vault at Yale.

Kevin Phillips says that the "imagery that the Bushes have painted – Maine summer cottages, the gray-haired grandmother, the cowboy attire – has emphasized comforting family values, but has distracted us from the fact that the family has used up all its resources to create a political dynasty that has gained the White House to further its family and ideological agenda. This would have horrified America's founding fathers. They, after all, led a revolution against a succession of Georges."

Prescott Bush had a bit of trouble in the 1940s. While American soldiers were fighting the Nazis in WWII, a few of the companies Prescott managed were seized under the Trading with the Enemy Act, because they were fronts for Nazi industrialist, Fritz Thyssen, a financier of Hitler's Third Reich.

So, let's start to add it up.

Prescott desecrated a Native American gravesite and helped fund the Nazis while they were killing our boys and trying to eliminate an entire race of people.

Good role model!

Prescott Bush, Jr.

The gods visit the sins of the fathers
Upon the children.
Euripides
484 BC - 406 BC

Then there is 41's brother, Prescott, Jr. During the embargo on China, his company was the only U.S. firm allowed to do business there, exporting communications satellites. He recently retired as the Chairman of the USA-China Chamber of Commerce, which might be one reason China isn't part of the "Axis of Evil".

The president's uncle concedes that he sometimes relied on his name to open doors, but he says any deals he made were the result of his own hard work. Sure, and I have a bridge in Brooklyn that I would be willing to sell you...cheaply.

"You can get a meeting because of it, you can meet a lot of people because of it," he said in a recent interview in Chicago, where the U.S.-China Chamber of Commerce has its headquarters. "But I don't get a lot of business because my nephew is president or my brother was president." Some experts and Wall Street would argue otherwise.

A name is not just helpful, it's essential, says Nick Larty, a professor of International Relations at George Washington University in Washington, DC: "Who you get access to in China Is pretty much a function of how important you are."

Along with access, the family name has also brought scrutiny to Prescott Bush's deals: He was criticized in 1989 for visiting China to meet with business and government leaders just three months after the Tiananmen Square massacre, in which army troops fired at pro-democracy demonstrators.

His Shanghai partnership with the Japanese firm Aoki in 1988 proved embarrassing when revelations surfaced that Aoki at the same time was allegedly trying to get business contracts by bribing Panamanian leader, Manuel Noriega, whom Bush 41 later ousted from power.

His connections to an American firm, Asset Management, came into question in 1989, when the company was the only U.S. firm able to skirt U.S. sanctions and import communications satellites into China.

When Asset Management went bankrupt later that year, Bush pulled off an arranged buyout through West Tsusho, a Japanese investment firm, which raised eyebrows. Newspapers reported that Japanese police were investigating West Tsusho's alleged ties to organized crime, but Bush declines to discuss those controversies.

"That's old news. It's in the past," he says.

But as we will soon see, it is a Bush Family tradition to just ignore the obvious. This entire generation of brothers seems to have a "deal" with Noriega. See 41's story.

George Herbert Walker Bush – #41

Some men just aren't cut out for paternity,
Better they should realize it before and not after
They become responsible for a son.
Lois McMaster Bujold
"Ethan of Athos"
1986

This Bush also has ties to Manuel Noriega. For many years, the Bureau of Narcotics and Dangerous Drugs (now DEA) wanted to have Manuel Noriega arrested for drug trafficking, but instead kept him on the CIA payroll.

For more than a decade, thousands of tons of cocaine poured into the streets of America through the Panama Canal while the US government looked the other way.

This destroyed the stability of millions of American families, and the repercussions to our society are still being felt today. But there is more of being in bed with drug traffickers with other Bush family members.

Let's back up a bit.

George H. W. Bush was born June 12, 1924 in Milton, Massachusetts. Anne Richards, former governor of Texas, said, "He was born with a silver foot in his mouth."

It was an image that he worked to maintain, lest people see him for who he really was. George Herbert Walker Bush was named after his grandfather. His mother called her father, Pop, and little Georgie became Poppy, a nickname he still carries.

He was a student leader at Phillips Academy in Andover and joined the Navy on his 18th birthday and earned a distinguished service record as a pilot. His plane was shot down, but he alone of the crew of three escaped from the plane before it sank. (He never elaborated on the plane's sinking.) He married Barbara Pierce in 1945.

After WWII was over, Bush followed in his father's footsteps and went to Yale and was tapped into Skull and Bones. Like his father, he entered a lifetime of "public service" and was as two-faced about it as his father had been. Bush would like us to believe that he was the first "compassionate conservative" president, but there were so many things that belied that title and the term is an oxymoron.

He tried and failed to be elected to politics in Texas, but was appointed to a string of high-level government positions. All of them set the pace for his illegal activities.

He was Ambassador to the United Nations, Chairman of the Republican National Committee, Chief of the U.S. Liaison Office in the People's Republic of China, and Director of the CIA. That was all before becoming Reagan's vice president and then president in his own right.

Let's see how some of those jobs influenced the way he did his various jobs. We already noted the connection between Prescott Jr.'s connection to Noriega, but it was #41 who kept the drug trafficker on the CIA payroll.

There were Prescott's dealings with China, when no other American company was allowed to do business there. Who do you think greased the wheels for that to happen? Yup, you are right. #41.

In 1991, President Bush bristled at the flurry of news accounts that questions the business ethics of three of his sons. "The media ought to be ashamed of itself for what they're doing," Bush complained.

"They (the boys) have a right to make a living, and their relationships are appropriate," added a White House spokeswoman in June 1992. These "boys" are adults so it probably wouldn't do much good to talk to them.

When one "connects the dots" in the myriad deals that these "boys" have done, it is clear that cashing in on influence has become a pattern of behavior extending through the Bush family beginning with Prescott and George Herbert Walker.

Honesty and integrity are two words that have never meant much to any of the men in the Bush family for generations. And, it doesn't look like that is going to change any time soon.

George Walker Bush – #43

It's not that he's mean.
It's just that when it comes to seeing how
His policies affect people,
George W. Bush doesn't have a clue.
Molly Ivins

Anyone doing any research for a report of George Bush would see him as a saint or a sinner, depending on the source. But, let's get the statistical things out of the way.

He was born July 6, 1946 in New Haven, Connecticut. He was educated at Andover Prep and went to Yale University where he was tapped into Skull and Bones. He was not particularly outstanding as a student…a strong C average, and he was a cheerleader in college, did not play any sports. In fact, he was rather rowdy and was drunk a lot and relied on his father to get him out of his many scrapes. He was a DKE – one of the frats almost kicked off campus. In 1968, he managed to get the DKEs placed on probation, which almost cost them their charter at Yale. See David Milch account, which follows.

In the early 70s, I found myself living in Kennebunkport, Maine, the summer home of the Bush family. The house is located on Walker's Point in the most beautiful part of the port.

While there, I happened to meet many of George's Yale-mates. I was not particularly drawn to them; they were loud and boisterous drunks and had a very condescending attitude towards the tourist trade, which makes up the lifeblood of Kennebunkport.

They could not believe I had attended a university in the hinterlands. I was the butt of many of their good-natured jokes, which mostly implied you couldn't learn very much there.

George's friends from Yale hung around for a couple of years continuing their boisterousness and obstreperousness. I learned a lot listening to them.

George's fraternity mates did not love him; he was a mean drunk, often cursing those closest to him. He was a quintessential male chauvinist whose reputation had so widespread throughout the Seven Sisters that his mates had to go south to Virginia to get him a weekend date.

There was a great deal of resentment when he was selected for Skull and Bones, but the fact had been preordained years earlier. He was not an ideal model to emulate.

His fellow students only knew George as the "mean drunk" (and were it not for his father's influence getting him into the Texas Air National Guard, he, too, might have been shipped to Vietnam). Yale students abhorred his manners and felt he was not a person to represent Yale or good enough for membership in Skull and Bones.

BUSH AT YALE,
PRESIDENT OF DKE
SENIOR YEAR

Skull and Bones is thought of as an incubator for future leaders. Bush's greatest problem was outdoing his father, who had been all-everything at Yale, captain of the baseball team, Phi Beta Kappa, Skull and Bones.

When Bush, Jr. drank too much, which was often, he would perform outrageous antics to upset his father. When he lost the election to the Yale Senate to Ralph Yarborough, the Yale chaplain, Coffin, told Bush "he had lost to a better man".

Bush excelled at the longest bar in New Haven. There is always one fraternity that creates a bad image for the rest. Yale's was DKE, which had this honor, and Bush and DKE spent time on probation for their antics.

He brought his share of shame to the DKE House, of which his fellow members were hesitant to divulge to me. "First loyalty and all that." He was called up on the charge of "branding" at the DKE House, and he defensively called it "not branding, but harmless cigarette burns".

Bush was a "red-neck" during his Yale years. He disdained the student "long hair" protests against the war, but even his father had his doubts. Shrub sought the companionship of his drinking buddies. The DKEs were the champions on campus.

A reporter called the DKE (Delta Kappa Epsilon) home to inquire about the "branding." David Milch was drunk and stuffed into the phone booth. He took the call. The reporter asked to speak to George Bush, and David replied "Speaking." The reporter told him he was calling about the branding incident. "Is it true?" asked the reporter, and David replied, "Yes, it is. Not only do we brand them, but then we bugger them." He hung up.

(David later became the creator of Deadwood on HBO and the network hit, NYPD Blues, for which he received an Emmy. He is a renowned author today in Hollywood.)

All hell broke loose and Bush knew instinctively that Milch was the culprit. The DKEs were threatened with expulsion and for a long time afterward the DKEs were called "the branders". George, as the DKE president, never lived it down.

One of George's favorite pastimes was upsetting his father. Anything he could say or do, he said it or did it, including challenging him to a fist fight when #41 was trying to get him out of trouble (again). While driving DUI, he wrecked a friend's car. The police cited him for DUI, a fact he tried to hide in 2000 and 2004.

The way Barbara, his mother, talks about him, one would be left to believe he was the ideal son, but all Bush parents have short memories concerning their children, as we shall see. I know from firsthand observation how distraught George made Barbara and her husband. But this is a bit of the way she never reined him in as a child. His daughters, Jenna and Barbara, are carbon copies of George.

I mentioned earlier, Bush, Sr. had his doubts about the war during these years. "I'm frankly lukewarm about sending more Americans to Vietnam" said then Congressman Bush.

At Ellington Air Force Base Bush trained under a 27-year-old Judo Black Belt, who was singularly unimpressed by his family background and abilities. "He was a mean SOB," Bush said.

Defense Secretary Udall later rated the pilot trainer in the top 5% of the pilots he trained. "He was no candy-ass," Udall stated later.

Bush showed his drinking prowess at Ellington. In a game called "Dead Bug" where the last man down (to land his plane) had to buy. Bush was always the first man down, and he could out-chug anyone in the squadron.

Bush was turned down for duty in Vietnam, because the F-102, which he flew, was termed obsolete. "I was heartbroken," he later said, but he was drunk at the time he said it.

In '72 he transferred to the Alabama Guard, ostensibly to work for the election of a family friend, Winton "Red" Blunt, who lost. Bush's attendance there is in doubt. The commanding officer can't recall him, nor can anyone else on the base at that time (1972-1973).

He also failed to show up for his flying exam, which may have been because he preferred to engage in his carousing and drinking proclivities. The new Air Force regulations called for absolutely no drinking to be allowed by any pilot on active duty. "Gentlemen, you are flying multi-million dollar aircraft," said the base commander.

Bush resigned his commission two days after the Defense Department posted this ruling. Bush would rather drink, so he resigned.

The only solid evidence that he was there was in a "newly discovered" dental exam, though he did earn the 38 points needed to complete his tour of duty. How is the unanswered question. When he wanted to go to Harvard Business School, he managed to get discharged six months early.

The president denies his deep ties to the eastern establishment and defines himself by his non-membership in the East Coast establishment, where his father has deep ties.

Bush scoffs at the hand wringing of foreign relations types, who worry about offending European allies. The edge and swagger of this approach will create many votes. Bush has scorn for the sherry sippers and the equivocators, who emasculated the all-male Yale. He was hostile until daughter, Barbara, was accepted, and he even had the Yale President, Richard Levin, stay at his house.

Bush is not the callow preppy he once was, and has answered the challenges he has met in his life. That's in the past. I admit to doing foolish things then, but I don't talk about them. Some may have broken lesser men. He conquered his alcoholism and drug habits, no easy things to do. There are many war stories, especially for the privileged, in a world that is no longer what it once was. Rove was able to present Bush in the more favorable light.

THE 43ᴿᴰ PRESIDENT

People who love Bush think he has done a great job – on the war in Iraq, education, the environment, and almost any other subject. But those people refuse to look at the real facts, much like Bush's parents and their parents before did.

Let's look at reality regarding different subjects and discover how he has duped the American people by his outright lies, deceptions, and backroom deals, which are impeachable offenses. It began with the election of 2000.

Bush was not elected in his own right; the conservative-leaning Supreme Court selected him. Nine people who made the decision for all of the 60 million-plus voters. Nine people who are not representative of the American people in that they are appointed and not elected by the people.

9-11 thrust him into the world's eye. It is also the place where he began to make his biggest blunders.

Most of the world was behind the U. S. when 9-11 happened. They were behind him when he ordered the invasion of Afghanistan to rid the area of the Taliban and a haven for Al Qaeda, but he just couldn't stop there.

He had to lead us into the quagmire that is Iraq – on trumped up charges that Saddam Hussein had WMDs and was in cahoots with Osama Bin Laden. People now call Iraq our second Vietnam.

See his remarks about the war.

November 16, 2002: "Our goal is the disarmament of Iraq. The dictator Saddam Hussein will give up his weapons of mass destruction or the United States will lead a coalition to disarm him."

March 19, 2004: "Our friends and allies will not live at the mercy of an outlaw regime that threatens the peace with weapons of mass murder", he read as the war began.

April 24, 2004: "Saddam tried to fool the UN, as he has for the past 12 years by hiding these weapons. It's going to take time to find them. [Years later, they are still to be found, and people who know say they never existed], but we know he had them and whether he destroyed them, moved them or hid them, we're going to find out the truth", Bush continued to proclaim.

May 29, 2004: "We discovered weapons manufacturing facilities (dated 1992) which were condemned by the UN".

December 16, 2004: In an interview, Bush dismissed the distinction between actually having weapons and planning to acquire them. "So what's the difference?" he asked in answering the question about whether Iraq had WMDs or was just trying to acquire them. "If he were to acquire the WMDs, he would be the danger."

Bush must think as Karl Rove does: Americans are a bunch of sheep who will believe anything he cares to tell them. It's very sad for this country's citizens to be so regarded.

Our president has succeeded in pulling a "Rush Limbaugh", he has divided our country into two camps, red and blue, and he has the distinction no other president in memory has enjoyed – love him or hate him.

Both sides are equally passionate. It's an amazing sight to behold. Bush is not the great communicator that Reagan was. Bush is the great polarizer. His approval rating is jumping up and down like a yo-yo.

People are complaining he has injected too much religion into politics. He clearly favors the rich over the poor.

His Medicare bill rewards the pharmaceutical companies more than the price-challenged poor who seek relief from the high cost of drugs. His family has a long-standing relationship with Merck. That is how Dan Quayle became 41's running mate.

Unlike his father, who could not convince anyone that he stood for anything, 43 is the polar opposite. "Cocky, arrogant, bone-headed, too dependent on Karl Rove for advice", have become the words of choice to describe George Bush; he has become a lightning rod for both Democrats and the GOP. He is a divider and not the uniter he claims to be.

When he went to England to help Tony Blair shore up his sliding fortunes and base, he sparked the largest political debate and protest ever seen in England. One columnist wrote, "He was the most unpopular visitor since William the Conqueror in 1066." The Mayor of London, Ken Livingstone, said, "I actually think Bush is the greatest threat to life on this planet". He also says that he refuses to recognize George W. Bush as the lawful president of the United States.

Bush's greatest problem is that he feels, as many evangelicals do, that they have a pipeline to the truth! There is no monopoly on the truth!

My sister said a fellow Chicagoan, J. Schwartz, placed a sticker on his van, which read "punk-assed chump" and he's passing them out. Schwartz is so frustrated by what he feels Bush has done to this country, "I feel my sticker says it all," he said.

All George has done is to blow the budget and put our future into debt. He has starved vital programs and he has emptied the treasury to the point where there is no money to reform healthcare and support entitlements. Bush, two weeks before Hurricane Katrina devastated New Orleans, crossed off $71 million in his budget earmarked for strengthening the levees there. It was another cost cutter to free more monies for the war in Iraq.

What will the future president do when the aging baby boomers begin clamoring for their Social Security benefits? Bush has removed any doubt of his being a servant to U.S. corporations! Molly Ivins says Bush is a wholly owned subsidiary of U. S. corporations. All the regulatory changes to roll back consumer worker protections have become plainly visible.

The world will have 13 billion people by the year 2100 and millions more will starve and be denied the simple rudiments of life. Bush is not concerned about dying infants in the world.

He has given his evangelical constituency the right to protect the pre-born. This resonates with his fundamentalist base, never mind that these babies must be fed once they are born; and our country has denied funding to anyone promoting abortions, or using artificial birth control methods, such as the morning-after pill all over the world.

He signed the partial birth abortion bill and opposes gay marriage – "No deal!" says Karl Rove. But gays are angry, Karl, and don't forget…they vote!

When asked who the greatest thinkers were who influenced him, Bush responded, "Christ, (thereby locking in millions of more votes), because He changed my heart". If you believe that, George, then what would Christ do about workers, women-led homes, and welfare recipients, who are no longer eligible for assistance? What would He tell a child who is hungry?

His former attorney general, John Ashcroft, when asked, replied "We have no king but Jesus!" Bush and Ashcroft are dangerous for they let others think for them, especially Ashcroft, who, as Shakespeare said, "has a lean and hungry look".

Both belonged to the circle that includes Condi Rice and the likes of Karen Hughes. "What is most important," said one Christian activist, "he is one of us".

Bush haters say he is too quick to interject his own moral beliefs into the decisions he makes. They are tired of his arrogance, tired of his leaning on a higher power.

It's not that people care that he has a higher power; he just needs to understand that most of us do, as well. It just may not be the same higher power and that is what makes America great.

Rancor rules the halls of Congress. Democrats complain they are shut out of critical legislation, such as Medicare, prescription drugs, and the energy policy overhaul.

(Cheney is still refusing to hand over his papers on who and what was said about energy in a conference before Bush took office in 2000. Was Rove a member? Was Kenneth Lay?)

Sen. Ted Kennedy (D, MA) and Congressman George Miller (D, CA), early supporters, are now bitter adversaries. It hearkens back to Reagan years when he was forced to reverse his tax cuts of the early 80s. The worsening deficit leaves few alternatives.

Young, polarized voters not eligible from the 1980s may become the keys to the winner in 2008.

The Democratic base still seethes with Bush's "theft" of the 2000 election and a wave of literati protest appeared during the 2004 campaign.

Books written by Al Franken, Michael Moore, and Molly Ivins are best sellers leading the critical revolt. There has been no machine available to desensitize the classic Al Franken. His and Michael Moore's books lead a burgeoning anger, a seething virulent anger caused by the lies and exaggerations of the Blond Bitch, Ann Coulter, Bill Riley, and Laura Ingram. All are liars! Worse – prostitutes!

It is said that David Conti has a new book of 33 pages on Bush lies. Coulter calls them elitists, revolutionaries, and "traitors" for not supporting Bush's views. Coulter leads a hard-core fascist group in Washington, DC, and they have a firm grip on the media. [The Tucson Daily finally got fed up with her and canned her recently. Unfortunately, they replaced her with Tony Snow, Bush speechwriter and FOX News commentator.]

Franken says her books confirm only the facts they know or need to know. His books are popular because she is good at this.

MSNBC fired Michael Savage, the right wing host, for telling a gay caller, "you should only get AIDS and die" This was going too far.

Father Charles Coughlin, in the 1930s in agreement with Henry Ford, said hateful things about the Jews. He gave the nationwide audience reason for fueling an even more intense hatred of Jews.

Attacks from both sides are long on ad-homonyms, and in the bitch's case, short on substance, a sounding board for hate of Democrats. George Soros, one of the richest men in the world, poured millions into a failing effort to defeat Bush.

When asked whether he would spend all the money that he had to defeat Bush, he said, "Yes, I would!" He went on, "if it could be guaranteed."

Democrats cannot afford to ignore Rove's "thin green line". Even tiny numbers of voters can turn the outcome. Rove and his forceful boss are playing for all the marbles, all the votes out there.

They increased GOP registrations in the South, and in the key battleground states of Pennsylvania, Illinois, Michigan, California, and West Virginia. Because of important issues unique to these states, they siphoned off Democrats into their camp, or so they claimed in 2004.

Both Rove and Bush were looking for El Dorado – a mandate in 2004. They did not get it.

Neil Bush

False words are not only evil in themselves,
But they infect the soul with evil.
Plato
427 BC – 347 BC

Neil served as director of the Silverado Banking, Savings and Loan in Denver from 1985 to 1988. During that time, the now defunct thrift made over $200 million in loans to Neil's two partners in JNB Exploration, his abysmally unsuccessful oil company.

The failures of Neil and his two partners were unable to pay off these loans to the tune of $132 million, because of Silverado's failure! (Neil was entirely dependent on his income from these two men during this period.) Silverado's closure was delayed until George Bush I was elected president in 1988. The failure of Silverado cost U. S. taxpayers over $1 billion.

During the next two years, an expert hired by regulators found that Neil "suffered" from an "ETHICAL DISABILITY" (There's that Prescott Bush morality factor surfacing in his grandchildren), and he was fined $50,000. Neil's estimated $250,000 in legal bills was reportedly paid via a banking industry lobbyist, who was fighting to get banks deregulated.

After the Silverado fiasco, Neil started a new oil company, Apex Energy. A family friend, name not stated, arranged the $2.35 million loan through a Small Business Administration program.

When news of this loan leaked out, the SBA found out that the companies behind the loan were technically "insolvent". It gave Neil 30 months to liquidate, which left Apex and its loans for others to worry about.

If Apex can't be sold for more than it owes, ultimately you and I will have to pay off his loans! Apex's only asset is an oil lease, which Apex purchased from Neil for $150,000 before he bailed out.

The resolution came just after the 1992 election. Go, Bush family! Screw the country!

Neil isn't bothered. His life goes on.

He divorced his wife of 23 years (for his mother's assistant) leaving her broke. Don't worry about Sharon, though. #41 and Barbara have agreed to buy a small, modest home for their two grandchildren. When the children reach 18, Sharon has to leave the house. And, she has to clear her things out of the house in Kennebunkport.

But, hey, it was Neil, not Sharon, who had several affairs. It was not Sharon who contracted a venereal disease.

John Ellis "Jeb" Bush
Governor of Florida

When the character of a man is not clear
To you, look at his friends.
Japanese proverb

A University of Texas grad, Jeb worked at a Caracas, Venezuelan bank before settling in Miami. In 1980 he worked on his father's effort to defeat Reagan. Jeb was about to learn that being one of George's sons means never having to circulate a resume.

Money flowed through the Right Wing Cuban community in the 1980s. A former federal prosecutor told Mother Jones that when he looked into Jeb's lucrative business deals with a now-fugitive Cuban, and he determined Jeb was either crooked or stupid, probably a little of each.

Look at some of the acquaintances that Jeb has. Then think if you did the same thing but did not have a famous father in high places, where would you be today? Not a governor of any state, but behind bars. That you can be sure!

JEB AND ARMANDO CODINA

When Jeb arrived in Miami, the Cuban developer, Armando Codina, hired him as a leasing agent. A few years later, they became business partners and purchased an office building in a deal partially financed by a savings and loan, which later failed.

The $4.56 million loan was granted in a way that neither Codina's nor Bush's name ever appeared on the loan papers as the borrowers (is this even legal?). When the regulators closed the Broward Savings & Loan in 1988, they found the loan in default. It had been secured by the Bush partnership.

Since Papa was now running for the presidency, the regulators had only two options after re-appraising the building. They decided it wasn't worth as much as was owed on it.

The regulators reduced the amount Bush and his partner owed from $4.56 million to just $500,000…and they were allowed to keep the office building! Taxpayers picked up the $4 million tab.

Jeb declared he and his partner were victims of circumstances.

JEB AND CAMILO PANDRERA

By 1984, Jeb was the head of the Dade County GOP, and it was as the party chairman that he coddled and nuzzled up to the con man, Camilo Pandrera, the finance chairman who raised GOP money from the Cuban community.

(He had been a henchman of Fulgencio Battista and made his living as a developer who specialized in deals with the corrupt HUD Development Corporation in Miami.)

In 1986, Pandrera hired Jeb as the leasing agent for a vacant commercial building, which Pandrera had built for $1.4 million in HUD loans, even though HUD knew there was a glut of office buildings in Miami.

Pandrera brought some hefty baggage with him (as other hangers-on in the Bush clan have done).

In 1982, four years earlier, Pandrera, along with another right wing Cuban exile, Hernandez Cartaya, were indicted for looting Jefferson Savings & Loan in McAllen, Texas.

They were accused of embezzling $500,000 from the thrift. (Cartaya was also accused of drug smuggling, money laundering, and drug running.) The case would never go to trial!

Soon after the indictment, FBI officials got a call from someone in the CIA, warning that agent Cartaya was one of their own – a veteran of the Bay of Pigs invasion – according to a prosecutor who worked on the case.

In short order, the charges against Pandrera were dismissed and the charges against Cartaya were reduced to a single count of tax evasion.

(Assistant U. S. Attorney Jerome Sanford was furious and filed a demand with the CIA, under the Freedom of Information Act, for all the documents relating to the agency's interference in his case. The CIA, citing "national security", denied his claim.)

The Jefferson Savings affair occurred four years before Jeb Bush met Pandrera. It is possible that he missed earlier reports, but he hardly could have passed over the next batch of stories involving Pandrera's questionable practices, because they were spread across the front pages of Miami's papers in 1985, just months before the two teamed up.

These stories, in Jeb's hometown paper, alleged that Padrera had improperly influenced a local politician – the Dade County Manager, to be precise – who's been made a secret partner when Padrera ran into trouble getting a parcel of land re-zoned.

The property was promptly rezoned and the county official made a quick $127,000 profit when Pandrera sold it to an offshore Pandrera partnership. A fugitive Miami attorney, who had already been indicted for laundering drug money, controlled it from Panama. The official resigned, and Pandrera was not charged.

The 1985 scandal did not seem to lessen Jeb's enthusiasm for Camilo Pandrera. Jeb enthusiastically accepted the task of finding tenants for Pandrera's empty HUD property. Padrera, the government officials involved, and Jeb all refused to answer questions about the scandals. Pandrera no doubt was guilty. In 1989, he pled guilty to charges that he defrauded HUD of millions during the 1980s.

You are a product of the associations and friends you make, Jeb, but this one was stupid.

JEB AND MIGUEL RECAREY

With a glut of office space, it was no small event when International Medical Centers became a tenant at Pandrera's HUD property. IMC leased nearly all the space in the big building and was, at the time, one of the country's fastest-growing HMOs and the largest recipient of federal Medicare funds.

Miguel Recarey, a character with a host of idiosyncrasies, ran IMC. He carried a 9mm Heckler & Koch coach semiautomatic pistol under his suit coat and kept a small arsenal of AR15 and Uzi assault rifles at his Miami estate, where his bedroom was protected by bulletproof windows and a steel door. (He fears his friends more than he does his enemies.)

Recarey had a longstanding relationship with Miami godfather, Santo Trafficante, Jr., and had participated in an ill-fated attempt against Castro in the 1960s. Recarey's brother, Jorge, also had ties to the CIA, so it's no surprise IMC crawled with former spooks. IMC was described as "a criminal enterprise interfaced with intelligence operations."

Good choice, Jeb! Daddy and Grandpa would be so proud!

He never closed one deal and he made $75,000 (out of the $250,000 he was promised).

Jeb's help was needed by Recarey to close the biggest fraud in HMO Medicare history. Jeb phoned top officials in Health & Human

Services (HHS) to get exemption for IMC. It was critical for the scam. Without it, their patient load would only be 50%, with the balance being private paying patients.

Recarey preferred the steady flow of federal Medicare money. In 1987, HHS Chief, McLean Haddow, (later an IMC employee) testified Jeb had directly phoned his then-secretary, Margaret Heckler, and it was a call that swung the decision to approve IMC's waiver. The patient load swelled to 80% and the money poured in. At its height in 1986, IMC was collecting $1 billion from Medicare!

Jeb would not discuss this with Mother Jones, insisting he had worked hard for IMC and earned his $75,000. He admitted the phone call, but said the waiver was not granted on his account.

"The allegation of a connection," Jeb wrote, "is unfair and untrue." (Yeah, Jeb, would you like to see the swampland I own in Okefenokee?)

Trouble began to brew for IMC despite Jeb's connections. A low-level HHS special agent, Leon Weinstein, found Recarey was defrauding Medicare by overcharges, false invoicing, and outright embezzlement! (How much money do you need off the top, Recarey? To the greedy man... "all nature will not suffice." - Seneca, 55 AD.

Weinstein had been following Recarey since 1977 and as early as 1983 he believed he had enough info to make a case. His superiors were less receptive (they needed the extra cash Recarey was funneling in their direction) and they took no action! [Bribery: the offering, giving, receiving or soliciting of anything of value in order to influence the actions of a public official. *Oran's Dictionary of the Law*]

But he kept digging and in 1986, he renewed his investigation of Recarey and IMC and again his superiors blocked his probe! "Washington just refused to pursue my evidence," he said. "They threatened me and my job if I pursued IMC." He dug in his heels. "I had 'em this time, and I told my superiors I would fight, as I had nothing to fear."

Had it been up to HHS, Recarey would still be working his fraud. Former organized crime strike force attorney, Joe DeMario, says

"Recarey was bribing union officials, but HHS never said a word to us." Before Recarey's trial began, DeMario's investigators caught him wire-tapping in an effort to find the whistleblower. So DeMario indicted him on these charges, too.

A lawyer for Recarey referred to the bribe money as "commissions". Recarey skipped the country before his trial on wiretapping charges. Before he fled, the IRS expedited the $2.2 million tax refund, which Recarey said he had coming.

Weinstein retired in disgust and tried to file a qui tam suit (Latin for "who as well as", a lawsuit based on an informer's tip. If the government collects a fine or penalty from this kind of lawsuit, the informer gets a share.)

HHS continued its fight against him and later accused him of stealing HHS documents before leaving his job. When the court supported Weinstein, HHS took over his lawsuit and shouldered him out. The case is unresolved to this day!

Since his flight, Recarey lives comfortably in Caracas, Venezuela, in a well-guarded fortress surrounded by an unapproachable moat. Officials are aware of his presence, but "we can't do anything until Venezuela turns him over to us. I'm not supposed to be talking to you," the general counselor said and hung up on me.

Pete Stark (D, CA) of the powerful Ways and Means Committee has written angry letters to the Venezuelan Ambassador in D.C., demanding an explanation for the six years of inaction on the Recarey case. [Bribes, man! Maybe $1 million or so will corrupt many officials.]

JEB AND THE CONTRAS

It may be for the role IMC may have played in Oliver North's secret Contra supply network. In 1985, the same year Jeb Bush was dialing for dollars with HHS officials, for IMC's Medicare facilities, Jeb also carried a hand-held letter from Guatemala's Dr. Mario Castejon to the White House directly to his father's office in the Executive Office Building. The letter requested aid for the Contras (bloodthirsty villains and killers of Guatemalans and Nicaraguans in the name of democracy versus the supposed elected fascist dictatorship government.) Bush penned a note on his letter directing him to Oliver North.

Here is insight into how Jeb got support in the Cuban community in his run for governor. Sick and wounded Contras were brought to Miami by insurgent leaders, Adolfo Calero and Felix Rodriguez, where they were treated with no charge! Weinstein was not surprised! "My investigation led me to conclude there may have been a deliberate attempt to obstruct justice – because Recarey, his hospitals, and his clinics were treating wounded Contras from Nicaragua and part of the $30 million a month he was given was used to set up field hospitals for the Contras." (One more bloody dictator supported by the unclean hands of the U.S., who killed thousands of innocent Nicaraguans with Oliver North's aid.)

JEB AND MANNY DIAZ

Manny runs a commercial nursery in Homestead, Florida. His sidekick, Charles Keating, Jr., is now in a California prison. Diaz became a Keating insider, confidante, and benefactor (in the $6 billion Lincoln Savings scam) in 1987, just as Keating's empire was beginning to crumble.

Keating and his attorneys transferred a large chunk of prime Phoenix real estate to Diaz – for $1! And before Keating filed for personal bankruptcy, he transferred is $2 million mansion on the island of Cat Bay in the Bahamas to Diaz.

Jeb was then Florida Secretary of Commerce. He arranged a private meeting for Diaz with GOP Governor Bob Martinez. Promptly afterward, Diaz landed a $1.72 million state highway landscaping contract despite the fact that he had no highway landscaping experience.

Howls of protest and charges of political influence peddling from other contractors arose. Officials said it was done hastily because they wanted to spruce up 113 miles of highway for the Pope's visit.

Did Jeb know about Diaz's business association with Keating? (Was he bribed, too?) Did he have any reason to believe Diaz could do the highway job?

The head of Bush's re-election campaign in Florida is silent.

JEB AND ORLANDO BOSCH

Orlando is Jeb's best friend. He's a terrorist accused of blowing up an airplane, killing 75 people in Cuba. Jeb's daddy thought so much of him that he gave him a presidential pardon!

Bush Family Members

> Children might or might not be a blessing,
> But to create them and then fail them
> Was surely damnation.
> *Lois McMaster Bujold, "Barrayar"*
> *1991*

Besides being brothers, Jeb and George W. have this in common: All their children have been in trouble with the law! Jenna and Barbara were caught drinking with fake ID cards. And how about the hookah pipe at Ashton Kutcher's house? I guess when your relatives have the drug connections they have, you can get some pretty good stuff. Oh, yes, these girls were campaigning for their father. So much for walking in the steps of Christ!

Then there are Jeb's kids. George P. Bush, called Ricky Martin Bush, who is a huge hit with little Latino teenyboppers. His girlfriend's parents liked him far less after he drove his car onto their lawn and left huge circles in it in a fit of rage. John "Jebby" Bush was literally caught by police with his pants down having sex with a teenager. What would happen to your 16-year-old son, if that happened in your hometown? Yeah, mine, too.

Then there's Jeb's daughter, Noelle. She has had several accidents, but has never been tested for being under the influence, even though she was taking the drug, Xanax.

Apparently, Jeb had already covered up THREE other arrests. She spent three days in jail and was sent to a treatment center where she was busted for sneaking in cocaine. Did Daddy's friends give cocaine to you, Noelle?

Unlike most Americans who commit crimes, ranging from sexual misconduct to felony prescription fraud, the Bush kids never go to prison. Prescott would be so proud!

Then how about Jeb's wife, Columba? She was embarrassed after she got caught smuggling almost $20,000 worth of clothes and jewelry into America after a trip to France. She said that she made an "awful mistake". She said that she realizes being married to Jeb comes with some responsibility. It also has a hell of a lot of 'privilege'.

She claims that Jeb was very supportive of her. Of course, he was, Columba, you just made a $20,000 "mistake", which you paid for by personal check immediately. Jeb says these are family matters.

That was good. Do you think you could get your husband to reimburse the government for the millions that he and his buddies have scammed from the American people? Now, that would be a real coup!

Plans are now floating in the air for a presidential run by Jeb in 2008. The Apocalypse is near than we think. Armageddon is right around the corner.

LAURA BUSH

Laura and a girlfriend were driving down a back road at about 50-55 mph. They were chatting and laughing the way all 17-year-old girls do.

Laura failed to see a prominently displayed stop sign and drove right through it. She rammed into the driver's side of a '65 Chevy, killing the driver instantly. The driver was Michael Dutton Douglas, her former boyfriend and classmate at Lee High School.

His father was following right behind him and was an eyewitness to the accident and the first outsider on the scene. An investigation ruled that it was an accident. Laura had simply not paid attention.

She was not cited nor was she charged with vehicular homicide.

THE BUSH CHILDREN –
THE TWINS: JENNA & BARBARA

One would think the twins (whose birth was difficult) would be honored to be the daughters of a president. Not these two! Jenna, in particular, has been 43's cross to bear. When Jenna was first arrested for underage drinking at age 16, Barbara Bush told George, "It's payback time." (George is the cause of many of the gray hairs on her head.)

None of the Bush children received the discipline they should have received. Jeb, Neil, George, and their parents all share the guilt in this area. Columba, Jeb's wife in particular, has set a bad example for her children.

"The girls are all noblesse and no oblige," one reporter stated. They show no interest in the world, which they and their generation will soon inherit.

Jenna was caught at age 16 using a fake ID. One month after 43's inauguration, she was in trouble again. William Ashe Bridges called her from his jail cell where he had been incarcerated for D & D. She went to his cell and asked if he could be released. The Secret Service was upset and stated that it was their job to protect the girls, not to spring drunks from jail. Three months later, Jenna was caught sipping a beer on 6th Street, the enclave of 100 bars in Austin.

Jenna has openly accused her Secret Service men of harassing her and keeping her "from living her life." She got another ticket for underage drinking that night.

The girls recently turned 21 and that sigh of relief you heard came from the White House.

Barbara has caused her parents fewer problems. She is a National Honor Roll student and was the homecoming queen. Jenna was chosen as the one most likely to trip graduation night.

What amazes onlookers is the fact that these two felt they could go out in public with fake IDs and drink and not be recognized. Laura has forbidden reporters and photographers from interviewing the girls. At home, they stay in their rooms when state dinners take place, losing an invaluable chance to meet the rulers of other countries. Like their father, they are maturing very slowly.

I can understand why Jenna and Barbara have been turned off on politics. Anyone, who has read *Giant*, Edna Ferber's depiction of Texas, would be pretty skeptical about the show put on in Texas. Karl Rove, Tom DeLay, and others are not exactly role models in the cesspool, which passes for politics in Texas.

Their father was not the greatest father during the formative years. Up to his 40th birthday, he was probably drunk most of the time. The constant stream of politicians with their hands out and schemes to benefit themselves had to be distressing to watch.

It is good their father overcame his dependency on alcohol and drugs. It is very difficult to believe it happened all in one day, however. Other than smoking, these are two of the most difficult addictions to kick.

Other than Saint Paul being struck off his horse on the way to Perseante, one is inclined to believe it is a slow process, which takes years of meditation and prayer to do so. One might more likely believe George stumbled on the road to wisdom.

Life, as Aeschylus said in 460 BC, "is made up of pain, which slowly, drop by drop, falls upon the heart and brings wisdom."

SKULL & BONES

Flowers & Hacky Sack

For this is the true strength of guilty kings,
When they corrupt the souls of those they rule.
Matthew Arnold
1822-1888

GAMES BLOOM ALL OVER THE Yale campus every spring. Daffodils compete with crocuses for favor until lilacs take back their never relinquished crown. Then Tap Nights come along; pell-mell yearly rituals where six major secret societies elect their members on the same night in April.

In April of 1966, it was John Kerry, and in 1968, George Bush joined him in the same mysterious group, Skull and Bones. It is the ultimate secret society on the Yale campus, and its past members are the most famous graduates of this institution of higher learning.

Skull and Bones is no common club. The 2004 presidential election matched these two former Skull and Bonesmen. Both candidates sprang from the same echelon of society, the upper class. They joined a group of 800 former members, still living. Many had obtained eminence, if not greatness, in their chosen fields. There are many conspiracy tales about the group known as 'an international Mafia' to the 'Brotherhood of Death'.

The Tomb, constructed in 1955, is their famed meeting place and each year former members gather. Among them are three former presidents, two Supreme Court justices, scores of Cabinet members, and numerous senators and congressmen. President William Howard Taft named two fellow Bonesmen to his Cabinet.

The CIA is facetiously called 'the Employer of Last Resort', as so many Bonesmen were enlisted and participated in its longstanding skullduggery. If you couldn't get a job elsewhere, you were always welcome. In the Time, Inc. Empire, Henry Luce and Briton Hadden were Boners. Many top secrets were discussed in the Tomb, says McGeorge Bundy.

At Tap Nights, where former Knights mingle with the new prospects, advisor Bundy, luminary of the CIA, was fascinated by discussions at the Tomb and how deeply the 'level of penetration' went into U. S. and foreign affairs. And how openly they discussed the Iran-Contra affair. The level of trust was startling to the new members. It was as, if you could get in, you could be trusted.

Some members were guilty of self-aggrandizing. The 2nd and 3rd generation Bonesmen, who campaigned to get in, and once in, developed an almost religious fervor to be Bonesmen. Many Bonesmen are more circumspect, 'not wanting to get into trouble with these guys'. [It's just another one of the games men surround themselves with, just another fantasy.]

On April 28, 1967, George W. Bush felt the tap on his shoulder and for weeks it touched off a great furor on campus. Many of the class of 1968 were offended by his selection. To them, George was a bounder, a wastrel, a lady's man, a poor student, a hard-drinking alcoholic, and a mean-spirited drunk, who simply did not deserve this accolade.

[In the late 1960s Kennebunkport hired a 20-year retired former military policeman as its police chief. He marched to the tune and was an obeisant pawn of the local selectmen, who were concerned about all the 'hippies' in town. This man turned the port into a fascist state. I saw one man put in handcuffs and marched off. His offense – he dropped a candy wrapper on the ground. The chief drove his police car around like an avenging angel looking for unwary prey. The chief was enthralled by the Bush family, and it was said that he caught George driving drunk many times, but cited him only once. A fact George tried to hide in 2004.]

George may have been a 'legacy'. His father and grandfather, Prescott, were Bonesmen. Many of the Yale Class of 1968 infer, to this day, his selection was unwarranted and a slur on Yale University, and many of those classmates became Democrats in protest.

In retrospect, David Allen Richards was the one who tapped George for the Bonesman honor. "I went up to him, smashed him on the shoulder, and said, 'Get to your room!' He did. I was embarrassed, as I was a fervent Democrat," said Richards.

Richards was Class of '67, intersecting the two candidates. "We didn't want all the members to be Lacrosse players, so we opted for a mix, different backgrounds, nationalities, and the like. I don't think George was particularly interested in joining, but he was a legacy," Richards continued. "Reports were his father wanted him to join." The Bones were so secretive about Bush's time in Bones that the usual scrapbooks have been sealed so Knights cannot read them.

Bones was a departure for George. No alcohol was allowed in the Tomb. [Later on, in his Air Force days, George had the nom-de-plume of being able to drink anyone under the table.]

Much of the time is spent in debates and life histories where George was rather a dim bulb. When he gave his life history, his father detailed his war experiences, his marriage to Barbara, and his hope for public service. His son, on the other hand, spoke only of his father in rather God-like terms.

The Tas, members call the Tomb, sits on High Street in the middle of the Yale campus. No non-members – barbarians – are allowed inside. Dozens of skulls and skeletons adorn the walls. There is a mummy and gravestones. One is entitled, *Tablet from the grave of Elihu Yale* (the founder) taken from the Wrexham graveyard, and war memorabilia.

The 'boodle' or dining hall is most impressive. Portraits of illustrious former Bonesmen adorn the walls. William Howard Taft, Supreme Court Justice Morrison White, Kerry's classmate, Dick Pershing, killed in the Tet offensive in 1968, and President George H. W. Bush are among the portraits.

The Skull and Crossbones are everywhere, from the crockery to the exit signs. Light shines through the gaping eye sockets of skulls bordering otherwise elegant light fixtures. 'Boodlehall' is played around the grand fireplaces, which double as goals for the violent soccer-like game.

One of its best players was John Kerry, and Dick Pershing, David Thorne, and Fred Smith were close behind and played it as often as possible. Thorne says, "They made up the core of the group and Freddie Smith, founder of FedEx, is a maniac." Thorne added that Dick broke his toe once, playing the game.

When he joined S&B, Kerry bonded closely with the other Knights in the Tomb and often steered conversations towards Vietnam and other politics. Bones was and is a meaningful part of his life, and he helped to resurrect the once influential Yale Aviation, a unit founded by Bonesmen in World War I. Kerry remains very close to his 'guys' and would go out of his way to help if one of them got into a jam. [Thorne became Kerry's brother-in-law when Kerry married his twin sister, Julia.]

William 'Chip' Stanberry ('66) was Kerry's partner on the debate team and they were close members of Bones, but Kerry had a difficult time being one of the boys. It was rare for him to hoist a beer with them, and some felt he was aloof. In the Tomb, however, Kerry relaxed and became one of the boys.

The origin of Bones is, to this day, a mystery. It was said that William Russell (later a Civil War guard) was dismayed when Phi Beta Kappa, the leading secret society in 1832, had been stripped of its secrecy during the Anti-Mason hysteria of that day. He then founded Bones on the basis of a secret society he knew in Germany.

The group included Alphonso Taft, the future Secretary of War under Lincoln. The Bones were founded on a legend. The Greek orator, Demosthenes, died in 322 BC and Eulogia, the Goddess of Eloquence, arose to the heavens. Bones was originally the Eulogia

Club, because the Goddess Eulogia returned to take up residence with them in 1832.

This would explain the importance of the number 322 to Bonesmen. Many have used it in a code, and Thorne uses 322 in his telephone extension. W. Averell Harriman (1913) used it as the combination lock on his briefcase, which he carried on diplomatic dispatches during WWII.

Both Eulogia and 322 are important symbols in the Bones' initiation ceremony. The ceremony itself is very hush, hush, top secret, in the CIA parlance so often used by Bones members.

Soon after his initiation, the new knight is assigned a Bones name to which he will be referred from then on. As a member dies, his name may be passed on to a new knight. The word 'magog' is given to the knight, who has seduced the most women. William Howard Taft surprisingly earned this distinction.

A Supreme Court justice, Potter Stewart, chose 'Crappo' and Dean Witter chose 'Thor'. Kerry was named 'Long Devil' as the tallest man in his class. When Alan Cross, now a doctor in North Carolina, was initiated, he became the tallest.

Bush couldn't decide on a name, so he became 'Temporary', a name he holds to this day. Some Knight practices are better left unsaid, as they are too perverse.

Women were admitted in 1991. William F. Buckley, true to his well-earned image, obtained a court order blocking the initiation of the Bones' first female members, claiming that admitting women would lead to 'date rape'. Only a true, sexually repressed conservative could dream up such a charge. Since then, 81 women have been admitted, despite lobbying against it by Bush's uncle, Jonathan. Neither of the Bush girls nor Kerry's daughters have been tapped.

For some members, it remains the highlight of their lives and they are lifetime devotees. All members gain numerous benefits from one another.

When Bush graduated, he called a Bonesman looking for a job. Robert Gow couldn't accommodate him at the time, but he still took him on as a trainee. In 1977, when GW formed his first company, his seed money came from Uncle Jonathan Bush, who raised over $500,000 for him and secured another $100,000 from William Draper, another Bonesman. He was let into the lucrative Texas Ranger deal by still another Bonesman, Edward Lampert, which netted him over $14.6 million, when the group sold the team. He bought a mansion with part of that money.

One of 43's first gatherings at the White House included fellow Bonesmen. One of them, Stephen Adams, had spent over $1 million on billboards in key states during the 2000 presidential campaign, and Adams had not even met GW, but was a fellow Bonesman.

One of his early Cabinet appointments was Robert McCallum (Bones, '68), head of Justice. Bonesman David Wiseman and McCallum filed pleadings in U. S. District Court that would make asserting an executive privilege that would make information on presidential pardons more secret than in the past. When #43 was governor of Texas, he tried to pass a law, which would have made it a crime to criticize the governor. Head of the Security & Exchange Department was Bill Donaldson (Bones, '53). Edward McNally (Bones, '79) was tapped for General Council of the Office of Homeland Security, and Rex Cowdry (Bones, '68) became Associate Director of the National Economic Council.

Also appointed to high posts were Evan G. Galbraith (Bones '50), James Boasberg (Bones, '85), and former Knoxville Mayor, Victor Ashe (Bones, '67). Then there were Fannie Mae's Jack McGregor (Bones, '56), and GW's cousin, George Herbert Walker III (Bones '53), who became Ambassador to Hungary.

When they gathered together at the White House, the only difference from meeting in the Tomb was the availability of liquor, courtesy of the president. Bonesmen say GW values Skull and Bones as an extension of his family – the Bush-Walker web includes at least 10 or 12 members. Frederick Smith (Bones, '66) was forced to withdraw because of illness.

John Kerry has attended meetings and arranged a tour to Arlington National Cemetery on the 25th anniversary of Dick Pershing's death. When Pershing died, Kerry wrote to his parents, "He was so much a part of my life and the love, concern, and compassion we shared as Knights can never be replaced."

Chip Stanberry (Bones, '66) said, "It was fine for us to get together after 30 years and still feel a connection to Bones." When Kerry has time, he stops by the Tomb, as do other members.

Jacob Weisberg received a call from Kerry in 1986. He showed up at the senator's office wondering why he was there. Kerry made small talk and then tapped him for Bones. He had not known Kerry was a member. Weisberg asked Kerry, as a liberal, why he supported an organization not open to women. Kerry then listed his efforts over the years to let women into Bones. Weisberg then told Kerry he was not interested, and Kerry asked him to think it over.

When he called Kerry back, his call went straight through. He rejected the offer, much to Kerry's disappointment. Members say Kerry considers Skull and Bones an important part of his college education and a source of many lasting friendships. A glance through notable figures in Kerry's life reveals only the Bonesman he knew from the time he was tapped. He railed against fellow Bonesman McGeorge Bundy in 1971 for his support of the Vietnam War.

Kerry's family carried the name, Forbes, but he was never part of the establishment, and David Thorne said their group of 1966 was not the 'elite establishment type'. Kerry achieved everything he did on his own. He had no millionaire friends to 'cut deals', like Bush had. Kerry's life is one of intellectual achievement, not who you know. "That's just how he was," Thorne concluded.

When asked about Skull and Bones and why Kerry won't discuss Bones, Thorne said, "The Bones face-off is simply a source of amusement. It's kind of an amazing coincidence, and too much elitism is drawn from it."

The accusation of the mysteries surrounding Bones draws a laugh from Thorne. "I don't think it is relevant to his run for the presidency.

Like marriage or divorce, it's a private matter and important to both him and Bush." Certainly neither party discussed Bones in public.

When Tim Russert asked Kerry about Bones, he deadpanned, "It's so secret, we can't talk about it." He gave the same answer in 2004.

Despite political differences, most Bonesmen took the 2004 election as a matter of pride. As they see it, Bones has a representative in the White House. It was a win-win proposition for Skull and Bones. If there is a Goddess Eulogia in the heavens, she has smile on both of them and on us, too.

DICK CHENEY

A Man in Waiting

Crime does not pay...as well as politics.
Alfred E. Newman

THIS IS A LESSON THAT Cheney has learned very well. He has made a lot of money in illegal transactions, maybe not as much as his boss, but just as smarmy and illegal. He often thumbs his nose at criticism just as he did when he called Senator Patrick Leahy the "F" word. His 'friendships' smack of improprieties, as when he went duck hunting with Justice Scalia. If Kerry had done something like that, Cheney would have been all over him.

As neo-cons go, Cheney is at the top of the heap. He got his start with Nixon, and he and Rumsfeld have been together for most of their careers. But Cheney also has to be examined apart from the others. Why, you ask?

Because Cheney is the second in command, that's why. If something should happen to Bush, Cheney is our president! So, who is this man that Bush put so much stock into? The other question is who is leading whom?

If you are the CEO of a company, does the person under you make all your important decisions? Of course not. Bush kept the same ticket in the 2004 campaign. For that reason, Cheney deserves the same scrutiny as Bush does, and Lynne, his wife, who follows her ventriloquist husband.

Cheney is a quiet, soft-spoken, unapologetic Republican. He spouts the company line like the pro that he is, but what is he really like, and what does he believe?

We will look at that famous duck-hunting trip with Justice Scalia. We will check out Halliburton, where Cheney was CEO, and his connection to it. We talk a lot about Bush's war record, but what about Cheney's? He received four deferments to attend college. Also, Cheney has had several heart attacks. Is it good to have that in a man who is just a heartbeat away from the presidency? On January 28, 2006, Cheney was hospitalized for "dizziness." Let's take a look.

Dick Cheney – A Good Guy?

The problem with political jokes is they get elected.
Henry Cate VII

That's the appellation William Safire has tacked onto the end of Cheney's name. I cannot see this, personally. Cheney is a hard-liner of great depth and opposes much more than he supports. He most of all influenced Bush on the tragic path that he chose in Iraq. To the weak-kneed Bush, Cheney speaks from the mountaintop, and that's a dangerous position for anyone.

According to Nixon speechwriter, Safire, Cheney, in his dealings with his secret energy task force, probably topsided by the oil and gas lobbyists. Safire has known Cheney since "their buddy-buddy" days in the tainted Nixon administration. It was under Nixon that Cheney (and Safire) tread the dark alleys of deceit together and learned their nefarious ways.

Safire touts Cheney from those days as "thoughtful, calmly conservative, non-pompous, decisive, and he answered all my phone calls." Cheney is now fighting to keep secret the identity of the courting of his wife, Lynne. He was fascinated by her free lifestyle and by her book, *Sisters*, a defense of lesbianism. She was the flip side of his life coin.

Scalia-Cheney Chumship

Recusation: Any justice or judge shall
Disqualify him in any proceeding in which
His impartiality may be questioned
Oran's Dictionary of Law

Antonin Scalia isn't backing down in the face of criticism that he should stay out of the case, which involves his "chum" Cheney. Recusing himself so that not a whiff of scandal should arise would be the honorable thing to do. That is why 'recusing' was added to the agenda of the law.

Scalia told a gathering at Amherst College, February 11, 2004, there is nothing improper about the Mississippi duck-hunting trip, and nothing in the case would present conflict for him. And he told an audience of 600 people "this was a government issue. It's acceptable practice to socialize with the executive branch official when there are no personal claims against them."

But, if it looks like a duck, and talks like a duck, it is a…? That's all I will say right now. Quack, quack.

But there are a lot of issues going before the Supreme Court in the next few sessions. For example, Cheney wants to keep private the details of closed-door White House energy sessions that produced the administration's energy policies. The administration is fighting a lawsuit brought by watchdog and environmental groups that say industry executives like Ken Lay may have helped to shape these energy policies. As rumored, was Ken Lay on Cheney's energy task force as were other Enron execs?

Paul Rothstein, a law professor at Georgetown University, said "although the lawsuit does not seek money from Cheney, it would be a mistake to say the vice president does not have a personal stake in the suit. These are reputation stakes, career stakes for Cheney. To a man in his position, those things are as important as money, and in the long run they may mean more than money." Rothstein asked Scalia to recuse himself. "I'm surprised he stuck to his guns. I hoped he would have seen the light," Rothstein said. "Scalia has some of the arrogance that goes along with being a smart GOP executive."

There was a movement all across the nation's newspapers and law circles to have Scalia recuse himself in the case. But Scalia did not, and the Supreme Court ruled in Cheney's favor.

Big shock! But, considering these are the same people that narrowly put Bush and Cheney in office, that gave them the presidency instead of having our votes decide, why should we be surprised?

Cheney: Asset or Liability?

The greatest of faults, I should say,
Is to be conscious of none.
Thomas Carlyle
1795-1881

Cheney is from a state with three electoral votes. He has a minus charisma quota, although he does buttress Bush's weaknesses. Forty-three percent favored keeping him on the ticket in 2004, but Cheney and Halliburton continue to drag Bush down.

The Department of Justice instituted a probe to investigate the contracts in Iraq and Cheney's trips with Justice Scalia. It is not doing much to brighten the image of this administration. But Cheney stands by his faults and thinks he has none. He is exactly the type of man that Carlyle was writing about.

Cheney said, and stands by his assertion that Saddam had WMDs, despite all the evidence to the contrary. "And he will use them against us and our allies" he told a veterans group in August of 2002. He still shouts the shrill message, "Saddam had weapons of great power the world has never seen" in 2005. He made the same comment early in December 2005.

Cheney is a good fundraiser and base motivator. "It's a serious time, and he is a serious boy," says a Bush advisor. "That's politics," Cheney says, amused by the Democrats attacks with his half grin and the shrug of his shoulders, his signal, "C'est la vie."

Dick Cheney continues to show utter contempt for the U. S. legal system. He is adamant in this refusal to release the names of the energy group gathered in 2000 to discuss the needs of the country and to plot a course of action. The case was put in the hands of the Supreme Court and, surprise, surprise, they found in Cheney's favor! Cheney states the records are a matter of "national security" and must remain sacrosanct.

Justice Scalia and Cheney have been on two widely publicized hunts. A question of propriety on Scalia's part has been raised but he, like Cheney, feels they are above the approbation of any criticism, and Scalia contents their friendship will not interfere in his decision in this important matter.

But Scalia was one of the judges who found in Cheney's favor. Kinda makes you wish you had a judge in your pocket when you have to do something you don't want to have to do, doesn't it? Scalia should have recused himself, but back to the "energy panel". Insiders are taking odds on three of the group members in question. All three executives were at the bankrupt Enron Corporation, which folded owing $74 billion, give or take a billion, to its creditors. Ken Lay waits to be sentenced.

In 2002, Michael Kopper, a former deputy to Andrew Fastow, the chief financial officer, pleaded guilty to a variety of charges. The next month, Enron's former treasurer pleaded guilty and received a five-year sentence. Fastow and his wife, Lea, came next. Fastow is considered to be the mastermind behind the incredible fraud perpetrated by its executives. With Fastow's guilty plea, only Kenneth Lay, the president, remains to be indicted. (He was indicted)…

Skilling has been charged on 36 counts. He has been released on $5 million bail and had his passport revoked. If found guilty, he cold face the rest of his life in prison. Also accused on many of the same counts is Kenneth Causey, Enron's former chief accounting officer who resigned in 2002. (They received 25-year sentences and are eligible for parole in eight years.)

On the Washington inside scene, the betting is 9-5 on Ken Lay, Andrew Fastow and Jeffrey Skilling being members of Cheney's energy board. There seems to be little doubt this betting has an inside track. Betting is 3-1 on Ken Lay escaping indictment.

On January 23, 2004, Halliburton repaid $63 million to the government. Its employees illegally and improperly received the money in a bribe; it was a kickback deal and was exposed in a routine internal audit. "We will bear the cost of the potential overcharge," said Randy Hart, president and CEO of Kellogg, Bong and Root, the Halliburton subsidiary to which the contract had been awarded.

Just in case you spent the last four years on a deserted island with no news coverage, Cheney was CEO of Halliburton before he became vice-president. Is it any wonder that they got the cream of the crop jobs in rebuilding Iraq? As long as these men profit off the war in Iraq, is there any chance the war will end soon? Certainly not, if Bush and Company have their way.

Dick Cheney:
The Real Force Behind Bush?

Practical politics consists of ignoring the facts.
Henry Brooks Adams
1838-1918

The president respects Cheney's judgment. They eat lunch together every day to discuss intelligence, Iraq, and terrorism, its global connections, and the spook's input into the mix. Cheney consistently takes a dim view on the terrorist threat, says they are only malcontents.

Beginning in the late summer of 2002, Newsweek has related how, on the eve of the invasion, Cheney declared, "We believe Saddam has reconstituted nuclear weapons" (he later said he meant "program" not weapons. There is a vast difference between the two words.)

He repeatedly said Saddam had ties to Al Qaeda –many months later we are still looking for WMDs and it has been proved that Saddam hated Al Qaeda. These suggestions hinted at a tie between Iraq and 9-11 and might even have been involved in the 1993 bombing of the WTC. Neither has been proved to be true.

As late as September 14, Cheney insisted that hijacker Mohammed Atta had met with an Iraqi Intelligence officer in Prague in April 2001. This has been widely discredited by Intelligence officials as untrue.

A few days later, Bush sheepishly corrected Cheney. There was no tie between Iraq and 9-11! Cheney still sticks to the lie.

ENVIRONMENT

Is Gail Norton Another James Watts?

The case of the center for use
This song of the birds from birth
What is near two guides' heart in a garden
Is anywhere else on earth.
Dorothy Francis Gurnee

SOME PEOPLE HAVE DESCRIBED GAIL Norton as "James Watts in a skirt". He was the Interior Secretary under President Reagan who ate his food all the way back the kneecap for this remark about his department: "I have a black, a woman, two Jews, and a cripple. And we have talent." He also coined the beauty, "Jesus is coming back and he is angry because we have not harvested the bounty He left to us." At least he had the courtesy to resign (but he made $500,000 securing public lands for building contractors years later).

"Amusing labels can fully capture why the current Secretary of the Interior is unfit to be trusted with our national parks, monuments, and other public treasures," Dale Kendall, founder and director of Community Rights Council, a nonprofit law firm, writes.

Gail Norton's record as a lawyer supporting the rights of polluters and corporate interests shows the reasons why. She began her career in the James Watts Mountain States Legal Foundation litigating on behalf of cattlemen, miners, and oil companies. She is a strong advocate of opening the Arctic National Wildlife Refuge to oil drilling.

As a member of the conservative organization, The Pacific Research Institute, she has helped craft litigation to enhance individual property rights at the expense of community interest. Then her record gets even better!

As the Attorney General of Colorado, she implemented a "self auditing" procedure that allowed polluters to evade environmental fines and promoted legislation that would have enshrined an extreme view of that "takings" clause of the U. S. Constitution. That is the last sentence of the Fifth Amendment, which says, "…nor shall private property be taken for public use, without just compensation."

Norton's absolutist views on property rights and her hostile attitude toward environmental protection place her far outside the mainstream. She promotes a radical interpretation of that clause and also on "right to build on one's property" and suggests that "we might even go so far as to recognize a homesteading right to pollute or make noise in an area."

If the country adopted her views, we would have to (1) pay polluters not to pollute or (2) repeal most of our health, safety, and environmental laws. We can do neither and still keep this country safe and beautiful for future generations. But Norton prefers a second choice.

She says, "If the government must pay compensation when its actions interfere with property rights, then its regulatory actions must be limited."

What laws would you repeal? Laws which minimize effects of pollution on residential areas? How about laws to keep adult bookstores away from our schools? Or maybe it's the laws that maintain parks and wilderness areas for recreation.

Norton manages nearly 500 million acres of public domain, which includes national parks, monuments, and wildlife refuges. These lands are already in trouble from pollution, have a maintenance backlog, and are being pursued by development. Big timber, oil and gas, mining, and grazing lobbyists have already filed stale, frivolous or otherwise defective claims of property interest.

Norton also administers the Endangered Species Act, under which she is entrusted to protect our wildlife and plants. You can imagine her feelings when these animals go onto private lands. Norton would take away the laws to say that habitat modifications on private lands must not harm protected species. In early January 2006, Norton announced a review of the EPA.

Finally, the Interior Department is charged with holding polluters responsible when they harm publicly- held national resources. How well do you think Gail Norton would enforce these laws with her antipathy to regulatory solutions and her advocacy of a right to pollute? Is Gail Norton another James Watts? No, she is far worse, unbelievably so.*

Liberals vs. the GOP

"Poor shad. Poor salmon.
Where is thy Redress?
When nature gave thee instinct,
Gave thee the heart to bear this fate?"
David Thoreau and his brother,
John Lowell, in Massachusetts,
watching a dam, which blocked the
spawning of shad and salmon

What's so terrible about being a liberal? When asked what I am, I proudly reply, "I am a Democrat and a proud liberal!" Nothing can make a Republican blanch more openly than this reply.

I care about people and the land. The GOP cannot understand why you're not in favor of raping the land, and not sounding like Reagan's former interior secretary, James Watt. He really believed Jesus was coming back soon and would be very angry with us for not using all the timber and minerals, which the land provides.

Any competent psychiatrist would state Watts was certifiable. His extreme religious beliefs caused him to be unable to draw logical

---

* Norton resigned 3-10-06.

conclusions. Such men, they state, make poor choices for any position of authority and like many extreme fundamentalists, they must be regarded with caution. They do not wish to support any plan to limit clear cutting of all forestlands or despoiling virgin lands in a mostly futile search for energy. The release of chemicals into the air is unabated. Smokestacks generate more of these poisonous emissions controllable by introducing scrubbers. "But the costs are too high," the GOP says, "for the corporations to do so." It would hurt their bottom line.

In the meantime, acid rain continues to fall, releasing more deadly arsenic into the soil and the underground aquifers, which slowly contaminates the water table and is especially dangerous to newborn infants who may suffer lifelong disabilities.

Our wetlands are disappearing and the GOP does nothing to stop their destruction. Wetlands are vital to purify the soil from the excess phosphates of bad farming practices and barely 25% of our wetlands are left. Along the shore, the destruction is worse, as year after year people build houses in tidal areas. Some homeowners have rebuilt two and three times, and who pays? We all do, as the government pays the bills of reconstruction. All this is caused by our uncontrollable desire to live by the water.

The Clean Water Act is taking a beating as Bush refuses to protect streams, rivers, and oceans. The Supreme Court has been on his side (surprise!) since 2000. They ruled in 1991 under Bush #41 that wetlands are protected when providing habitat for birds, which they all do.

Bush has further opened lands to the mining corporations to explore and mine for gold, using deadly arsenic as a wash, further polluting our virgin lands. Wyoming is being turned into one giant oil and gas well!

These lawless entities operation on the principle of the bottom line. If it makes money, do it! Remember "corporations have no soul." They answer only to their bottom lines.

The recent farm bill of more than $85 billion will go mostly into the jackets of large corporations that already own and run the majority of farms. They are responsible for over-fertilizing their lands, which in turn create a cycle that pollutes streams and rivers. In turn, this hurts fish and destroys wildlife. Much of the destruction from Katrina is attributable to the loss of wetlands in New Orleans.

Economically, the GOP has raided the reserves of Social Security of $2 trillion with total disregard of the aging baby boomer generation. In 10 years, we will face an economic disaster of incredible proportions, and Bush's tax cuts will have wiped out any hope of lessening the disaster.

Someone has to be a liberal and protest the continuing rape of our land. I take it as a compliment when the GOP disagrees with me on this issue. There are two sides! The GOP's money considerations and the liberals' desire to protect and share the land and save the economy of the future for our children and grandchildren.

This, too, is a religious issue and should be treated as such. Rape is punishable in every state in the Union.

The Bush Rape of the Environment

We won't have a society if we
Destroy the environment.
Margaret Mead

The defenders of wildlife have released a comprehensive evaluation of Bush's implementation of the Endangered Species Act (ESA). It leaves little doubt this administration is out to destroy our most important law, protecting living nature.

Interior Secretary Gale Norton has willfully violated, on at least 76 occasions, that ESA rulings told them were all but certain to be illegal. Put in another light, it means that twice each month, starting January 1, 2001 through October of 2003, Norton's officials have knowingly violated ESA. They have willfully violated direct court orders that would protect an endangered species.

One judge said, "Their attitude is ludicrous and preposterous. The Federal Government is not above the law. What's going on here is not the way the government should be working."

Why are they breaking the most fundamental of all law? Follow the money!

The Bush Administration is pursuing an incomprehensible path:

- Giving unto the special interests even when it violates the law.
- Ignoring a court order if the stakes are sufficiently high.
- When found guilty of violating a law, using taxpayer money to pay the miniscule fine.
- Using the payment as justification for breaking a law elsewhere.

They knowingly violated our laws 28 times in the past 24 months. On December 23, 2003, Bush continued his assault on the environment. I did not hear anything in the Bush State of the Union message pertaining to their violations of the law. They are smug and serene in their actions. Tyrants in disguise.

Bush's Assault on the Earth

"Forgive me, dear Lord, that I am so meek
And gentle with these butchers!"
Barry Lopez
On those who desecrate nature

With the 2002 election victories, the GOP directed its heavy artillery towards the environment. No tree, river, scenic view or unspoiled plane is safe. No traces of gold or silver would be left unmined.

Again there will be snowmobiles in Yellowstone National Park and oil drilling on Padre Island. The National Marine Fisheries will ease salmon restrictions in the Northwest. Washington State will dump rules on logging and energy conservation.

Most recently, Bush and Norton opened 58 million acres of forest to exploitation by loggers and are destroying the last great stand of virgin timber in the Tongass Forest of Alaska and in its road-less areas put "off-limits" by President Clinton.

Opponents are alarmed that bolder measures in the coming months will affect air and water restrictions. New efforts to allow Alaska's Arctic National Wildlife Refuge (ANWR) to be explored for oil are tied to the new energy bill due for passage in 2005. It passed both houses but is up for review in the Senate, where it has stalled.

In response to protests, the wimpish White House spokesman, Scott McClellan, said, "There are a number of 'alarmist groups' out there trying to promote fear in order to boost their own fund-raising."

"The air, forests, land, and waters are God's gifts to us, his people. We have an immense obligation to protect them now and for the future," said the Indians.

"God will be sad if we do not exploit these treasures." When God sees what Bush has done to His treasures, He will be much sadder.

Bush is waging a Great War on God's work, which took billions of years to create. Why aren't people protesting and rising in anger over these policies? They're standing around shaking their heads and wringing their hands as these gifts are destroyed. Once destroyed, they are lost FOREVER.

Recently, the bill introduced by John McCain and Joe Lieberman to limit greenhouse gases met Bush's stern disapproval. The Bush plan for water would reduce the volume of water protected by 20% and leave the exposed land open for development. Bush wants increased exploration for oil and gas across the West.

In Wyoming, oil wells are sprouting like sagebrush across the unspoiled land. One of Bush's greatest crimes is his lack of attempt to curb acid rain in the East. It leads to destruction of the forest and pollution of lakes and streams. He refused to join the Kyoto protocol.

Democrats, by a margin of 72%, favor curbs to help regulate environmental protections and safety practices in business, but Bush contemplated no efforts in either direction. He has learned from the mistakes made by Newt Gingrich back in 1994. Back them, resting on a House majority (which Gingrich called and termed a mandate), he launched an attack on the regulations governing mining, oil drilling, air and water pollution as part of his Contract with America.

All of his measures were quickly derailed in committee or vetoed by President Clinton. Gingrich really believed in his supposed mandate to pass anti-environmental measures and "he ended up painting a huge bull's-eye on his back," said Scott Stoermer, director of the League of Voters.

Bush allows criticism of his policies to 'slide off his back', smiling all the while. He presents the ever-positive image of the 'good guy leader', who would do no real harm to anyone.

This is the primary quality of the calculating leader, something that Bush strives mightily toward. "Damn the torpedoes, full speed ahead."

"Bring them on," he intones from his God-given pulpit on high. Many Americans are oblivious to the rancor he creates. What Americans do not fathom is that Bush does not only wish to govern, but also he and his henchmen wish to rule! There is a difference! In Europe, Bush is called Emperor Bush.

The GOP is also employing subterfuge, identifying themselves as conservationists in an attempt to bring people around to the GOP point of view. Instead, go to Oregon, as Bush did (to encourage logging) and announce the Healthy Forest Initiative, a judicious thinning of the forests to prevent forest fires, using ecological research as the excuse. It would provide a reason for the logging of trees 30 inches in diameter to make it easier to circumvent the environmental impact statements. Logging interests would get the last word on which trees were cut down.

Bush's recent end run around polluting smokestacks by amending the clean air act to allow older plants to avoid installing costly scrubbers. Bush said it would make older plants pollute less, but critics say it's a way for these plants to continue polluting.

Nine states have sued to block the proposal and it faces a strong battle in Congress. How much more crap will Bush employ to cripple the environment before people scream loudly? Enough! Enough! Enough! You SOB. (or is that traitorous to call Bush a SOB?).

Senator Pete Domenici (R-NM), chairman of the energy committee, manipulated the ANWR bill to become an attachment to the energy bill. This stopped the Democrats from filibustering, forcing Bush to back down on raising arsenic standards in water.

Fortunately, several court rulings have gone against Bush and helped to deter his program. They are:

1. Logging another 58.5 million acres of land declared road-less acres under Clinton
2. Halting the drilling for oil off the coast of California
3. Stopping efforts to drill for gas near Utah's arches and Canyon Land National Forest.

Groups are fighting Bush appointees to Agriculture and Interior. "They know what they are after and have been on a mission since they walked in the door," said Gloria Flora, a Clinton supervisor in the Lewis and Clark Forest in Montana. "They know what they want to change, and the environment will suffer from these changes," she concluded.

Lobbyists for every corporation faxed their legislators' offices saying, 'we need to get all we can out of 2003.' "The election of 2004 was getting close and the GOP was worried about their possible creation of new election issues," said Philip Clapp, president of the Environmental Trust. "They could not imagine Bush winning a second term in 2004."

Ruby Johnson Jenkins, who routinely exercises by taking 10-mile hikes through forests near her house, is doing her very best to save the 30-inch trees in the forest near her home. She has done this for years. "I have to," she says. "I consider it my forest, not theirs."

Bush and the GOP tend not to agree. More atrocities approved. The Bock Range in Southern Utah was opened to oil exploration; rights to drill were sold to oil companies. This is the same pristine area that President Clinton attempted to have declared a preserve in 1999.

The Bush machine continues its rampage across the West. Utah joins Wyoming as a state to be trashed in the GOP's efforts to find oil and gas. Remember, "they want to rule, not govern."

We need to omit the plan to drill for oil in the Arctic National Wildlife Refuge (ANWR), which is tucked handily in the energy bill. If Bush and his cronies get their way, it will endanger precious wildlife in the area and endanger the environment, while doing nothing to affect gas prices until 2025 and then, not by much.

Bush's Assault on the Nation's Forests

The clearest way to the universe
Is through a forest wilderness.
John Muir

Oregon Representatives Earl Blumenauer, Darlene Hooley, Peter DeFazio, and David Wu have protested to Interior Secretary Gale Norton, following the disclosure that a Reno, Nevada-based group retained to draw up a Steens Mountain plan having mining industry ties. Richard DeLong of Enviro Scientists is treasurer of he California Mining Association and its vice president, Opal Adams, are on the Board of Trustees of the NW Mining Association.

DeLong has described derailed mines as "victims of radical environmental groups and ill-informed local governments." He also discussed ways and means to "minimize the effects" of environmental groups. This is the first time an outside group has been brought in.

We are concerned that many agencies, through no fault of their own, lack the resources, ability or capacity to administer contracting endeavors. "They said as more and more functions of the federal government are contracted out, key expertise within these agencies will be lost."

The government contract pays Enviro scientists $670,000 to complete the plan on 1.6 million acres, which could be handled by the government. BLM documents for the plan refute Elaine Brong that the company "only maintains and serves as an advisor". BLM documents show they "will review input from groups and individuals (and, if favorable, will allow the mining to proceed). The lawmakers also question Brong's assertion that the ties to mining are mere professional affiliations and are not considered conflicts of interest."

What are they then? The lawmakers questioned Norton's statement that the draft version of the Steens plan now approved by the BLM will open 448,000 acres to mining. These companies use arsenic washes to get to the gold, which remains behind, destroying the environment and babies' lives.

Do these questions overshadowing the contracting process raise concerns about the preferred recommendation? How can you, Secretary Norton, assure the public the plan is based on both the law and the public good? (I can hear Watts applauding her in the background.)

These issues about the fragile Steens Mountains are important to both citizens who live in that area and thousands of Americans for whom the Steens Mountains are a prime destination for its pristine environment and recreational opportunities. (448,000 acres is the max, which can be allowed.) Remember what Seneca said about greedy men in 55 AD.

COURTS

Bush 1 – Democrats 1 –
GOP's Attempt to Stack the Courts

Laws alone cannot secure freedom of expression;
In order that very man present his views without
Penalty, there must be spirit of tolerance
In the entire population.
Albert Einstein
1879-1955

BUSH'S WIN WAS THE APPOINTMENT of Charles Pickering (who once lobbied for a cross burner as an appeals judge), ending a two-year filibuster by the Democrats to keep him out of this lifetime appointment. Bush used his recess-appointment powers to seat Pickering, a federal district judge in Hattiesburg, MS, on the 5th U. S. Circuit Court in New Orleans in an effort to placate the right wing of his constituency.

This contemptible act on Bush's part was another slap in Democratic faces who feel that Pickering is too far to the right and anti-civil rights, to boot. It's one more reason to work harder to criticize Bush as president. The Democrats are still angry with Pickering over his reduction of a sentence of a man convicted of a cross burning near the house of an interracial couple.

He has also worked for the MS Sovereignty Commission, which worked to preserve segregation in the South. Trent Lott said the nomination was held up by "special interests" that have unfairly smeared the reputation of a good man! This from a man who has had ties to the Klan.

In the second case of the day, a "victory" for the Democrats! Rep. Kathryn Harris, the Florida election official in the 2000 election that certified 537 votes which gave 27 electoral votes to Bush (and the Supreme Court decision to do likewise), would not run for the Senate. Rove told her he was afraid it would cause too many angry Democrats to turn out and reduce the GOP's chances of carrying the State of Florida.

John Roberts – The Right Choice

In another stroke of political genius, George Bush reached out and plucked John Roberts to be the next Supreme Court Chief Justice. Roberts, a summa cum laude graduate of Harvard Law School, is a candidate par excellence for the position. He is a former clerk under the late Justice William Rehnquist, but more notably under Judge Henry Friendly on the U. S. Court of Appeals who may be considered his mentor.

Friendly, who died in 1986, was regarded as the greatest appeals court judge of the 20th Century. He became a role model for Roberts. Friendly never rushed his decisions; he carefully weighed the facts and the law, gave close attention to precedent, and was intellectually honest, "almost brutally so", TIME tells us.

Roberts has had but a marginal flirtation with political activism and is not the hard-line ideologue the Right had hoped for. They were disappointed in a lack of "red meat" issues in his dossier.

Virginia Law School Dean John Jeffries, Jr. says, "He will be sensitive to precedent and will be unlikely to march in step with Justices Scalia and Clarence Thomas."

Roberts is enormously self-confident, but he is not showy or arrogant. He is a devout Catholic, who thinks for himself about church doctrines. He and his wife adopted two children when she was unable to conceive.

His self-esteem is more of the quiet kind, which allows for a presence of humility, a rare quality in DC, where the march of egos is overwhelming. He graduated in three years from Harvard, a mark of his intelligence.

Roberts is very intense in a low key way, but he is a driven worker, who, after graduation from law school, was hospitalized to recover from the ordeal of 14- to 20-hour days he spent studying. He has appeared before the Supreme Court 39 times and spent a lot of time shuffling the note cards in front of him, his only sign of nervousness. His only fear or slight neurosis is losing his voice in court, a fear he tries to abate by carrying boxes of cough drops in his briefcase.

Democrats were in awe of his nomination and were hard pressed to find points for attacking Roberts. They hoped to challenge him concerning his pledge to follow legal rulings, stating his record creates doubts about his commitment to privacy rights, particularly on the issue of abortion where his wife belongs to an anti-abortion group.

In Roberts' favor are rulings he made in his representation of the special voting rights of native Hawaiians and his representation of environmentalists trying to preserve Lake Tahoe – made not because he was a pro-Green, but because Judge Lazarus had a scheduling conflict. In Roberts' arguments before the Supreme Court, he was not partisan; instead relying on sound, legal arguments. He took umbrage with those who tried to make the Justice Department make ideological arguments.

At the heart of the debate were Roberts' views on "judicial activism", a criticism levied by congressional Republicans, when they believe judges go too far in deciding social issues rather than leaving those choices to elected legislators. After George Allen (R-VA) met Roberts, he said he was pleased by Roberts' view that judges should interpret the law, not make law. Allen said they did not discuss abortion.

Some Senate Democrats cautioned against "judicial activism", although their definition refers to judges that would ignore precedent and overturn more liberal Supreme Court decisions of the 1960s and 1970s, such as Roe v. Wade (abortion ruling).

Roberts reaffirmed that precedent plays an "important role in promoting the stability of the legal system." He also said judges do not have a commitment to solve society's problems.

Roberts was confirmed and now serves in the highest judicial post in our country. With the death of Rehnquist, Bush made Roberts the Chief Justice to replace him.

CONSERVATIVES

Conservatives Upset at Bush's Spending

All words and no performance.
Philip Messinger
1583-1640

WHEN YOUR OWN PARTY BEGINS to complain about the money you are budgeting, something is amiss. George Bush himself has emphasized the need to reduce spending, but the budget has increased to $2.31 trillion since October 1, 2003. $2.31 trillion!

Bush said it's for fighting terrorism and the wars in Iraq and Afghanistan, but also expanding relentlessly are such huge programs as Social Security, Medicare, and Medicaid, which go automatically with inflation and higher medical costs.

Conservatives are vexed most by the 31.5% increase in discretionary spending, which constitutes one-third of the past budget. It covers defense spending, domestic security, school aid, and everything else, save Social Security. During the Clinton years, this spending grew 3.5%. Compare!

Among the issues paining the conservatives is the enactment of a $400 billion, 10-year enlargement of Medicare and $87 billion in aid to already gorged farm programs. Brain M. Reidl, Heritage Foundation budget analyst, says, "two-thirds of all farm subsidies go to large farms and wealthy agri-businesses, most of which earn more than $250,000 a year." Reidl concluded, "Congress could guarantee every full-time farmer a minimum of 185% of the poverty line ($32,652 for a family of four) for only $4 billion per year – one-fifth the cost of direct subsidies in the new bill."

There is $40 billion more for veterans' benefits and for the Air Force to lease tankers and buy important refueling equipment, all of which add up to millions of dollars.

Soothsayers say the election of 2004 was the most important issue. Many field victories could have been purchased with the aid of increased government spending, all passed by a GOP Congress. The future looks bleak to Douglas Holley Eakin, who has said, "the Medicare bill could cost $1.72 trillion during its second 10 years." The U. S. budget is out of control, say investment bankers at Goldman Sachs. They have projected huge deficits for the next decade.

There is growing frustration within the GOP House. Members are saying, "We're no longer fiscal conservatives, not with these growing deficits and big out-of-control entitlements."

"I feel," said one, "September 11th has clouded our vision and we must begin to clear very soon." Some say our vision became clouded way before 9-11. Brian Riedl has shone a spotlight more than once on the excessive spending of this administration. He said, "In 1995, the GOP shut down Congress, and it came off as petty and mean-spirited, and the voters blamed the GOP and House Speaker Newt Gingrich.

"The GOP was his politically," Riedl said, "and Gingrich doctored spending cuts, the new third rail."

"In a recent Cato policy report," says The Times, Mr. Crane goes back even further to Reagan's 1984 re-election effort and its 'Feel Good Morning in America' program. He argues it missed an incredible opportunity to capitalize on the ever-popular Reagan. They could have laid out specific ideas to shrink spending programs rampant in the federal government.

Now he blames Bush for the collapse of the GOP. He ran in 2000 not calling for a single spending cut, a point Mr. Bolton, the budget director, does not dispute. He campaigned on favoring limited government, but its policies have put lawmakers in a bind, caught between their loyalty to the president and their fiscal principles.

Some voted for and some voted against; nine GOP members voted against the Medicare bill. Barbara Musgrove, a freshman voter, did, too. "To have to say no was tough," she added.

Democrats were gleefully looking on and enjoying the divisions among the GOP. Mr. Crane, for one, wished Bush had a privacy foe. "There will be a battle for the soul of the GOP in 2006 and 2008," he predicted, the free marketers who have been sold a bill of goods by Bush and the limited-government types.

Conservatives Against Bush

Benjamin Disraeli, the greatest political leader of the 19th Century in Britain's House of Commons, had little love for conservatives. He stated, "Conservatism discards prescription, shrinks from principle, disavows progress. Having rejected all respect for antiquity, it offers no redress for the present and makes no preparation for the future."

Could we find a better description of the Bush Administration? All over America, conservatives are bolting from the GOP. They feel the party has drifted so far from its moorings of honesty, practicality, and common sense as to become unrecognizable to many of its rank and file.

Angry letters of protest against Bush's policies and actions have flooded the offices of publishers across the nation. The Internet is jammed with angry comments against the president. The little boy, who was never corrected by his mother, Barbara, for always wanting his way (and always getting it), is finding he cannot always do this as an adult. These protests are all in agreement that America faces a unique array of critical issues that are not being faced with competence, honesty, and integrity. The political discourse has fallen into dysfunctional disarray.

Some critics of Bush have been questioned for disloyalty (my way or the highway) and branded as "Rethuglicans". And on the far right, there is a sinister alliance against the president put on by moveon.

org. Most have been repeatedly questioning if you leave the GOP, where will you go? It is an electorate grown weary of the Bush/Rove posturing and phony politics, which fail to address the serious issues created by the Iraq War.

It's still a two-party system. Ralph Nader and Ross Perot supporters tried and failed to make it otherwise. Now it could change into a virulent third party, even though they have come and gone over the years. In closed states, like Oregon and others, one must declare party affiliation before voting, losing part of their power of even a single ballot to protest. So the only way open is to switch parties and no matter how repugnant the choice may be – become a Democrat.

You may have trouble finding a fiscally conservative group to join or one that favors individual rights and one that favors death with dignity, gun ownership, and freedom of speech or sexual orientation. These are all dear canons to Republicans. Bush left all those canons behind months ago as he forged his blind-sided policies.

Abraham Lincoln harkened the Republican dream as one of the last, best hopes on earth. Governor John Winthrop proclaimed the Puritan Experiment as one of religious freedoms dear to all Republican hearts. Ronald Reagan and the GOP could not escape its destiny (to lead the world).

The GOP under Bush has become shortsighted and no longer empathizes with the working man and the poor (as if they ever did – he who has the most toys wins, because this is the only goal of this capitalistic society). Bush too has aligned himself with the religious right, disdaining science, and fostering the creationists' view of the fanciful tale of the Earth's creation in seven days. When people failed to salute, he switched to Intelligent Design, both tales having no scientific basis for belief. Ninety-nine percent of all scientists believe in evolution.

The U.S. faces an incredible host of obligations in the world. We did not need a war in Iraq to compound the problems besetting us. The world waits our every move with baited breath; we are its last great hope. (We are not informed that Iran was the true enemy if we wished to fight a war. They have worked on the atomic bomb for as long as 20 years, a frightful issue for the U.S. to face.)

We cannot solve any of the world's problems from an ideological rigidity. The world is no longer liberal, conservative, Republican, Democrat. (Oh, Adlai Stevenson, where are you now when we need you? We may lose for want of a single statesman.) The late lamented Barry Goldwater said, "Our country was one in which vigorous debates between men of good conscience, who had an opposite view, can and do produce policy."

This one statement makes the Bush Administration a cruel farce, where if one dissents, he becomes a traitor no longer worthy of citizenship. What would the people of Athens, Greece have said in 450 BC if such Bush policies were proposed? He, like Socrates, would have been cast into exile and the city gatherings on corners to discuss the politics of the day would have been dispersed.

The Bush policies involve disrespect, arrogance, and outright lies and dishonesty from the Rove-Cheney machine. It is folly to suppose such policies represent discourses between nations. All we ask for is honesty from the Bush government and the men who run it. Americans must learn to live within their means, whether this means more taxes or spending less money and learning how to save in the process.

It's like the ad where a man on a grass mower shows us his $200,000-plus house, his new car, and says he has a membership in the local golf club. Then he says he is in debt up to his eyeballs and can't even pay the interest on his loans. He ends, "Won't somebody out there, please, help me?"

Our spending is out of proportion and our consumption of the world's resources is grossly out of kilter. Our balance of payment had a deficit recorded for its second highest in the second month in a row in December 2005. It can't go on like this forever.

We also must become a nation of proudly standing individuals, people without shame for how we got there. Unless we do so and admit to our shortcomings, our time at the top of the hill will come to an end. Our free market has never tolerated extremes for very long; always it moves toward the center.

It's easy to forget our racial prejudices, the Ku Klux Klan, and the liberal attitudes of the 1920s returned in spades during the 1960s. I hope and pray the U.S. will return to those qualities that once made us a great nation.

The Pork Bill

George Bush signed the energy bill, touting it as his answer to the energy crisis of the 21st Century. What he didn't mention were the little surprises therein: $10 million for a study on riding bikes to work, and $1.2 million to experiment with hydrogen-powered boats and tourist boats in the Grand Canyon. It would also have the Department of Energy design a feasibility study of using mustard seeds as opposed to chicken fat in making bio-diesel fuel. No cost estimate was given.

The bill contains hundreds of millions in the credits to build more nuclear power plants, $2.6 billion in subsidies to drill for more oil and gas, and $2.9 billion for coal companies to invest in cleaner-burning fuels.

It orders double the amount of Ethanol to 9.9 million gallons produced, even though producing one gallon uses 30% more energy than it produces.

Worst of all is drilling for oil in the Arctic National Wildlife Reserve in Alaska, and the bill does nothing to reduce our dependence on foreign oil but it does set aside monies to study alternative energies. Wind power, solar power, hydro, geo-thermal, bio-mass, and landfill gas are mentioned but no money is set aside for studies, but $1.3 billion for tax credits.

The re-election of George Bush has been a disaster on all fronts. The environment, civil liberties, healthcare, energy, and drug laws. The crime of taking us to war without any real justification is surely a sign worthy of treason and is an impeachable offense. Let's all work toward the 2006 election, if there is no groundswell for impeachment.

Grover G. Norquist –
Super GOP Foe of Welfare Programs

Grover G. Norquist has a master's degree in business administration from Harvard and a bachelor's degree in economics, also from Harvard. He has been a staunch Republican all his life. P. J. O'Rourke, the Democrats' oldest foe, is a huge admirer of Norquist, as are most of the neocons. "He is," O'Rourke says, "the courageous leader for tax cuts for the wealthy." Newt Gingrich is also a great fan of his.

There is a glaring error in his personal philosophy. Why is he so opposed to government programs that help the poorest, most downtrodden, most helpless members of our electronic society? Is he not aware of the affects of the computer revolution, the changing economic status of millions upon millions of people? The uneducated masses have been forced into a state of helplessness to a point where they are unable to care for themselves. Welfare allows them to keep their heads above the raging torrents that surround them. He may have become a shining beacon to Gingrich and the others but to many, he is the unrepentant Scrooge.

Grover G. Norquist –
Biographical Sketch

Grover G. Norquist, a native of Massachusetts, has been one of Washington's most effective issues management strategists for over a decade. He is president of Americans for Tax Reform (ATR), a coalition of taxpayer groups, individuals and businesses opposed to higher taxes at the federal, state, and local levels. ATR organizes the

TAXPAYER PROTECTION PLEDGE, which asks all candidates for federal and state office to commit themselves in writing to oppose all tax increases. To date, President George W. Bush, 222 House members, and 46 Senators have taken the pledge. On the state level, six governors and 1247 state legislators have taken the pledge.

Mr. Norquist also serves on the board of directors of the National Rifle Association, the American Conservative Union, and as president of the American Society of Competitiveness. He wrote the book, *Rock the House*, an analysis of the 1994 elections.

In the past, Mr. Norquist served on the Advisory Commission on Electronic Commerce and on the National Commission on Restructuring the Internal Revenue Service. He served as an economist and chief speechwriter with the U. S. Chamber of Commerce from 1983-84, and on the campaign staff for the 1988, 1992, and 1996 Republican Platform committees. He served as executive director of the College Republicans and was closely associated with Jack Abramoff.

In the words of former Speaker of the House Newt Gingrich, Grover Norquist is "the person who I regard as the most innovative, creative, courageous and entrepreneurial leader of the anti-tax efforts and of conservative grassroots activism in America . . . He has truly made a difference and truly changed American history."

P.J. O'Rourke says, "Grover Norquist is Tom Paine crossed with Lee Atwater plus just a soupcon of Madame Defarge."

Mr. Norquist holds a Masters of Business Administration and a Bachelor of Arts degree in Economics, both from Harvard University. He lives in Washington, DC.

Bush-Norquist Plan

The Bush-Norquist plan is simple in its complexity – reduce the states through GOP tax cuts to states of insolvency. They are succeeding. Each tax cut enriches the rich and makes the poor poorer. The states, by law, must state a yearly budget. On December 22, 2005, Congress passed an almost $500 billion budget. Social programs were cut, and home health care, Medicare, and Medicaid would be frozen for on year. The $12.6 billion cuts in the student aid loan program passed. To do so, they have no recourse but to cut the safety nets put in place by FDR and Johnson in the Great Society. Next, they create a false crisis in Social Security and call for a cut in benefits to balance their dwindling reserves.

One answer is to cut the size of benefit checks when a better answer may be to raise the $90,000 tax ceiling, which enables the very rich not to pay any Social Security taxes. In this one act, the false crisis would disappear into 2080 or more. (The GOP sees that act as a "tax" and refuses to consider this most logical of all answers to the lying net of the Bush-Norquist plan.)

The Social Security crisis is just the first of many crises that will arise. Bush-Norquist seeks to control the economic bases of the US. To our fading educational system (now 24th in the world and being surpassed by China and even Taiwan), they have cut the Pell grants that enable the poor – and prisoners – to attend college. Food stamps have already been cut beyond the point of poverty and are harder to bear.

The least far-reaching programs of all are being cut. Space travel and exploration has become too expensive. We can't afford to fix the Hubble Telescope, they say, the greatest scientific achievement on our part since the moon landing.

Every NSF cut is the price we pay for having a president who is proud of the fact that he was a "C" student. Bush was exposed to the finest possible education at Yale, all that money can provide. He became an ostrich, put his head into the sand, cut classes (in which he might have learned a whole lot more of a practical philosophy). He opted for carousing with the boys and out-drinking the best of them. He was very proud of this fact.

Bush's NSF cuts and his ignorance of the charge of the Far East in economics, mathematics, and science achievements belabor any thinking person's mind. It is readily apparent when he cut Merck's overseas tax liability from $35 billion to $3 or $4 billion. The Bush family has a great deal of Merck stock. It explains how Dan Quayle became the VP under his father. They, too, are beholden to Merck.

Norquist lacks an open mind in many areas, especially in economics.

Bush Hirings

One of Bush's biggest failures was his attempt to hire Bernard Kerig as director of Homeland Security. Along with his many unearthed love affairs and shady business deals, he is responsible for promoting the Taser, which has killed more than a score of suspects.

The Taser Corporation gave him generous stock options to promote Tasers when he was a police commissioner in New York City. Kerig reaped $6.2 million for options he received when working for Taser.

Kerig was a partner of former New York Mayor Rudy Guiliani before his sordid past caused his resignation from his appointment and partnership.

Doonesbury Strikes Again

"Mr. Cigarette" is listening to the cigarette companies complain that Bush has helped and gotten into bed with big oil, big steel, big sugar, and others. What about us, they wondered? We shouldn't have to. Last month, our good friends at the Justice Department overrode their own lawyers, reducing a potential $130 billion industry settlement down to a very affordable $14 billion.

Here's the beauty part. It didn't even have to be negotiated! How can we ever repay the Bush Administration for its interference – we can't really. So they will just have to settle for a big wet one from us at big tobacco!

Flash to the White House…yeech! Hasn't he ever heard of soft money?

Voice in the background: We'll follow up, sir.

James Tobin

When will all the dirty tricks end? The GOP has spent $722,000 to provide a defense for GOP official, James Tobin, who is charged with four felonies ("I'm innocent of these charges," he maintains.). He is accused of conspiring with a GOP consultant to jam Democratic and labor union get-out-the-vote phone banks in November 2002. A telephone firm was paid to make repeated hang-up phone calls to overwhelm the phone banks in New Hampshire on election day, 2002.

John Sununu, the GOP candidate, became NH's newest senator in a very close race. A top NH party official and a GOP consultant have already been indicted. The party agreed to underwrite Tobin's defense because he was a long-time supporter, and he assured them he had not done anything wrong.

Bill Clinton

Bill Clinton was a better conservative than George Bush is. In fact, Clinton was the best conservative the GOP has had in the last 40 years. The GOP has to return to solid GOP values, a revolution that returns sanity to fiscal and foreign policies and one that believes in clean air and water are all conservative values. They are threats to climate change and bad science. They would never start a war of choice, a revolution that takes the GOP from those who value wealth and power over health and dignity, one that returns to personal responsibility by supporting children and schools, works for community and neighborhoods.

A revolution, which brought us the national parks and which Eisenhower warned us against – the military industrial complex – would suck the lifeblood out of our future and founded the EPA (yes, the EPA!). The GOP has to move forward to build a future based on basic human values.

A vote for fear is a vote for failure.

JOHN KERRY

Why Kerry Lost

FOXIFICATION OF THE NEWS BY journalists is a scary trend. "Fox's right wing partisanship is having two effects," says columnist William Raspberry. First, its popularity – It outdistances its competition, even MSNBC and leads other cable companies that mimic it. The second is far more dangerous – It threatens to destroy public confidence in the news (plus Bush's phony no-existent 'news' copy here and in Iraq).

Fox is fiercely partisan (though they deny it). It is right-wing talk metastasized into cable. Rush Limbaugh, for instance, doesn't try to be evenhanded. He does it with a wink and a nod to his right-wing audience. Even his audience knows how right wing it is, and we in the media certainly know it is. It attempts to sell that what FNC presents as just another set of biases that routinely drive the Network's news machine and, by extension, The New York Times and other newspapers'.

[Most recent polls show Fox's rating plummeting and lagging behind, of all things, Internet blogs and alternative news sources! Bill O'Reilly has lost half of his audience.]

It makes all of us seem to be grinding our own axes and none need to be taken as serious purveyors of the truth. If all of the major networks and papers are seen as left-of-center counterparts of FNC, why accept them as authoritative sources?

At risk is infallibility. Even the best reporters make mistakes, but the mainstream news at least tries to get it right, even when after the fact, they admit errors. (The Dan Rather flap (which really was true), but its sources were tainted and became a battlefield of warring biases.] You sock them and they sock you and both feel it's a good day's work. Come to think of it, look at the stories on Social Security! It's happening there, and you become less sure about Social Security's worth.

Fox is more than an annoying pest. Bill O'Reilly has thousands of devotees who swear by his every word (no matter the jibes by MSNBC). His latest claim nears sacrilege. "There is a war on Christmas. The latest liberal plot is to ban the sacred Christian holiday."

Fox has an average viewing audience of 1.1 million and is far from being the most watched in prime time; CBS – 12.4 million; NBC – 8.3 million; and ABC – 9 million. Fox isn't the big bully in the schoolyard and not even the big journalism kids know what to do about it.

Kerry lost and now we are faced with four more years of messianic militarism, corporate giveaways, and civil liberties infringements. Would or could the Republic survive? It's a dismal project to contemplate.

How could Kerry have lost? "Let me count the ways", to paraphrase Elizabeth Barrett Browning. People have never seen a tide of such hatred as that directed against Bush. He was vilified by anyone of importance in the entertainment business and laughed at by all of the intelligentsia of the country. He couldn't wipe without help, it was said.

Here is an account of a few of the many things that were wrong with the Kerry campaign. I was writing "Will the Republic Survive Four More Years?" during the campaign and tried to pass along some of my ideas to Mary Beth Cahill, his campaign manager. I called her on the phone and tried to give her my ideas, but she was on a conference call at the time and would call me back later. She never did call back, though I left six messages for her with my number. She probably did not give much credence to my call, as she did not know me from Adam.

I have worked on elections since 1976, and I felt I could have made a contribution to the campaign. As it turned out, I could have influenced John to get off his elite Eastern bandwagon to which he had attached himself, and to which Mary Beth had pledged as the only way for him to be.

One of Kerry's biggest failures lay in his inability to challenge the common sense of the American people. He did not speak clearly and forcibly to half of our country that was looking for the words of at true leader, words like he spoke to his men on his swift boat. These men followed him into battle unquestioningly with full faith in his ability to lead them. Mistake #1 – He failed to answer immediately the false charges the GOP made about his courage and the validity of his wounds.

Karl Rove was following up on the same campaign he waged in Georgia against Max Cleland, a true American hero. Rove insinuated Cleland had fathered a child by a black woman. The truth was he and his wife adopted a fatherless child.

Rove employed the same tactics against Tom Daschle in South Dakota, hurling innuendo against his character. Daschle failed to answer these scurrilous charges. Both he and Max lost to non-entities of an incredibly low order of intelligence that defend creationism.

Even as we complain of their tactics, one has to admire how Rove has marshaled his troops 'on line'. They seem to be following a script and all together parrot the same philosophy.

The Kerry campaign, on the other hand, was disjointed, with many groups espousing their own philosophy and agenda. They lacked a herder with a long whip to get them into line.

Liberal has become a dirty word that traces back to the second election of FDR in 1936. George Lakoff argues that two different models of the family – the 'strict father' family and the 'nurturing parent' family – divide liberals and conservatives. It shapes the difference of opinion on everything from tort reform to same-sex marriage to school vouchers. "These neat dualisms in our politics are simply irrelevant to nations with no history of a two-party system," Lakoff stated. "The trick," as philosopher Richard Yorty states, "is to talk about labels without prefacing the word with the self-deluding word 'mere'." It's one of Rove's favorite words, and he used this logic to denigrate the word 'liberal'.

Behind Kerry's loss was the specter of Roe vs. Wade. The conservatives made it a basic part of their political philosophy. "Abortion and Hollywood's shameless lifestyle were jammed down our throats," one conservative stated.

Democrats, especially the eastern elite types, were prone to referring to Midwestern fundamentalists as 'hayseeds' and they laughed at their religious pretensions. The emphasis on same-sex marriage, when the country was far from ready to accept anything other than one man-one woman, was a turn off for Kerry and a move toward Bush. "It's in the Bible," fundamentalists stated. [It isn't.]

Conservatives were turned off Kerry on the issue of entitlements and opted for individual responsibility. Teachers, wearing Kerry buttons, taking liberal stands on many issues, teaching evolution and laughing at creationism, upset many Christians.

Eliot Spicer stated, "Kerry lost because we have to do a better job of speaking bout the moral and spiritual values, which have always been a part and characterized our party." Many of the middle class voters for Bush failed to vote in terms of their economic interests and fell for the Rove dialectic on Bush being more concerned about these than Kerry was.

People have always voted in terms of their hopes and resentments, and Bush relied heavily on these resentments more than Kerry did. He distracted the voters' interjections of irrelevant issues, such as slavery, civil rights, free love, free masonry, and same-sex marriage. Hard work, patriotism, faith, and integrity were ignored in the Democrat's campaign to a large degree. "They are not only religious in character, but also they are part of our nation's creed," said Eliot

Spicer. "The GOP and Rove usurped all these issues from Kerry's campaign."

Kerry thought he got his message across – but what was his message? Kerry aides attacked Clinton aides. The National Committee staffers lobbed bombs at the WONK's policies, and they in turn complained about inept political consultant aides. Aides on the phone with Kerry contended with aides in DC. They turned on each other rather than working together under one banner, "Anyone but Bush!"

On the GOP side, all toed the line. There was never any deviance from Rove's carefully scripted campaign issues. They were well orchestrated to the nth degree – and it worked, because Kerry failed to offer a compelling message. No one had a counter strategy to combat the many GOP attacks on Kerry. All the false claims, distortions, and outright lies, which they often said with a straight face, went largely unanswered or answered too late as on the swift boat issue. People believed these boldfaced lies and voted for George, the guy they would like to "hoist a beer with."

Day after day, week after week, Bush called Kerry a flip-flopper! Kerry never really answered, but the war in Iraq had many instances of Bush's flip-flopping, which cost the lives of young soldiers. Why wasn't Kerry on top of these issues? They questioned Kerry's patriotism, his war wounds, and tried to say it was grandstanding. "Kerry was running up and down the Delta with bullets pinging all around him and his men."

This was grandstanding to Karl Rove, who made an issue about Kerry's war wounds. Is there no end to Rove's menialty, his total unconcern for the truth? Rove's mendacity and his concupiscence are beyond the limits of belief. He is an evil man devoted to a single cause, the election of Bush – and it pains one to see that it worked.

Kerry became a slave to polling data and the guidance of Mary Beth Cahill, and he used this research too literally. There was an insurmountable gulf between these 'highly paid' consultants and the volunteer Kerry forces. They pressed Kerry for the values he would bring the presidency, but he failed to provide the needed ammunition for their cannons. He spoke in terms of specifics rather than principles crying out for expression.

Jay Leno's humor was deadly to the Kerry cause. "Kerry would have conceded earlier, but he had not met with the French, Germans, and Russians to discuss their views on the election's progress." (Bush became the first president to increase his lead in both houses in an election year.)

Maureen Dowd was critical of Bush's strategy. "He has divided the country along the fault lines of fear, intolerance, ignorance, and religious rule." The election result showed Rove was correct on these issues as a way to win the election.

The greater issues of why Kerry lost are (1) He did not hold Bush's feet to the fire on the issues of trade (a massive trade deficit balance of $600 billion in 2005), civil liberties, the war in Iraq, WMDs, and economic justice. The move to increase the scandalous minimum wage from $5.15 an hour failed again when Bush did not promote the issue, and Kerry ignored it. (2) "The Democratic progressives have allowed the party to be pulled apart and to the right by corporate interests and their preferred 'swing vote' policies," chimed Ralph Nader.

"As a result, Kerry's message became a blurred hodgepodge dismally vague to the voters as he listened to Mary Beth Cahill's restraint tactics. They were lined up against a prehistoric Tyrannosaur, and they were hurling marshmallows at him. The policy should have been centered on Bush's jugular."

Kerry did not face up to all the issues. He was soft when he should have been angry at Bush's lies. He even lost the advantage he gained over Bush in the debates. He had Bush on the ropes and couldn't finish him off.

The activists in the party were fed up with Kerry's blandness. Kerry retreated on too many issues – Social Security, welfare reform, and the biggest one of all, unemployment and, in tandem, the deficit. He never commented on the growing control of the media by Fox Network's Rupert Murdoch and the corporations' control of 70% of the media. Kerry threw in the towel on these issues when he should have been warning the public how they were controlling the news and their minds and emotions.

The Democratic Party, as a result, fell into a decadent, decaying, headless monstrosity and completely lost its center, the most important part of the campaign. "Without a heart, not only was the party dead, because it is the force we rely on. Is this not true?" asked Noam Chomsky.

And, in turn, Nader called Chomsky and Barbara Ehrenreich 'scared liberals'. "They all lost their chance to stand up for justice, and it became a fatal omission," Nader concluded.

Other Issues Kerry Missed

Caroline Gordon, a voter, said, "I thought we were going to show the rest of the world we weren't brainwashed, but the results showed otherwise. We should all be afraid of the consequences." People all over Europe were horrified and very, very disappointed. "Europe can now see a world crisis and economic collapse looming on the horizon. If this happens the GOP will be destroyed forever," said Anatole Kaletsky of The London Times.

Backtracking to the reasons for Kerry's loss, David Browder said, "Day after day passed without Kerry answering the swift boat charges. He made no reply. His acceptance speech was only so-so – it created no bounce. He did not take up his advantage created in the debates. I could see Bush was vulnerable, his tenacity and the clarity of his and Rove's policies carried him along very nicely. Even the awesomely bad economy and the scarcity of his promised jobs, the war in Iraq, all he overcame. The 9-11 became his fortress and helped him carry the day." He carried all the Red states, and the East went for Kerry. It just wasn't enough.

Iowa surprised me greatly. I thought the lady in Des Moines encapsulated the whole state's stand when she said, "Bush has lied to us and I'm going to vote for John Kerry." Late returns proved both of us to be wrong!

Kerry was a bad messenger and he under-performed in every demographic grouping – youth, women, Hispanics, African Americans, Catholics, and Jews. The Democratic Convention became an exercise in false enthusiasm, and it carried over into the campaign. (We are going to need a more viable candidate in 2008.)

Spicer said the election was a triumph of GOP values (many of which were usurped) and a repudiation of the Democrats. "How could this be so?" he asked. "Democrats have always prided ourselves as being the party of the people, of their working values, and more about farmers, opportunity, inclusion, and responsibility. But we failed to make our stands persuasively enough. The GOP captured and co-opted our value mantras and made us sound like we stood for nothing. We failed to unmask the GOP claims, and this just should not have happened," Spicer concluded.

Bush experts were able to stop the introduction of the emergency contraception pill in cases of rape, and stop it from being sold over the counter. "It's murder," they say, though it is an unsupported idea, and a few pharmacists refuse to sell it on this basis. They a have set themselves up as purveyors of morality. It's one more instance of religious ideas jamming up the expression of free ideas and the taking away of citizen's rights. Bush also flat-funded Title X, which pays for birth control for the poor, and he has spent millions on his abstinence program, which is a glaring failure. Forty percent of 16-year-olds have had sex.

To Bush's religiosity, Europeans scoff at "his direct line to do God's work on earth." Bush is on record as having said, "The U.S. is a citadel of Godly righteousness", and he agrees with End of Days fanatics, who preach Armageddon is coming sooner than we think. (William Benton, founder of the Seventh Day Adventists, said the same thing in 1843, but we are still here.) These are the same 20% who believe the world was created in seven days, is flat, and fossils were placed in the ground by the Devil to confuse Christians.

Their justification for these beliefs: "It says so in the Bible", a book more mythology with scarce scientific documentation. They are seeking out the anti-Christ and see him in animal rights, women's lib, and vegetarianism. "He is among us," they say, and "these are his works." The Rapture will occur any day now; "be prepared you sinners and blasphemers of Jesus." There are other unsubstantiated beliefs that only the "faithful" are privy to, but they are myths! The Bible promotes mythology and the Rapture.

These ideas do not sit well in Europe and even the Catholic Church is concerned with falling attendance in the once-Catholic countries of France, Germany, and even Italy, seat of the new Pope Gregory XVI. They rail at the new Catholic purge of demons, asking, "Who has ever seen one?" It's a Middle Age carry-over to the present. I doubt the extremely conservative Pope Benedict will have much influence over his and others' dying religious thoughts and beliefs.

Pope Benedict faces other challenges. The forged Shroud of Turin was debunked as a 15th or 16th Century answer to the questioning Middle Ages priests against the selling of indulgences as a way to heaven. More and more Catholics today are ignoring the basic tenets of the church on birth control and divorce. There is a strong movement for women to be ordained as priests but there is little hope for change under this pope. What will he do with all the pedophiles recently exposed in the Church?

Wendell Wilkie accused FDR in the 1940 election of being a warmonger. What can we say about George Bush? Kerry failed miserably for not attacking Bush as a liar about the Iraq War and starting it upon the manufactured lies of the neo-conservatives around an escapee from military obligations.

Bush has been an alcoholic, a drug abuser, an incurious zealot, and a puppet dangling on the strings of Dick Cheney and Karl Rove. Did Kerry attack Bush on any of these issues? Hell, no!

Why did Kerry ignore all of Bush's vulnerabilities? Ask Mary Beth Cahill. She was the one who pointed Kerry on the 'path of righteousness' when it should have been the path of anger. Did they ever find one WMD, John?

Bush characterized Kerry as a windsurfing expedient hollow-man! What did Kerry do? He laughed. He did not protest when Karl Rove's group hurled mud at his war record and reviled him as a flip-flopper. (Rove believes if you throw enough shit at the wall, some of it is bound to stick.)

Kerry stood grinning at this organized slaughter of his character. No end was too evil for them to employ, no road of condescension too low for them to travel. They did to him what they did to John McCain in the South Carolina primaries when they accused him of fathering a black child. (John, too, grinned and did not fight back. By the way, he lost, too.)

Why did he not stress the real issues Bush gifted him with? Jobs, the economy, GOP indiscretions – they were all 'Big Bertha' issues. Why didn't he try to raise the ire of the voters against Bush? Again, Mary Beth Cahill with her insistence on the good, level fight, worked against him. When you fight with a saber tooth tiger, you need fangs, too, John!

Why didn't he use TR's Big Stick and not listen to Cahill's coterie of tea-drinking liberal advisors? Instead, he should have been stirring the pot to boiling as Rove kept it at that temperature for months and months. Why weren't the vituperative powers of James Carville more widely used? I often visualized him tearing Bush's failures to shreds, but he never was used for this purpose. It was a major error on Kerry and Cahill's part. Bush needed to be labeled for the phony he is, and Carville was the man most able to do the job.

Rove turned out to be the master planner. Like Julius Caesar, he turned away the hordes of approaching Gaul armies. He was able to distract voters from the main issues – abortion, the war, no WMDs, the economy, jobs, and all the social issues which affect our lives. And the great issue turner – same-sex marriage, supported by Kerry's home state of Massachusetts.

Rove's dirty tricks extended to the Catholic Church, an institution for which he has no love. He was able to get priests and bishops to campaign for Bush from their pulpits. He used late-term abortions, the morning-after pill, and same-sex marriage as issues to convince Hispanics that Bush was their man and his stand on abstinence was the only one to follow. And all contraception was evil. Armed by these issues, many Latinos sadly voted for Bush.

The GOP's organization included carpools to get out the vote. The elderly registered Republicans were contacted by phone to make sure they voted. Bush picked up surprising strength in Las Vegas. The Democrats have counted on Nevada where 70% of registered voters voted against the nuclear waste dump in their state.

On the positive side, Sheila Leslie's (D-NV) win increased from 57% to 63% of the vote and also picked up some seats in the Reno area, which insured control of the legislature by the Democrats. Harry Reid became majority leader with Daschle's defeat. In South Dakota, the minimum wage increased by a mandate vote and the Education Fund easily passed; yet Daschle lost.

One of the biggest Bush lies is his claim that the United States has world-class health care. Investigators Donald Bartlett and James Steele, in their book Critical Conditions, places our country far down the list of industrial nations at 16th. They framed Bush's claim 'a great myth'.

Democrats have become marginalized, identified with Hollywood, liberal movie types, East Coast elites – sushi eating demos, Seattle weenies, and red-necked hillbillies – Mike Rave, another Rovite, said of Bill Gates, "He should buy Canada and build a big house on it." The GOP is vulnerable and Democrats need to hit them in these areas.

Kerry did not take advantage of the warfare in the GOP. Powell told Bush, we need more troops in Iraq. Bush said we didn't and Rumsfeld agreed with Bush. Kerry never hit on the Mussel Shell Missile boondoggle. Billions spent on Reagan's pet with little or no results. Kerry didn't criticize Bush for his budget cut of $100 million for our science program and never made the issue on stem cell research, where Bush was truly vulnerable.

Our woeful scores in math and science would have been a good fire to light under Bush's education program. He ignored Bush's cuts in the Global Feeding program, when it was under-funded to begin with. Millions are starving on our over-populated Earth, and Bush asked for $80 billion more for the Iraq War. What an area for Kerry to criticize, but he didn't.

Kathleen Parker scored a few good points. "He lost touch with the ordinary American working man. Hollywood types or platforms extolling Kerry's qualities didn't cut it, and they are not friends of the working man. When one flies over the Midwest, he should not point down and say 'I love you stupid, red-neck morons.' An aide used these exact words on Kerry's plane."

[It was another example of why people felt Bush had their best interests at heart, against an alien effete in the Harvard-Yale culture. It was despised and just not tenable.]

Other reasons for Kerry's loss were outlined in The Orlando Sentinel. Kerry's men called Bush supporters obtuse, shortsighted rednecks. This is slanderous talk in the South. People there are very concerned and care just as people do in the North. They respect the religious convictions of Northerners and like that to be reciprocated.

Kerry's support of stem cell research along with the intelligentsia of our country was another setback in the South. There, Karl Rove made the Christians believe it was a form of murder of the unborn and the morning-after pill more of the same. Both were amazing presentations of ignorance. His claims were absorbed by the scientifically challenged, and they voted for Bush.

Kerry blamed his loss on the following factors, of which 9-11 was the decider, he said on a "Meet the Press" program. The release of an Osama bin Laden tape erased Kerry's last stab at victory. (Carefully hidden away by Rove waiting for the moment of its greatest impact. It didn't just appear out of the blue, as the GOP told us to believe.)

Kerry did admit he "made mistakes". Make that hundreds, John, possibly thousands. In retrospect, it was a poorly run campaign guided by a woman living in her own dream world of reality. There should have been savage thrusts, the tearing, rendering, and severing of flesh, blood staining the floors and walls. There was gentle cooing; instead, Rove had many laughs at Kerry's inept, lightweight jabs with no force behind them.

Kerry says the slurs against his Vietnam record could have been dealt with more forcibly. He feels he did well against a sitting president in a time of war. He minimized the scope of the Bush victory as being less than a mandate. He said, "If half the crowd at an Ohio State football game had voted for me, I would be talking about my State of the Union message." And he failed to challenge the flawed Ohio vote, which afterward we learned was fixed in the GOP's favor.

Homosexuality was another issue behind protests, along with gay marriage. Both candidates were with the Bible's teaching they heard as children. One man-one woman was their credo and song.

All the wedge issues were firmly clasped to the GOP bosom, one would believe. These were the Democrats' issues, but Rove had the GOP campaigning as if they were their own. The Catholic Church was against Kerry on a single issue – abortion. The bishops in a case or two threatened to excommunicate Catholics who voted for Kerry – shades of Ireland where such practices are common. It is a powerful deterrent to the truly faithful. I was amazed to see this happen in our country.

The filibuster is, and always has been, a tool to safeguard the USA from one-party rule. Someone should tell Frist the next presidential election is three years away, and it is too early to be campaigning for the nomination. To bring religion into the issue as Frist has done is a gross violation of the Constitution's separation of church and state. I think he should hire a new set of advisors. Frist also saw the light of reason in Terry Schiavo's eyes – a good trick, as the autopsy showed she was blind.

Election Reflections

Criticism of the Democrats included the Endangered Species Act and its 30-year effort that ended up taking 27 species off the list. People found out it took conservative principles to solve these liberal problems and in turn they blamed Kerry.

The Democrats stumbled badly and failed to win the catch-up game. By September, there was no clear viability in the Kerry message. This hurt the morale of all the campaign workers, who believed in their heart and soul that Kerry was the one. "I don't know shit about Kerry," said one staffer. "I don't know where he stood and why he had taken that stand," said another. "What are his main issues?" asked one young woman. Why he was the alternative to Bush was never clearly stated.

Of Kerry, James Carville said, "He spoke in litanies, not narratives. Churches have litanies, but politicians must have a clearly defined narrative, and Kerry failed to furnish one. Jobs, healthcare, security issues, the Iraq War, WMDs, all could have been part of a compelling narrative. Bush was vulnerable in all these areas."

The comment Barry Lopez made about the forest industry's clear-cutting policies is applicable here. "Forgive me, dear Lord, that I am so meek and gentle with these butchers." I tried to tell Cahill this on the phone, but she wouldn't listen. I was the tree falling in the forest where no one could hear it fall.

There was no fire in Kerry's words. He failed even to appear angry, when all nature was crying out in agony for Kerry to attack vehemently in the many areas where Bush was vulnerable.

In an interview later on, Ralph Nader said, "I blame the Democrats, especially Progressive magazine. They were so freaked out by the mantra, 'Anyone but Bush' they did not make any demands on Kerry to speak out more forcibly. They totally abdicated their responsibility to create a fierier candidate and the craven image Rove and

Bush had made of Kerry. I will never understand why he waited three weeks to attack Bush's slander of the swift boats."

Bush mugged all protests raised against him and the GOP policies, and Kerry never made an issue of this censorship. Bush was not in favor of open discourse, and Kerry never made this the kind of issue it should have been. When Bush spoke in Charleston, West Virginia, protestors wore anti-Bush t-shirts with Bush in a circle and a red line drawn through his name. Police told them to take the shirts off, cover them or get out. (It was a fascistic moment. The only thing lacking was the police were not wearing brown shirts.) Police then told them they were in a 'no trespassing zone'. Some were hauled away, jailed, and later released after Bush left town. Firsel, one of the protestors, was told he was unpatriotic and did not deserve to see Bush ride by.

Scenes like this were repeated in every city in which Bush campaigned. Dissent was not tolerated, and attendees at his speeches were carefully screened to keep out any dissenters. Young voters, who felt they had a right to protest as a democratic right, soon learned otherwise. Again, Kerry did not make an issue of this closed society of Bush's; and he missed the opportunities Bush presented to him.

Greenspan urged a tax cut in 2000. He was afraid of the looming deficit, but more concerned by the rising costs of Medicare and Medicaid. "His call was a favor to Bush, but we should not accept this as a reason for the tax cuts," Paul Krugman said. "It's like a game of 3-card Monte with Social Security being a part of the right's strategy for dismantling FDR's New Deal."

The tax cuts are a part of Grover Norquist's philosophy, "Starve the beast," he says. "If there is no surplus to feed the beast, it will die." (He was referring to the whole social welfare program of FDR and Johnson's Great Society.)

"First, they advocate tax cuts using whatever rationale might work – supply-side economics, inflation, budget economics, whatever. The resulting deficits become arguments for reducing government spending. Bush has employed this strategy in his first term," Krugman stated.

Bush and Greenspan justified tax cuts with sunny predictions, saying the budget would remain in surplus. His advisors knew this was an outright lie; they knew the tax cuts would cause large deficits, budget problems, and they welcomed that prospect. In fact, Bush celebrated the initial slide into deficit. In the summer of 2001, he called "plunging federal revenue" incredibly positive news! "This will put a straight jacket on federal spending," he said.

They had to convince the voters that the tax cuts were easily affordable and could not be reversed now. Their assumptions were false. Greenspan tried again to come to Bush's aid insisting in March of '05 that we should deal with deficits "primarily if not wholly", by slashing Social Security because "tax increases would pose significant problems for economic growth."

Is this true? "Hardly," said Krugman. "America has prospered for 50 years under a level of federal taxes higher than the ones we face today." Clinton's tax increase in 1996 ushered in an economic boom, so why are tax increases out of the question, many ask?

There is growing evidence that the theory behind the tax cuts was very wrong. According to Norquist and the neo-conservatives, they can use the large deficits caused by the tax cuts to derail social programs.

The remainder of Bush's second term will present problems for him when the growing deficit becomes his Achilles heel. His criticism will not come from his compliant Congress. Bush takes too much freedom on the issues. His prevarication is legendary. He's not the brightest bulb in the ceiling, as many have noted. He is bloodthirsty and incompetent in many areas and most unpopular on the world stage. His recent attempts to mollify France and Germany were failures. He is still called "Emperor Bush" in France. Europe remains stunned by his re-election.

Kerry said he was proud of his campaign, even of his 120,000-vote loss in Ohio. "I mean, millions of new voters came into the campaign.

I won the youth vote and I won the moderate vote." He remained upbeat after his loss. This interview underlined his effort to place himself as a leader of the Bush opposition, and he suggested he might run again in 2008, but he is beginning to think about it. He said he was happy the vote did not give Bush the mandate he sought.

Virulent protests against abortion were featured in many of the red states. In Kansas City, a poster of an aborted fetus was prominently featured. When police were called, they sided with the poster bearers, saying, "it was their right to protest in any way they wanted." It was just one more sign that Kerry would not carry the state of Kansas.

Bush controlled all aspects of the Right. He appointed judges to support his anti-abortion stand, helps items pass the Legislature, and packs social agencies with hard-liners like the anti-abortionists. Dr. W. David Hager has been heard to say, "abortion doctors should be killed." Hager is on the FDA panel on reproduction, and the FDS controls the flow of information over solid medical opinions, which they ignore.

An odious group from the Fox Network supports Bush. From Rush Limbaugh to Bill O'Reilly, Sean Hannity, the Drudge Report, they all lend their support to Bush's policies and enjoy harpooning the Democratic liberals. To them, all liberals are communists or worse. Social Security is socialistic in character and must be replaced, and all should be belittled at every turn.

[The louder these commentators scream against liberals, the more likely they are to be in violation of the law. Rush Limbaugh was unmasked as a dope and sex addict. Bill O'Reilly's accuser, who said that he harassed her and talked sex to her on the phone, recently purchased an $800,000 condo in a tonier section of 5th Avenue. (She got a kitchen, living room, and bedroom for $800 grand; about 540 square feet!) It is rumored she received $8 to $10 million to "dry up and blow away". O'Reilly's actions intone, "Do as I say, not as I do." William Bennett was exposed as being an inveterate gambler, waging hundreds of thousands on single wagers.]

They agree if you disagree. In Bush's eyes, you are un-American (a traitor to many of them) for having the temerity to criticize the president. Can Bush become a healer? I don't know. He is too busy being the Great Divider. His efforts against Social Security alone are disrupting the status quo, not a good sign. The deficit may bury him if not addressed.

The debates may have been a highlight of the Kerry campaign, yet Kerry never articulated a clear position on the Iraq War. The convention also skirted the issue, and there was no carry-over bounce. Kerry's continued insistence on rehashing his Swift Boat exploits in Vietnam ended up working against him. He should have mentioned it in detail one time and never brought it up as a campaign issue again (except in defense of his record, which he never did). Instead, it was repeated ad nauseum.

Rove stressed the skyrocketing Indian Rights issue (they are getting too uppity), Social Security, and a new health care plan. Yet Bush won by 21,567 votes, 30 more than he received in 2000! Nevadans were against Bush on Iraq, tax cuts, and the environment, and they still voted for him.

When you wear Spandex and ride a $20,000 bike, it just increased the distance between him and the people. That's the yearly salary of many people! Kerry might have done better walking down Beale Street in New Orleans whistling Dixie. He said he supported the people's goals, but where as the evidence?

Mollie Ivins called the Swift Boat flap a comedy. Never before have so few lied so effectively in disgracing Kerry's fame. Mary Beth Cahill should have put Kerry on point against this wild, rapacious, animalistic group but no one did. Couldn't Kerry see they were out to destroy him the very first day, not three weeks later? It was Mary Beth fighting against Lady MacBeth, and she could not be as ruthless as Lady MacBeth was.

Now we face more years of the messianic militarism of the neo-conservatives and their stooge, George Bush. Corporate giveaways, environmental rapes, civil liberty infringements are all too much for us to bear, no matter what Bill O'Reilly and Rush Limbaugh tell us daily.

Kerry also failed to challenge the common sense of the American people. He did not speak clearly and boldly to the half of the nation that was looking for the wise words of a true leader. [Adlai Stevenson, where are you when we needed you?]

Bush's war has radicalized the Arab World. There are thousands more terrorists than in 2000. Our 1st and 4th amendment rights are in jeopardy (by the Patriot Act), which gives the FBI the right to enter and seize without just cause or a warrant. Justice Brennan stated it succinctly. "Liberty is a fragile thing."

In December 2005, Bush admitted after 9-11 he authorized the National Security Agency (NSA) to eavesdrop on international phone calls and e-mails without seeking warrants from the courts. Congress is enraged and has called for investigation.

Zito Joseph, a retired psychiatrist, and Roberta Kimmel Cohn, an art dealer, spoke out for Kerry's electorate. They called those who voted for Bush obtuse, shortsighted rednecks, shooting-from the-hip zealots, and religious liberalists.

"People who support same-sex marriage, family values, are not necessarily homophobic and Stepford wives," they said. "Nor are they rubes who believe in a higher power – Neanderthals. There are many intelligent votes out there in the South, and they are not snobs like many Easterners." Kerry did not zone in on these people.

Davis Broder put in his two cents' worth; maybe it was a nickel's worth. "Bush won by 500,000 votes and the debacle of 2,000 votes voided. Bush won because he was able to galvanize his supporters (Rove's main job) better than Kerry. They had been working harder, longer (since 2000) and were far more organized than were the Kerry forces.

They marched and eventually defeated his labor forces, then trumped his aces. The congressional GOP gains in the 2000 election were surpassed in 2004. (Bush became the first re-elected president to increase his hold in both houses of congress). Unbelievably, a non-entity creationist candidate defeated Tom Daschle, so overwhelming was by the Bush victory. Rove and his partner, Ken Mehlman, spent $125 million and years of work identifying the Bush base in all the Red states. It worked.

Terrorism was another of Bush's trump cards. It was the edge from 9-11 and he never let that day stray from the voters' minds. He became the rock they could depend on. He told them again and again it could happen again, and they needed a strong leader, not a flip-flop-per like John Kerry. "He's da man," became a rallying cry.

He overcame job losses, autocracy, a poor economy, setbacks in Iraq, and same-sex marriage (he turned this in his favor), in which he took a civil union stance in Massachusetts by their okay of gay marriage. Any one of these issues could have defeated a candidate, who was less prepared and didn't have Karl Rove at his side. (After the election, Bush appointed Rove to the job he already has – Chief Advisor to the President.)

Broder called gay marriage a 'lightning bolt'. The country is not yet prepared to accept anything other than one man-one woman. "The issue united and elevated Catholics and the Evangelicals into the same camp for Bush," Broder added.

Allan Gyngell is the executive director of the Lowy Institute in Australia and does not show too much love for George Bush. Broder called him a 'hard export'. Like most Australians since WWII, he looks to us for support. Both major parties have sided with the USA, as do the public opinion polls.

Gyngell says, "public opinion has shifted since the invasion of Iraq". John Howard, the Prime Minister, sent 2000 troops anyway and has taken criticism for not calling them back home. He has been replaced as the party leader as a result. His replacement is regarded as having strong national security issues.

Gerard Henderson of the Think Tank Sydney Institute said, "H. W. Bush and Clinton were held in much higher regard than George Bush is. Henderson recognizes Bush's strengths, but they do not make many friends overseas."

"It's a matter of style," said Gyngell. "Australia is still working to overcome its past history with the aborigines and emigration." Condoleezza Rice puzzles them, also.

Australians are a happy lot. A booming economy, generous social services, budget surpluses, and a stable consensus-minded government. Its isolation from the rest of the world contributes to their easy-going attitude. "We have to get along. We don't have a choice," said Henderson. "We are pragmatic and ideological."

"We have an eye on China but see nothing but opportunity there. Many Australians do not like Bush and were rooting for Kerry."

'He's my mate; I'd like to buy him a beer,' said one Aussie, who worries about the conflict over Taiwan. An issue Kerry did not address. It could be bad news for all concerned."

Instead of the new frontier that Bush promised, Karl Rove offers a new back tier. As Bush rushes backward, stifling possibilities, stirring intolerance, and confusing church and state issues, state laws, and facts with faith. He also favors teaching evolution, along with creationism. The laughter you hear is from London and Paris.

Bush presents a picture of a paranoid Right, the issue Kerry worked hard to avoid. It's a scary, repressive reality, far from the positivism Kerry tried to project. Bush's new health plan is out of control, and the costs are adding $700 billion to an over-inflated budget.

In many ways, we are becoming a backward country. Doug Sosnik called it a "political disconnect". We favor isolation (not as bad as in the '30s and Senator Vanderberg (R-MI). Bush however, favors nationalism, chauvinism (a GOP characteristic), and Puritanism (another Bush promotion along with his religious fanaticism).

Bush and Clinton tried earlier for some control on religious issues, but it has grown out of hand. Bush now seems to favor the 'devils over the angels'. Carter had the evangelicals on his side, too, but he tempered it with a case for social justice, and he lived the life he preached, which Bush does not.

Kathleen Parker called Kerry "a propagandist, an unkempt perennially juvenile one." He is the face of one party. When a man like Ben

Affleck is your spokesman (who couldn't deal with Jennifer Lopez in his personal life) and an inarticulate one at that, you lose the regular folks. They are busy paying their bills, making house payments, mortgages, and the like. They would rather vote for the common man Bush represented to them.

They saw Kerry as a pampered darling from the New York jet set and bistro crowd.

It's all in one great nutshell for all to see and think about. Getting back to the real America will not be easy for the Democrats, say the evangelicals. "You have to believe before you can see", so they say.

To many, this was, as many issues in the Catholic Church are, a violation of women's rights, just as birth control is. More and more Catholics follow their own volition, and the election of Pope Benedict VI is seen as a set backwards into the Middle Ages, when the Church was an inflexible giant ruling over docile people. Times have changed, but Catholics lie moribund in an extremely conservative Church. Even my sister, Janet, a former nun, was upset at the election of Pope Benedict. She had hoped for a more open Church, now that Pope Paul was gone.

This next year or two will be the most important for the Democratic Party. They face men, like Senator Bill Frist (R-TN), who are trying to roll back the senate's rights to filibuster against legislative proposals repugnant to their sense of law. Frist is joining together with the Bush fundamentalists, saying, "This is an issue of faith". This is truly only in his mind and in other like-minded senators.

If the Democrats do not band together more than they have done, they face extinction as a political force. Much will depend on how closely the party unites behind the activist groups, such as MoveOn. org or America Coming Together. It is important that the Party outlines the issues and then unites behind them as they were doing on the Social Security issues, much to the chagrin of the GOP. The Democrats have remained firm in their position.

We need to study Karl Rove's tactics more carefully and emulate them as closely as we may. Rove began to organize and re-strengthen the GOP not long after Bush was elected in 2000. He trained 7,000 activists in 21 states, a veritable army to counteract any potential Democratic opposition to Bush in 2004. This army campaigned door to door. If no one was home, they left literature extolling the Republican Party.

Most importantly, they laid a single line from which they never deviated. When questioned, their answers were robot-minded restatements of what each of them had said at the last house they visited. They were well trained Charlie McCarthys, and Rove was their Edgar Bergen.

The party must make inroads with male Bush supporters, who voted 61-38 for him, and with women, who went 54-45 for Bush. We have to make a stronger stand against terrorism. Their vote was the highest for Bush, 86-14, higher than the moral value vote of 79-21.

Kerry gained support in some areas, however. African-Americans voted 89-11 for him (though Bush tried mightily to steal their vote, as he did with the Hispanic vote, where the margin for Kerry was much less impressive, 55-42). If you have Hispanic friends or live with them, talk up the Democratic Party, the party of the workingman. Every vote will be important in the coming elections.

Kerry was a hit with first-time voters, 59-40, but their turnout was poor. Work with your younger friends concerning the value of their vote, get them registered, and make sure they vote. Also stress the futility of the Iraq War. Those who disapproved of the 'Bush War' voted 87-11 for Kerry.

There was the political vote against Cheney (who, next to Rumsfeld, is the least admired) and the neo-conservatives, 60-40. The jobs and economy disappointments also voted strongly for Kerry, 80-18, but these are intangible factors to be determined before the election.

How many Democratic leaders go to Applebee's to eat? We must tone down our love for the high life, be seen – as John Edwards was – celebrating his and Elizabeth's anniversary at McDonald's. It becomes a matter of which image you would like to project. Back in

1755, Benjamin Franklin said, "Those who would give up essential liberty to purchase a little temporary safety, deserve neither liberty nor safety."

Ohio Election – August 3, 2005

Although the election was far closer than expected and their candidate lost, the Democrats said that this election established momentum for them for the 2006 elections.

Former State Rep. Jean Schmidt, 53, defeated Iraq War veteran Paul Hackett, 43, by 3000 votes in the heavily Republican Ohio 2nd District. It was the best showing of a Democrat in the 2nd District since FDR days. This very red district became bluer, said Emmanuel, a representative from Illinois, who is the chairman of the Democratic National Committee.

The vote was outstanding in the election where Hackett openly called Bush a chicken hawk and a "son of a bitch". Many would like to do the same thing but Hackett is the first one with the balls to do so.

Bush as President

Bush and Cheney continue their lies about uranium from Niger and throw in Tonkin Gulf, Contras, and Watergate to boot. He has unveiled yet another plan for victory in Iraq. It's comforting to know he has a plan. Unfortunately, he says, "We cannot and will not leave Iraq until victory is achieved. We will never accept anything but complete victory." He continues to claim the war was justified, and Saddam was an evil man. (Not a word about Iran developing an A-bomb, the real threat.)

Molly Ivins calls the Bush plan "a blue-bellied fare-thee-well, but it's a little too late."

Bush claims 40 Iraq battalions are prepared to fight at the side of our forces. George Casey, our commander in Iraq, puts the number at 1+. Will he ever tell the American people the truth?

It does not seem wise for Bush to opt for complete victory. The American people are aware the war is not going well. His claims on reconstruction are likewise hard to accept. There are charges of rampant corruption, which must be overcome. There is little real government order.

Bush claims (with some justification) the New Orleans' reconstruction will be the greatest effort we face. It is second to what we face in Iraq to restore the carnage and destruction we have brought to the Iraqi people. It is not as Bush claims, "another mission accomplished." No amount of "spin" by Bush will change this fact.

HISTORY OF THE NEOCONS

The History

You cannot have a proud and chivalrous
Spirit if your conduct is mean and paltry,
For whatever a man's actions are,
Such must be his spirit.
Demosthenes
384-322 BC
Third Olympic

IT IS INTERESTING AND MAYBE a little cynical that I chose a quote by a feminist to put on the cover of the Neo-Con section. When I chose this, I did not know who he was, but thought that the quote more than identified who the neocons are.

Conversely, this is the type of men that he had to deal with during his lifetime, and these men could still live in the 18th Century with its prejudices and property ownership (including the ownership of women) still intact. Life, for this kind of people, has not changed much.

Even Demosthenes warned about the example one portrayed by his actions. In "Bush Family Values", we looked a little about how the Bush family came about their rise in our government.

In this section, we will look at the build-up of "wrong-wing" values. While we deal with Nixon, it would be prudent to remember whom he put into control of the CIA. "Prudent", you remember that word, was one of 41's favorites, which he used excessively.

We invite you to read the following pages with "prudence." See where all the tentacles of this political octopus take you.

History of Legacy of
Richard Nixon & Henry Kissinger

Hegel was right when he said that
We learn from history that man can never
Learn anything from history.
George Bernard Shaw
1856-1950

REPUBLICAN SCANDALS

Lest we forget, Nixon has been dead almost 10 years. Not only did he leave us the legacy of Watergate (the break-in of the Democratic Party's Washington DC office to procure information), but he left a long list of men to follow in his footsteps. Nixon introduced us to Donald Rumsfeld, Dick Cheney, Pat Buchanan, John McLaughlin, and Karl Rove. Plus a host of characters that follow the policies of the think tank that brought us the Watergate break-in along with disrespect for human rights, i.e., The Patriot Act, and now the outrage of covert spying.

In the latest release of the tapes, we learn that Nixon did not like Reagan much and felt uncomfortable around him. He also found him "strange". It may be that Reagan's honesty (?) was offsetting to the devious Nixon.

Highest on the list of deviousness was Henry Kissinger. Shakespeare referred to Hamlet as a strange mixture of nature's forces, much the same may be said of Kissinger. Part devil incarnate, extraordinary prevaricator, Dracula-like in the shedding of American blood in Vietnam, and the natives' blood in Suharto's Indonesia and East Timor.

There was substantial rumor that Kissinger was bribed with mining stocks not to protest and to turn his head the other way while Suharto's invasion of terror proceeded in East Timor and resulted in thousands and thousands of innocent deaths.

On December 5, 2003, we read of another bloody caveat in his tainted blood-soaked laurel wreath –Argentina! Not only is there a standing warrant in Great Britain for the arrest of Kissinger as a war criminal, it has been revealed as Nixon's henchman, Kissinger gave tacit U.S. approval to the Argentine foreign minister in their 1976 war against the leftists, which cost 30,000 lives.

"We wish you to succeed," he was told. So, roughly speaking, Kissinger's policies caused the death of 56,000 in Vietnam, an untold number in Indonesia, certainly more than 100,000, and possibly one million or more in Cambodia. And now an additional 30,000 in the Argentine dirty war.

The revelation of the meeting between Kissinger and Navy Admiral Cesar Augusto Guzzetti on October 7, 1976 is the first documentary evidence that the Gerald Ford Administration approved of the junta's tactics. Their tactics led to the death or disappearance of 50,000 people from 1975 to 1983.

This document further complicated Kissinger's legacy over his connection (known, but not revealed) to human rights violations around the world. This includes Bangladesh, Chile, and Indonesia.

Kissinger's detractors have suggested he revived Old West lynching to atone for and explain his foreign policies. Kissinger also told the admiral, "Look, our basic attitude is that we want you to succeed," he stated in the seven-page transcript. "I have an old-fashioned view that friends ought to be supported," he said. "What is not understood in the US is that you have a Civil War. We read about human rights problems but not the context. The quicker you succeed, the better."

The Argentine military began its war against leftist guerillas and suspected sympathizers in 1975. By the time of the meeting between Kissinger and Guzzetti, the machinery of murder and violent disappearances had received worldwide condemnation, and the U.S. was considering economic sanctions.

John Dinges, an assistant professor at the Columbia School of Journalism, is author of *The Condor Years*, a book on military dictatorships of the Southern coup. In it, he says, "Kissinger actually encouraged human rights violations in full consciousness of what was going on and would vacillate once the US would not protest." The transcript also revealed that when Robert Hill, the US Ambassador to Argentina, protested the human rights violations, he was told, "It was being done with the full support of your country (the US)". Hill couldn't believe it.

Mutual Fund Scandal
Flashback to the '60s

He that is of the opinion money will do everything
May well be suspected of doing everything for money.
Benjamin Franklin
1706-1790

A big offshore fund began to funnel large amounts of cash into American mutual funds. It was an attempt on its part to gain "market timing" privileges not available to all.

The drama began in September 2003, when Canary Capital partners, an unregulated offshore hedge fund, began their escapades. Almost an identical scenario unfolded in the '60s. The culprit then was Bernie Cornfield. Remember that high-handed dude? Those concerned about Canary may benefit from the Cornfield saga.

Cornfield had several run-ins with the regulators before he died in 1965. He is remembered for creating that "fund of funds", the Super fund that invested only in other mutual funds. By 1964, this fund was "plowing" hundreds of millions of dollars into domestic mutual funds. That made Bernie – no one called him Mr. Cornfield with a straight face – the most powerful and most worrisome investor in the whole mutual fund world!

The smell of money was his *eau de cologne*, and unregulated status suited him best. Federal law prohibited one fund from owning more than 3% of another, but Cornfield was exempt from that limit. By 1965, he owned 50% of one popular fund and almost 30% of another. He also controlled a stake in the Templeton Fund, the Wellington Fund, and a number of others. He held more power over mutual funds than God!

After Senator John Sparkman intervened in 1968, the exchange commission proposed to not allow the fund of funds concept entirely and to bar any fund or share or offshore from investing in other American funds. They worried about one investor being able to exert "undue influence" on the mutual fund market. They also worried about the large amounts of cash, which needed to be held by the funds, billions of dollars.

There was prescience to the SEC charges, which followed. Though still disagreeing on the fund of funds concept, where they allowed unregulated funds to buy up to 3% of a regulated fund. The limit did not prohibit the abuses appearing today.

The ban on the fund of funds concept has been lifted, but along the way the idea of protecting mom-and-pop funds has been forgotten. Should defense be built today? Some regulators think it is worth re-considering.

"It puts a lot of pressure on the system when hedge funds are seen to fire hope cannons at the smaller funds," said Catherine B. McGrath, a former regulator.

Whether hedge funds should have access is being debated, for this is a market for those of smaller means. It is part of their response being made to today's scandals, which are now out of hand.

Watergate Revisited!

Politics, n. - Strife of interests masquerading
As a contest of principles.
Ambrose Bierce
1842-1914
The Devil's Dictionary

GOP snooping through tactical memos (a well-known dirty Rove trick) on Bush's judicial nominees has grown into a Capitol Hill uproar – with comparisons to Watergate, accusations of court tampering and conservatives attacking senior GOP senators. Already two staffers implicated in going to newspapers and conservative groups with memos stored on a shared judiciary committee computer server have been forced to leave. Secret Service agents are providing the capital (for) interviewing legislative aides, and some senators are calling for an outside investigation – perhaps by the FBI – and punishment, if warranted.

"We know the dirty tricks have long been infecting the nation's politics. But they haven't infected the Senate or our committee until now," said Sen. Edward Kennedy. He and Sen. Richard Durbin (D-IL) learned that some of his staff memos had been taken off the shared computer.

"At Watergate," Kennedy said, "break-ins required a physical presence, burglary tools, lookouts, and getaway cars. Today, all that's required for theft may be a computer and the skills to use it and the will to break in." Parts of the memos contain Democrat strategies for blocking GOP Bush appointees.

The politics of that strategy ought to be investigated," Kennedy said. "It is also illegal if a person steals, embezzles, purloins or knowingly converts to his use or the use of others without authority sells, conveys, or disposes of any record." I wish just once they would admit to one of their many felonies.

Only a small number of Senate GOP members were involved, "headed by Karl Rove" and none were committee members. A final report at the end of February will be issued. The other senators have criticized both Orrin Hatch, committee chairman, and Bill Frist in this. We are still waiting for this report in 2006.

Manual Miranda, the lawyer who was dismissed and resigned from Bill Frist's office, said he thinks he did nothing illegal.

Saxby Chambliss

A healthy hated of scoundrels
Thomas Carlyle
1795-1881
No. 2, Model Prisons

His victory in the 2002 election based on the impugning of the reputation and good name of a true American hero and is one of the great aberrations in American politics. He emerged as a leader on defense, budget, intelligence, and agriculture, by becoming a craven despoiler of a truly great American.

Since his election, the budgets of veterans' hospitals have been cut way back and some have been closed. This could never have happened if Max Cleland was still senator.

Chambliss won the election, not on his own merits, but by following in the footsteps of the bigot, Richard Russell, and the equally biased, Sam Nunn. He showed himself to be a follower and not the leader he claims to be. Remember the stand and comments on patriotism as being "the last refuge of scoundrels."

"Paradise Lost"

Mission Accomplished

2700 U.S. servicemen and women have lost their lives in Iraq by late 2006, 15,000 more are maimed for life, and 100,000 Iraqis have been killed.

WAR

I hate war as only a soldier
Who has lived it can,
Only as one who has seen
Its brutality, its futility,
Its stupidity.

Dwight David Eisenhower
34th President, 1953-1961
Commander, Allied Forces
European Theatre, WWII

Private 1st Class Tristan Wyatt

Bella, horria bello, Et Thybrim
Multo spumantem sanguine cerno.
I see wars, horrible wars, and the
Tiber foaming with much blood.
Virgil
70-19 BC

PRIVATE FIRST CLASS TRISTAN WYATT'S story is typical. He said, "When the rocket propelled grenades hit our armored M-113 battle taxi, it blew my leg right off!" He was standing at the rear of the carrier, loading an M-40 machine gun at that moment. The rocket then passed through Sgt. Eric Castro's hip, spinning him to the floor; his leg barely attached to his body. Finally it shredded Sgt. Mike Meinen's right leg, which was partially torn off.

Score three new seriously wounded, zero dead. They were lucky. Were they wrong, these men who do not lose their lives? The real danger to these men would be bleeding to death before their wounds could be attended. Medics won the frantic race, which followed. This is part of the unseen war in Iraq. There are many bloody incidents like this, but most of the tales are never told.

The Pentagon, which makes terse announcements when soldiers are killed, fails to mention the wounded. Photographers are not allowed to photograph the litters carrying the wounded to Walter Reed Hospital. The wounded are only a part of what has been happening in wars since the beginning of recorded history. They are mentioned only if another solder has been killed during the same incident.

The Army doesn't tell the family their sons or daughters have been wounded. April 2004 was the bloodiest month of the Iraq War. The numbers of wounded kept rising. Daily attacks against our troops tripled and came from every quarter.

No soldier knows when he will be fired upon – sometimes at point-blank range. More people have been killed trying to keep the peace than have died during the war, and the toll of dead and wounded rises daily. The numbers changed so much and so fast as I wrote this that I had to take out the numbers!

The improvised explosive devices now being employed have increased the ranks of the wounded, especially in the extremities. Most of the wounded men and women survive. Better protection, better medical techniques, and faster evacuation learned in Vietnam on the edge of the battlefield have drastically reduced mortality. A great help are the wound-sealing potions, which lessen the loss of blood. There are new techniques to decrease amputations, which are most important.

Maimed soldiers are routinely flown to Landstuhl Regional Medical Center in Germany, where they are stabilized before being flown to Walter Reed or Bethesda Naval Hospitals in Maryland.

The Air Force has flown 1513 battle casualties, but the overall toll is more than 15,000, including soldiers suffering from stress and other medical conditions. Half of all battlefield deaths occur in the first half-hour. In the current war, one out of every eight wounded dies vs. one in three in all earlier wars. Of the almost 4,000 wounded flown to Germany, only a handful have died. Small mobile medical units are on hand immediately to treat and assist the wounded.

Navy Captain, H. R. Bohman, a 30-year veteran and a surgeon, was one of an eight-member medical team that performed surgery eight miles from Baghdad – the closest medical units to the city – as the Iraqi capital fell to U. S. forces in early April 2003. Marines are alive today that would have died if they had to be sent back as far as his troops were in the first Gulf War.

"I'm on the brink of being able to walk again," said Tristan Wyatt, 21, the wounded man mentioned at the beginning of this article. An RPG sliced off his left leg just two weeks after his 21st birthday. Ten surgeries have removed several more inches of his thigh. At Walter Reed Hospital, he has been fitted with a replacement leg. Wyatt was excited when he was getting the high-tech German-made C-leg. The top-of-the-line C-leg is made of carbon fiber, costs $100,000, and has a hydraulic knee. "Cool," said Wyatt.

The Great Patriotic Deception – Jessica Lynch

Our subtle tribes repress these patriot throats
And ask no questions, but the price of votes.
Samuel Johnson
1709-1784

It seemed to be the manna that the Republicans were looking and praying for. A woman Army private had been captured, abused, and beaten in an Iraqi hospital. "An example of why we were there to depose Saddam Hussein," said Bush.

(Frank Rich, our eloquent commentator on social mores and issues, stated afterwards, "PFC Jessica Lynch wasn't really Rambo any more and is no longer the 'Mona Lisa of Iraqi freedom'.")

In the beginning, her story was a note of better things to come. Lynch rescued from a hospital by Marine forces, etc. She fired at the enemy, though wounded, emptying her weapon. All these stories proved to be false. Her weapon jammed, and she never got off a single round. She wasn't taking out "any man who got in her way."

The way her story plays out is one of great grandstand stories of heroism gone astray – all a figment of PR men trying to put a glad face on the war. There was "no blaze of gunfire" as told in The LA Times account, just as the enthusiasm over the premature carrier landing proved to be – "No Mission Accomplished."

Who runs the news in this country, you may ask? Jessica Lynch's story was a pop romance. "Boys back home were crying for a chance to marry her." It was Rick Bragg, the LA Times reporter at his most maudlin. When they tried to interview her at the hospital air base in Germany, reporters were not allowed to see her or photograph the flag-draped coffins nearby. (The White House wishes to shield us from the flag-draped coffins and does not acknowledge the 15,000-plus maimed and wounded.)

This is dangerous distortion of war's cruel reality. Bush did not go to the funerals of Lynch's soldier friends killed in the ambush, nor was he at the 700-plus funerals of others involved. It's up to Jessica now to put a good show on the road, but she complains and says she has done nothing, and that's for certain.

She's a demure, blond, country girl. "She hails from Palestine, West Virginia, and always wanted to see the world, so she joined the U.S. Army and ended up fighting for her country in Iraq, simply because she could not get a job a Wal-Mart. She has ended up with a sign outside Palestine, West Virginia, declaring it to be the home of a real American hero," says the LA Times and Rick Bragg.

Jessica and her companions, assigned to a Humvee, were ambushed, and the Humvee crashed, injuring her severely. In the firelight, which followed, her rifle jammed and as her companions died, she never got off a shot. The lies said she got off many, was captured, and taken to an Iraqi hospital, where she was cruelly treated. Then a rifle squad fought it out with hospital personnel in an attempt to free her; the PR unit in Baghdad said they almost succeeded, but it was an overblown attempt to make her into a hero, which she was not.

But the nation was hungry for one and the PR unit complied with a fanciful story of Iraqi barbarism and cruelty. It just was not true. The hospital treated her gently and bound her wounds as if she were one of theirs. She never said "they wouldn't take her alive" as The Times said she did. The BBC called it one of the most stunning pieces of news management they had ever seen. She remembers only that she spent 10 days in the hospital, where her 10 broken bones were treated with care by Dr. Harith a-Houssona.

She is effusive in her praise for her captors and their treatment of her. Witnesses told us that the Special Forces knew that the Iraqi military had fled a day before they swooped on the hospital. "It was like a Hollywood film. The Special Forces cried, 'Go, go, go' with guns and guns without bullets, blanks, and the sound of explosions. They made a show for the American attack on the hospital – action movies the likes of Sylvester Stallone or Jackie Chan."

There was one more twist. Two days before the snatch squad arrived, Harith had arranged to deliver Jessica to the Americans in an ambulance. But as the ambulance, with Jessica inside, approached a checkpoint, American troops opened fire, forcing it to flee back to the hospital. The Americans almost killed their prize catch! Dr. Greg Argyras, at Walter Reed Hospital, said her injuries were inconsistent with sexual assault of which Jessica has no memory. But all of her story in the LA Times is simply not true.

Jessica has been home now for some time. "I'm not a hero," she contends. As ever, the PR boys persist in trying to make her into one. But Jessica, being the hero she really is, is not about to lie. She told Diane Sawyer in an interview, "I was just a soldier in the wrong place at the wrong time whose gun jammed during the chaos. I'm not about to take credit for something I did not do."

Now, that's honesty, and that makes her a hero in my mind. She is still adulated by her peers. She led the Thanksgiving parade in West Virginia, and was chosen to christen Carnival Lines' newest ship, Miracle, on February 27, 2004 in Jacksonville, Florida. She was the Miracles 'Godmother' and will be part of its first cruise – to compensate her for her injuries.

Jessica has been granted an 80% disability pension. (Shoshana Johnson, a black fellow prisoner, got 30%, a difference of $600 a month.) Jessica also has a one-million-dollar memoir and an appearance on David Letterman. It can't get any better than this, even for a real hero.

Thoughts on All Wars

War may sometimes be a necessary evil.
But no matter how necessary, it is always an evil,
Never a good. We will not learn how to live together
In peace by killing each other's children.
Jimmy Carter
1924-

Down in the depths of the Pentagon, deep inside the War Room, older men join together in plotting and formulating the war effort, at the current time on several fronts, Afghanistan, Iraq, Haiti, Iran, and China. Oh, sure, they call some of them 'police actions', yet no matter what name you give to the gunfire, young men and women die.

Every generation of youth has had a war to fight. Some were necessary and others were questionable. Wars bring out the poetry in many young men. In the earlier wars, like World War I, when young men went off to battle, there was a huge possibility that they would not return to their families. Of course, that still exists today, but technology and field medical techniques have advanced significantly so that absolutism of death is not as accepted as it was in earlier wars.

Wilfred Owen was one of the young men of earlier wars who wrote poetically about it. He was WWI's greatest poet, and going off to battle for him was the thing to do. He was a not a pacifist. He and others embraced Horace's dictum: *Dulce et decorum est, pro patria mari*. "It is good to die for the honor of England" was their cry.

It did not take long for them to lose their romantic fervor – the grim reality of mustard gas, the killing fields, the shells screaming overhead. At the battle of Verdun, French soldiers refused to fight; but did at the point of the bayonet after many were shot as cowards. Verdun –1916 – two million dead, one million on each side. Most died taking and losing the same stretch of shell-marked terrain over and over again.

War to Owen meant young men dead and dying, "their ruined lungs froth-corrupted. It was a war full of blood and vile, incurable sores on innocent tongues." There, too, was Trench Foot, where feet rotted off from standing in the ever-present water in the trenches.

Owen's poetry was about 'the pity of war' expressed in dark word portraits, in which dead and dying young men were stripped of any glory or sentimentality. He died at the age of 25, killed just one day before the Armistice of 11-11-1918. Owen is a revered poet in England and became one in the U. S. during the Vietnam War. War's terrible truth was the same in the '60s as it was 40 years earlier.

Owen was born in western England near the Welsh border. He was entering the literary life as war clouds gathered over Europe. He, too, caught the war fever and wrote a poem, in which he glorified Horace's dictum. After training, he wrote to his mother, "I do wish to fight", and he got his desire. He escaped death a number of times, once when a shell threw him into a ditch and fractured his skull. He was committed to a war hospital, where he met Siegfried Sassoon, who had been shell shocked.

He was haunted by his blood-soaked dreams. He and Sassoon embarked on an orgy of writing and created some of Owen and Sassoon's best poetry. He wrote on one wounded soldier, "heavy like meat/ and none of us/could kick him to his feet". It was here that he wrote:

Dulce et Decorum Est*

Bent double, like old beggars under sacks
Knock-kneed, coughing like hags,
We cursed through sludge
Till on the haunting flares we turned our backs
And towards our distant rest began to trudge.
Men marched asleep. Many had lost their boots
But limped on, blood-shod. All went male, all blind
Drunk with fatigue, deaf even to the hoots
Of tired, outstripped Five-Nines that dropped behind.
Gas! Gas! Quick, boys! - An ecstasy of fumbling
Fitting the clumsy helmets just in time;**
But someone still was yelling out and stumbling
And flound'ring like a man in fire or lime...
Dim, through the misty panes and thick green light,
As under a green sea, I saw him drowning,
In all my dreams, before my helpless sight,
He plunges at me, guttering, choking, drowning.
If, in some smothering dreams, you too could pace
Behind the wagon that we flung him in
And watch the white eyes writhing in his face,
His hanging face, like a devil's sick of sin;
If you could hear, at every jolt, the blood
Come gargling from the froth-corrupted lungs,
Obscene as cancer, bitter as the cud
Of vile, incurable sores on innocent tongues,
My friend, you would not tell with such high zest
To children ardent for some desperate glory,
The old lie: "Dulce et decorum est Pro patria mori."*
Wilfred Owen

*Sweet and fitting it is, to die for the Fatherland
** Poison gas turned men's lungs to mush and damaged the nervous
system. A small dose incapacitated a man. When Owen recovered,
he was sent back to the front and while leading his troops across a

canal into the teeth of German machine guns. He was killed in the crossing.

His mother received a telegram on November 11th, the day before the war ended. Posthumously, he was honored with a medal for "inflicting considerable losses on the enemy." He led his men the best he could and wrote of their sufferings for later use. He wished to report honestly what happened there. He knew one had to "take part" to be able to do that. Owen and other poets wrote eloquently about the horrors of war.

Other people have talked about "cannon fodder" in sending a country's youngest and brightest men off to be killed …for what? A whole English generation perished in World War I.

NEOCONS

The Neocons

It is of no account whether they are told
To go quickly, quickly to go, or to go
Quickly. The important thing is
That they should go.
George Bernard Shaw
1856-1950

THE NEOCONS ARE THE NEW, war-loving conservatives. They are the men (and women) who are (it seems) setting back civilization a couple of centuries. Led by Grover G. Norquist, Dick Cheney, Donald Rumsfeld, and Paul Wolfowitz, they wish to roll back the social order of the New Deal. Their first goal is to obliterate Social Security.

The quote at the top of this page says it all. They need to go before there is no longer an America that we can be proud of in this world. This section will examine these men a bit more. We have left the obvious women, like Laura Ingraham and Ann Coulter, out of this examination on purpose. Neither is in a position to do any more than bitch about the "liberals", and it takes a bitch to know a bitch.

While this may be bad enough, they are not responsible for meeting world leaders and making deals with them that affect the nation and the entire world. So, saying that, who are these men who have so much to do with how the world sees and reacts to us? And how we react, or should react, to these men.

Leo Strauss –
Guru of the Neo-Conservatives

*To become a popular religion, it is only necessary
For a superstition to enslave a philosophy.*
Dean Inge
1860-1954

Some have compared Strauss as the champion of democracy; he is anything but. Strauss condemned what he called "extreme democracy". His lifelong pre-occupation was the safety of "the few" from persecution by the multitude (the great unwashed).

The philosopher, Socrates, asked, "These men are those who understand that religion is nothing more than a lie, deference to the ruling class?" a stance Strauss applauded. "Philosophers who tell the awful truth about religion," he argued, "will meet the fate of Socrates." Death!

The philosophical elite should curry information from "the gentlemen" (the cadre of 100 or more men whose desire to rule the world). These sons of prominent and preeminent families run the government and can be enlisted to enact "harsh laws with teeth in them" and with the help of the Supreme Court keep the great unwashed in line and make the world safe from philosophers.

"If President Bush's Neo-con advisers are indeed taking a page from Strauss's play book, this should not be a cause of joy or celebration among the friends of democracy," said David Larsen, Professor of Law at Georgetown University.

Members of the Neo-Fascists' Cabal

The perfect bureaucrat everywhere
Is the man who manages to make
No decisions and escape all responsibility.
Brooks Atkinson
1894-1984
Once Around the Sun, 1951

PAUL WOLFOWITZ

O fret not after knowledge – I have none,
And yet my song becomes native with the warmth.
O fret not after knowledge – I have none,
And yet the evening listens
To what the thresh said.
John Keats
1795-1821

This man Wolfowitz appears to be a bundle of contradictions, all of them inside of him. Calm outwardly, he is drawn as a champion of bold action. He speaks in a soft, somewhat quivering voice. He paces the world stage today like an expectant father, which he is in a sense – to an idea of world domination.

His idea has taken on life of its own and is acting like a delinquent child. This idea is causing its parent, Bush, no end of woe. It was Wolfowitz and Wolfowitz alone, as super hawk of this administration, that soon after 9-11, pushed Bush into the present strategy.

Wolfowitz, the chess whiz, fell in love with the idea of national greatness as a child, much as Caesar did after conquering Gaul and Britain (and there it should have remained). Wolfowitz is regarded as Bush's chief intellectual who, in the footsteps of a Tallyrand counseling Napoleon, counseled Bush to transform the war on terror into a campaign of regime change by ousting Saddam Hussein.

Charles Fairbanks, a fellow grad student with Wolfowitz at the University of Chicago, a haven of right-wing thinkers, says this of Wolfowitz. "He was smitten with the idea and grandeur of great

nations. He had been reading the historian Livy's History of Rome",
and they talked on a long drive back to Chicago from New York City.
"Wolfowitz was in love with the idea of political greatness. I think
in the same way the young Lincoln was. He talked to me for hours
on the ancient Romans, what kind of men they were and all they
achieved in conquering the known world of their day. I believe he
believes in evolutionary change rather than conquest."

He wanted Bush to spread the idea of democracy into the Middle
East, especially in Iraq and the Islamic world. The intellectually bereft
Bush, the man of little foresight, was pushed to the brink of war.
Wolfowitz has been characterized as obsessed with Iraq. Many feel
he is biased in Israel's behalf and is Israeli-centric.

Wolfowitz told Keller, "I don't feel it is unreasonable to think
Iraq, properly managed – it's going to take a lot of attention, and the
stakes are enormous, much higher than Afghanistan – that it could
really turn out to be, I hesitate to say it, the first Arab democracy."
Wolfowitz has remained optimistic concerning his goals and the use
of using military force to pursue this aim.

"I do not like the term 'hawk', because it suggests going to war
with just anybody", he told New Perspectives Quarterly in the summer
of 2002. "If there are political and diplomatic ways to achieve this,
I would approve them over the use of force. The result we want is to
protect American interests." Wolfie, as Bush calls him, has written
widely on U.S. national security interests.

He was born in Brooklyn, NY on December 23, 1943. His father,
a Polish Jew, emigrated to the United Sates from Warsaw in 1920. He
later became a math professor at Cornell where Wolfie sent most of
his youth. The U. S role and moral responsibility were often topics at
the family dinner table.

He studied under Albert Wohlsetter, the intellectual father of the
Cold War hawks. This includes Perle and Wolfie as members of the
thinking that led to the Korean War involvement, the Vietnam War,
Grenada, and other containments. He was a member of Team B, a 10-
member group appointed by the CIA, which questioned intelligence

reports on the Soviets. They assert Russia was an even grater threat than was supposed, but critics found these ideas to be exaggerated.

Dennis Ross criticized Team B, but mentioned Wolfie for special praise as being more "intellectually open." He helped to initiate maritime predisposition of ships. The strategy involved cargo ships laden with military supplies in the Persian Gulf. Twelve years later, it was the backbone of Operation Desert Shield in the Gulf War.

Wolfowitz served as dean and professor of international relations at SAIS, a division of Johns Hopkins University, which is widely regarded as one of the world's leading graduate schools in international relations with 750 students enrolled.

As dean, he led a successful capitol campaign, which raised $75 million and doubled the school's endowment. Under his strident leadership, he modernized a new faculty. Fellow hard-liners and programs were added to shift the school's focus from the cold war to the modern era of globalization.

Prior to becoming Deputy Secretary of Defense from 1989-1993, he served as under secretary of defense for Dick Cheney, a fellow hard-liner. He was responsible for reshaping strategy and forcing posture at the end of the cold war. Under his leadership, the policy staff played a major role in reviewing plans for the Gulf War and raised $50 billion in allied financial support and prevented Iraq from opening a second front with Israel. They also worked on regional strategy, the base force, and two nuclear initiatives that led to the elimination of thousands of Soviet nuclear weapons.

Under Reagan, Wolfowitz served for three years as ambassador to Indonesia and earned a reputation as an able ambassador and a tough negotiator on behalf of American intellectual property and as being a public advocate of political openness and democratic values. Jakarta was voted the fourth best-run embassy in 1989.

Prior, he served three and a half years as assistant secretary of state for East Asian and Pacific Affairs, where he was in charge of 20 countries. He worked to improve relations with Japan and China and played a central role in coordinating U.S. policy toward the Philippines that supported the transition period after Marcos.

The desire to oust Hussein was shelved until George W. Bush became president and became deeply concerned about WMDs, which to this day – in 2006 – have never been found! But they were used as a pretext for the US invasion of Iraq. Wolfie had been urging Bush to invade Iraq since 9-11. He did not feel that the Taliban and bin Laden were the greatest threats to our security. He was very disappointed that we were not greeted as liberators in Iraq, a big point of his invasion plans along with Rumsfeld and Cheney.

He has hailed the U. S. efforts in Afghanistan, which disrupted bin Laden's Al Qaeda terrorist network, as a success. He told The New York Times, "it showed the U.S. ability to employ a small force on the ground and leverage it in a dramatic way" (guided missiles were also used).

Bush always urged Wolfie to press his case. Since he left his teaching post at Yale to join the Nixon gang, he has served under every president, save Clinton. Only after 9-11 did he reverse his position to remove Hussein before he could ship his WMDs around the Middle East. Wolfie contends he does not work out of a set of principles but "in the national interest" and only he knows that that is! It's a nice catchphrase that is better than "bring them on" or "if you're not with us, you're against us."

After Bush entered his second term, he appointed Wolfowitz head of the World Bank, where he currently serves.

DOUGLAS J. FEITH

In Bush's first administration, Feith served as Under Secretary of Defense for Policy and Works, planning guidance and force policy, Department of Defense relations with foreign countries, and the Defense Department's role in U.S. government inter-agency policy making. He promoted Perle's brainchild to promote Turkey under Perle's international advisors. He and Perle were the only stockholders. Perle was paid $98,000 a year and Feith, $60,000 yearly. Both supported Bosnia in 1992.

For 15 years he was an attorney of Feith, Zell, PC in Washington, DC with offices in Israel that handled, as their primary client, the Israeli military.

From March 1984 to September 1986, he was a Deputy Assistant Secretary of Defense for Negotiations Policy. He also served on Perle's National Security Policy Committee as a special counsel. In 1981-82, he worked as a Middle East specialist. His writings on international law and foreign and defense policy have appeared in The New York Times, Wall Street Journal, Commentary, and The New Republic. He is a contributor to a number of books. He holds a J. D. (magna cum laude) from Georgetown University and an A. B. from Harvard.

Feith was one of the neocons' hatchet men. He is no longer part of the Bush Administration.

ANDREW H. CARD, JR.

Andrew Card, Bush's former chief of staff, was highlighted in a biography on First Gov, the official Web site of the White House. It said, "On November 26, 2000, Andrew H. Card, Jr., was appointed to be Chief of Staff in the presidential administration of then Texas Governor George W. Bush. Mr. Card was chosen because of his impressive service record in the public and private sectors, including service in the administration of two former presidents."

From 1988 to 1992, Card served in President George H. W. Bush's administration as assistant to the president and deputy chief of staff.

From 1992 until 1993, Mr. Card served as the 11th U.S. Secretary of Transportation under President George H. W. Bush. In August 1992, at the request of President Bush, Secretary Card coordinated the administration's disaster relief efforts in the wake of Hurricane Andrew. Later that year, Card directed President Bush's transition office from the Bush Administration to the Clinton Administration.

Prior to being named chief of staff for the administration of Governor Bush, Card was vice president of government relations for General Motors until 1999. His private sector background includes work for Chrysler Corporation, Ford Motor Company, and General Motors Corporation.

Andrew Card graduated from the University of South Carolina with a Bachelor of Science degree in engineering. He attended the United States Merchant Marine Academy and the John F. Kennedy School of Government at Harvard University and has received numerous honorary degrees and awards.

A native of Holbrook, Massachusetts, Andy and his wife, Kathleen, have three children and four grandchildren.

RICHARD PERLE –
MISCREANT EVILDOER IN THE BACKGROUND

All that is necessary for the triumph of evil
Is that good men do nothing.
Edmund Burke
1729-1797

I was taken by Perle's appearance the last time I saw him on C-Span. The first time he had dark circles under his eyes and the malevolent look of a hit-man character on the Sopranos. The second time he had been made over – no dark circles, a new wardrobe – and he looked at least 10 years younger than his real age.

Perle is the don of hard-liners in the Bush Defense Department. Until recently, he was the chairman of the Defense Policy Board (DPB) and a shaper of U.S. foreign policy. His central conviction was, he told The American Spectator in the November-December 2001 issue, that "it is fundamentally to self-defense that we act preemptively to forestall attacks on our country." This conviction, shared by

Wolfowitz, Rumsfeld, and Cheney became one of the guiding foreign policies of the Bush II Administration.

Eric Alterman called Perle – along with Wolfowitz – "the primary intellectual architects of Bush's foreign policy." His commentaries have revealed a striking pattern.

Thomas Amestad wrote in US News and World Report (11/25/2002), "He often seems to telegraph touch positions before they become accepted wisdom in the White House." He is open to attack by those who do not share his hard-line positions or approve the course of America's recent foreign policy, which took an amazing turn by the U.S. invasion of Iraq and the toppling of Saddam Hussein.

Perle was born in New York City on September 16, 1941 and his family later moved to California, where he went to Hollywood High School. He became a friend of fellow student, John Wohlsetter, whose father was an intellectual leader of Cold War nuclear strategy. He later became a mentor to Perle and Wolfowitz, among others.

Perle got a Bachelor of Science degree at University of Southern California and his Master's degree in political science at Princeton. From 1969-1980, he was aide to Senator Henry "Scoop" Jackson, a centrist Democrat who was fiercely anticommunist and who believed in supporting democracies abroad, even it if implied military force (as the twig is bent, so grows the tree).

Under Jackson, Perle became one of Washington's most powerful figures, who worked to develop a hard line against the Soviets. Perle wrote a novel, *Hard Line*, published in 1992, in which policymakers were engaged in a battle of ideas. "They fought not with AK-47s, but with memos, position papers, talking points, leaked news breaks, and wore dark suits." It was unrestrained warfare; there was no rulebook.

Perle served as assistant secretary of defense for international security policy under Reagan. He established a reputation on nuclear matters, where one of the initiatives became Star Wars. He was an ardent supporter of the plan and rallied against all the liberal critics.

Perle was an extreme critic of all nuclear arms-control measures and was against limits on ICBM, feeling that both kinds of weapons were necessary to counter any threat of the Soviets. In an article in The New York Times wrote on March 16, 1987 of Perle's retirement form the Defense Department. "In 6 years he (Perle) has dominated administration policy on arms control talks and trade controls on high tech exports. The common passion in these pursuits is an abiding mistrust of the Soviet Union."

Perle replied that he had tried to keep the U.S. from signing a "single arms control agreement that damaged our security." The article concluded the "guiding light" behind Perle's work was mistrust. Perle had a role in blocking the Salt II nuclear arms agreement with the Soviets.

Asked to name his most important contribution, Perle said, "I have kept the U.S. from signing any arms control agreement that would have threatened our security." For the second Bush II Administration, Bush nominated Perle to be the U.S. Ambassador to the United Nations. After stormy debate, his position was confirmed. He presently serves in that capacity and continues to stir up controversy at the UN as he has done in other positions. John Bolton replaced him in a controversial appointment.

DONALD RUMSFELD –
PENTAGON WARLORD

As we know, there are known knowns.
There are things we know. We also know there are
Known unknowns. That is to say we know there
Are some things we do not know. But there are
Also unknown unknowns, the ones
We don't know we don't know.
Donald Rumsfeld
February 12, 2003
Trying to backpedal from a
reporter's question about WMDs in Iraq

It's almost as if Donald Rumsfeld is trying to out-hawk Wolfowitz or vice-versa. It is certain the war in Iraq is the result of both men having the easily suggestible president's ear.

Rumsfeld is a meticulous worker, deciding which troops will go and where. He worked for months with generals and admirals, inculcating them in the drill, working, and reworking the plan for invading Iraq.

General Tommy Franks wrote the plan but that misses the point, because Rumsfeld became the architect. Initially the invasion would start in Kuwait, then switch to Turkey and the North and from Jordan in the West.

Paul Bremer said on NBC's "Dateline", "We did not really see the insurgence coming." This from the man appointed by Bush to oversee Iraq. If they missed that, what else did they miss?

Bush sabotaged these plans with his arrogant disregard for diplomacy. "You are either with me or against me" has become extremely passe.

Disputes arose on the size of the invading army. Franks wanted 250,000, Rumsfeld, 100,000. While Rumsfeld accepted more, he remained in charge! "He wants to go after the WMDs," said an officer. But he hasn't forgotten the SCUD missiles.

Rumsfeld felt that once the shooting war started tanks and armored vehicles should rush ahead and be in Baghdad in weeks, not months. He was correct – Saddam's forces refused to fight. In a ridiculously short period of time the troops rode into Baghdad.

"The war is over – and we have won," cried an exultant George Bush, but he was mistaken, as a guerilla war ensued. Today almost more than 2,500 are dead and 15,000 maimed and wounded.

Once we were in Baghdad, there were no plans for a follow-up on what to do. The Iraqis rioted and tore down and burned their infrastructure. Far worse, no soldier ever knew when he would become a target for rifle fire or carefully placed bombs.

Rumsfeld's carefully laid battle plan was losing out to a rag-tag force of Iraqis determined not to give up their country. The question arises – who is to blame for this debacle? Since Rumsfeld took the lead, we have him to thank.

A good battle planner, he failed to have a plan to win the hearts of the people, and until he does, good and fine young men and women will continue to get blown up and die. As of February 2005, almost 2500 have paid for Rumsfeld's inability to unite Iraq on our side.

Could it be possible that:

1. Iraq can never be a democracy?
2. The Iraq civilization reached its zenith in Mesopotamia?
3. The Middle East cannot be converted to the American ideals of life?

We would find out June 30, 2004, but after that election date, nothing much changed. People were being taken hostage and beheaded. The American-led government passed power to the Iraqis who seem unable to control their own people. Civil war has broken out in many areas. There is much chattering about how, at least, Saddam kept relative peace there.

Rumsfeld's path to power has followed a most circuitous route. During WWII, he attended five different schools in four different regions of the United States. He sold and delivered newspapers and magazines, raised chickens, watermelons, and cantaloupes. He dug clams in the Pacific Northwest. He was in a hurry and in 1962, he ran for Congress. He was in DC at the age of 30, during President Kennedy's last year in office. He was noticed from the start and he became one of the Young Turks in the House along with fellow House members, Gerald Ford, Dick Cheney, Bob Dole, and George Herbert Walker Bush. He and his pals formed an informal club.

Rumsfeld served four terms before joining the Nixon Gang. He rose through menial tasks but his approach was far from conventional. He was appointed NATO ambassador and maintained close ties to Allard Lowenstein, the famed liberal organizer. They scratched one another's backs.

From the beginning, Rumsfeld is seen as tough and transparently political. He was so organized he caught Gerald Ford's eye. When Nixon resigned, Ford brought "the long knife" Rumsfeld back form NATO to the totally disorganized White House. He was equal to the task and kept his sharp knife, which he has maneuvered to keep rivals in line.

Rumsfeld kept a secret agenda. "One never knows what he is thinking." He is the greatest insider of them all, if you can believe it. More so than the devious, ever plotting Henry Kissinger. With Rumsfeld's urging, Ford appointed Dick Cheney. And the rest is history.

As the end of George W's first administration drew near, there were loud cries for Rumsfeld's firing or resignation. True to Bush's insensitivity to the masses, he gave Rumsfeld a pat on the back. And today in 2006 he's still head of Defense.

CHALMERS JOHNSON

Although tyranny, because it needs no consent,
May successfully rule over foreign peoples,
It can stay in power only if it destroys
First of all the national institutions
Of its own people.
Hannah Arendt
The Origins of Totalitarianism

Chalmer Johnson's book, *The Sorrows of Empire*, makes many salient points for cogitation, lays it all on the level. We have 736 known military installations in countries around the world (Saipan leads) and numerous secret bases.

We are in favor of 50 to 56 regime changes and are led by men like Paul Wolfowitz, whose mantra is "I don't care how many of them don't like us, just as long as they fear us." Where do we get the cannon fodder now that we have used up and disrupted the lives of the National Guard – again, I ask, where is the Army that a $430 billion Defense budget supports?

There are more blacks than Caucasians in the Army, and the women's army is composed of 40% minorities who rule. Jessica Lynch joined the Army because she couldn't get a job at the Wal-Mart the next town over.

The Soviet Union's collapse had four causes and we are now facing the same ones. It may deter Washington's secret policies built around the idea of the U. S. ruling the world (just as Rome did). It justifies the expensive Star Wars and will keep other countries from landing on the moon – it will some day be one of our military bases.

The U. S. may not be able to rule alone and may have to take on coalition partners like who? Tony Blair and Colin Powell (now Condoleezza Rice) are persona-non-grata in Europe, and England has lost any standing she once may have had.

Europe knows Powell lied to the UN in his speech there – he knew Iraq had no WMDs and no ties to 9-11 or Al Qaeda. It's all part of the conspiracy the U.S. is using to gain the support of other nations.

Britain ruled India with Indian conscripts and a few division of her own as they tried to civilize the natives (India had 5 million) and bring the English culture to that land's ancient culture. Not a bad concept, save for the hundreds of thousands of Indians they massacred and allowed to be massacred in the interval. Religious disputes raged; a parallel is Iraq, where two or three religious groups were at war with one another. Now, the Kurds have been included in their new constitution.

President James Madison warned of the loss of the republic. "Never place all the responsibility in the hands of one man." Yet we did just that. We gave Bush absolute power to declare war on Iraq. We are now in danger of losing the Bill of Rights and the Constitution. Bush is known as the "little emperor" in England, and the largest demonstration turned out in protest of his visit there to bolster the government of his "pet poodle" Blair, who makes Neville Chamberlain look like a diplomatic genius by comparison.

KARL ROVE

WHEN WILL THE AMERICAN VOTERS wake up to the insidious evil Karl Rove represents? [In his new job, you never see Bush without Rove toiling to one side.] Rove used the same reprehensible tactics against Ann Richards in the Texas governor's race by impugning her character with hints of lesbianism and her support of gay issues.

The man has few, if any, scruples, which all add up to a lack of character. He lies, insinuates, manipulates, and uses any little matter at hand to destroy the Bush challengers. Look at what he has done in the past.

He and Tom DeLay make a good pairing. Both live at the bottom of a barrel of unconsciousness unparalleled in history. We can add the hired guy, Jeff Gannon (Guthert), a gunslinger hired to ask fluff questions at the daily news handouts. He helped in the smears against Daschle in South Dakota. Anything he says is an out and out lie, causing people to take Bush's side. Since 2003, he has been invalidating the efforts of honest people.

Rove's Mystery –
A Largely Unknown Story
Now Known as the Plame Affair

Let me see if I have this straight. President Bush is on record as saying, "He would fire anyone who ever intentionally revealed a covert operative's identity" (a charge, which George H. W. Bush called an offense punishable by hanging).

Did Karl Rove identify Valerie Plame as a CIA operative? Here the waters become very murky, and a war broke out, which TIME called "five years of political warfare in concentrated form."

Ken Mehlman, the GOP national chairman, said Rove was the victim of "blatant partisan political attacks". But was he? Scott McClellan had called the notion that Rove was involved "ridiculous". The first President Bush called anyone who exposed intelligence assets as "the most insidious of traitors."

Bush quickly backtracked on his earlier statement of "firing anyone who had leaked Joseph Wilson's wife's name and blown her cover", stating instead, "anyone who had been convicted of doing so" and added, "this is a serious investigation."

The story began to unravel back in 2003 when Valerie suggested Wilson as the logical choice to send to Niger to see if Saddam Hussein was actively involved in the purchase of yellowcake uranium for building nuclear weapons. Joseph Wilson IV, a flamboyant ex-diplomat, left the foreign service for the greener pastures of business consulting. He is a veteran of political wars.

The Bush Administration intent on selling the story of WMDs posed by Iraq's weapons program is no small deal. They would soon turn it into an effort by Saddam to go nuclear.

Wilson spent a week in Niger, talking to local officials about these allegations. He came to the conclusion that the yellowcake charges were totally unfounded. He reported his findings to the CIA. His report never reached the White House.

This saga might have ended right there, but Bush, Cheney, Rove, and other officials decided to make the yellowcake charge a piece of the weapons charge, which included nuclear weapons. On his march to war, Bush rebuffed concerns from some at the CIA. He included the yellowcake charge in his State of the Union address in 2003 with the now 16 famous words, "The British government has learned that Saddam Hussein recently sought significant quantities of uranium from Africa."

Wilson was floored and became very furious at Bush's charge. He set out to refute Bush's words, working through his back channels. He told The New York Times' Nicolas Kristof of his findings in Niger on May 6, 2003. In so doing, Wilson caught the attention of Cheney's office and others involved in the war program.

Bush has always found himself on the defensive about WMDs. Wilson was not alone. Democrats, reporters, and a few former officials publicly wondered had Bush led the country into war based on the flimsiest of evidence? Even on outright false intelligence?

Cheney's office set out to cut off the legs of their critics, Wilson in particular. By the time The Washington Post published Wilson's allegations about the intelligence (without naming Wilson as the source) on page 1 of the June 12, 2003 edition, and just one month before the Plame Affair was made public, Wilson was on Cheney's radar screen.

The more Wilson pushed the issue, the more determined the White House and Bush became to push back against a man they thought was an irresponsible provocateur.

At this point Wilson acted mainly behind the scenes. On July 6, 2003, he penned an op-ed in The New York Times, writing a forceful answer to his White House critics, "Some of the intelligence related to Iraq's nuclear weapons programs was twisted to exaggerate the Iraqi threat."

The Bush gang replied quickly in the usual Cheney mode. They used the simple rule of politics: kill the story before it kills you. Word spread by Cheney and Bush that Wilson was a Democrat, a supporter of Bush's political opponents, who was sent on an inconclusive mission that people in power knew nothing about. Then they went further.

Two days after Wilson went public, Robert Novak, the right wing columnist, told Karl Rove that he was hearing that Wilson had been sent on his mission at the suggestion of his wife, who worked for the CIA. "Rove replied, 'I heard that, too', said a lawyer, who heard their conversation. Rove said that Novak told him her name was Valerie Plame, the first time he had ever heard her name." (It seems incongruous that a lawyer would be nearby to conveniently hear this now very important conversation.)

On July 7, 2003, Bush and Colin Powell went on a trip to Africa, and Powell carried with him a memo on Plame, which he discussed with Bush. This is central to the case.

Officials are trying to determine whether the White House officials shared information on the State Department memo or from conversations with reporters on Air Force One, as Rove has testified. Now Rove defenders have come to his aid, saying he hadn't done anything to saying he hadn't done anything wrong, that Plame wasn't really a secret agent anyway or if she was, Rove didn't know that.

He only brought it up because he didn't want reporters to write a bad story about Wilson's false charges. Besides, it was a reporter who blew Plame's cover to him in the first place. (Novak - but I find it hard to believe that Novak would know something, which Rove didn't know.)

Orrin Hatch (R-Utah), that great defamer of Anita Hill, has sprung to the defense of Rove. "I don't for one second believe (Rove) would do anything like what his opponents are accusing him of doing. He is too 'decent' a person and, frankly, he is too smart." Pardon me while I regurgitate.

The issue matters because it's all part of the internal warfare going on in the Bush Administration, the intelligence committee, and the continuing debate over the Iraq War. The rights of the First Amendment, which guarantee free press, has become involved with a reporter being sentenced to jail and another being forced to reveal his source. [When prosecutor Fitzgerald finished his findings, only Scooter Libby was charged, not Rove.] The endless stream of ruthlessness and political prevarication provides ongoing fascination.

Many on the sidelines have long wishes to hang Karl Rove by his thumbs and let him dangle in the wind. They do not believe in the DC mythology, which states that Rove is unassailable. How could such a gentleman do anything wrong – visably, that is? He may have left a few horse heads here and there, a tarantula or a black widow or two, but to be caught "inflagre delicado" –impossible!

We are all well aware from his rigged elections in Texas and on the national scene. This is a man Nixon wished had been part of his team.

"Could he have become a spy?" TIME asks. Once you have lived for means of discrediting the opposition, any task would be permissible. Rove has insisted from the very beginning that he didn't know Valerie Plame's name or leak it, and he is fully cooperating with the probe.

It is demonstrably true that Rove didn't tell Cooper (ordered by TIME to turn over his notes) her name, but rather referred to her as Wilson's wife. (Since Wilson has but one wife and her name is easily available on Google or a host of other sources but not her affiliation, Democrats were led to believe that they had Rove this time. The GOP feels the new evidence exonerates him.)

Karl Rove has a reputation in DC that keeps everyone from getting on his bad side. When Rove sets out to get someone, he assails him. It may be his hatred for them that convinces him they are corrupt, vile, and dangerous. Destroying them is a special delight because he sees them as stupid and not worth any special consideration.

Wilson, by his disclosures, had placed himself directly in Rove's gun sights, but Wilson was not stupid. He is a former ambassador, who has a gallery of photos of him and past presidents, world leaders, and dignitaries of all kinds. Bush's father once called Wilson a "hero" for his service in Baghdad during the first Gulf War.

Wilson's charge was the most damning and damaging charge leveled against Bush's administration. It put all Bush's intelligence about the war in question. The CIA asked him to go to Niger to check out the yellowcake story. When his report did not contain the evidence Bush hoped for, he discarded Wilson's intelligence.

When Wilson's charge was levied, Fitzgerald was sent out from Chicago to learn how, after one week following the op-ed column appeared, Wilson's wife's cover was blown. How did the White House learn of her status and connection to Wilson in the first place and how did it come to be discussed with reporters? TIME says Special Investigator Fitzgerald has shown special interest in a classified State Department memo that was forwarded to the White House the day after Wilson's article appeared.

The memo was sent to Colin Powell, but he was traveling in Africa with Bush that day. The memo, dated June 10, 2003, identified Plame and discussed her role in sending her husband to Niger. The memo was requested by Under Secretary Mark Grossman after The New York Times and Washington Post began reporting on an intelligence-gathering trip to Niger by a former U. S. diplomat. Sending it to Powell was a way to censure Wilson for going public.

Fitzgerald has circulated the memo to those who have clearance on the case. He wants to know if they have ever seen it before, as he thinks it was circulated aboard Air Force One. It's part of the thorough way he does things. Some of the reporters traveling to Africa were told that a low-level member of the CIA sent Wilson to Niger. Fitzgerald asked them to look into this more deeply and report to him.

Fitzgerald was also curious if any member of Bush's staff had stayed at the White House while he was in Africa and if they had the memo. He also wanted to know if they had shared it before Wilson went public. Libby, Rove, and Rumsfeld all denied ever seeing the memo.

Rove said he had learned Plame's identity from someone, probably Robert Novak, who walked around during this time like a Cheshire cat that had swallowed a canary.

The administration spent the following week on damage control. George Tenet took the heat, stating the CIA should not have approved the uranium claim in Bush's address. Rove also spoke that week with Cooper, who also called Rove to inform him of his new assignment for TIME and to introduce himself. Cooper spoke to Rove in "double secret background".

Cooper then emailed his superiors, Michael Duffy and James Carney, afterward. "Rove's big warning – don't get too far out on Wilson". Cooper wrote that Rove had disparaged Wilson for a "flawed and suspect" explanation for the basis of the trip. Rove also said Cheney had authorized the trip, not the CIA director. This is a claim never made at this point by the cowed Wilson.

Cooper in his conversation with Rove added it was "Wilson's wife, who works on WIND (Weapons of Mass Destruction), who authorized the trip". Rove also implied strongly, Cooper said, "there's still plenty to implicate Iraqi interest in obtaining uranium from Niger". (Rove is like a bulldog – once the bit is in his mouth, he is reluctant to dislodge it. Cheney and Rumsfeld have this same problem.)

No one involved can explain why Plame's name appeared in the first place. Was Wilson tainted by his association with the CIA, whose agents were skeptical about Iraq's threat in the first place? In his book, *Politics of Truth*, Wilson denies Valerie authorized the trip. He maintained all along that Bush and Rove conducted a "smear job" on him. Surprise, surprise!

Rove's associates deny this, for all that's worth. I don't believe Rove would pass up any opportunities to impugn Wilson's veracity. Rove's lawyer, Robert Luskin, said Wilson not writing about his wife, Valerie, lent weight to charges that Cheney's office had deliberately ignored Wilson's findings. Luskin further stated that it was true about the yellowcake, but he saw Wilson as overstating the importance of his mission. Wilson still maintains that yellowcake should never have been included in the State of the Union address. Cheney maintains that Wilson's mission did not resolve the issue of yellowcake one way or the other.

Why does the issue of Plame's identity or who outed her have so much importance? The reporters may have been in the "loop" for some time. The Washington Post reported that Libby learned her name from a reporter, too. Tim Russert, under oath, told Fitzgerald about a call from Libby, giving him clearance to testify about their conversation, and he reiterated that he was not Libby's source.

"It would be better if Bush and Company were considered leakees, not leakers," Wilson says, It's just one more challenge Fitzgerald has to face in making his case. "It's one thing if Rove heard her name from a reporter that she was a CIA operative, casually confirmed that he had already heard that to another reporter (Novak) and incidentally spread the word to another (Cooper)." It's another story if the Bush gang made an effort to gather information on Wilson, then discovered that his wife was a CIA officer and carried it out as a strategy to discredit Wilson. This included outing Plame to a number of reporters. It's more former than latter, depending on which side you are on. It's still another thing to do the second and pretend, under oath, that you had done the first.

Did Karl Rove break the law? That is the question. He insists he did not identify Plame by name. A simple Google search turned up the name of Wilson's wife – Valerie Plame, the mother of twin boys. A court must decide whether Rove mentioned that she worked for the CIA with the specific intention of blowing her cover. Whether Cooper did not tell Rove she worked for the CIA undercover, what is certain is that Plame was still classified as a covert operative at the time of the leak and as recently as the late 1990s she worked as a non-official cover (NOC) officer. She was one of a select group of operatives within the CIA who are placed in neutral-seeming environments abroad, and they collect secrets.

They know the government will disavow any connection to them should they be caught in the line of duty. NOC operatives cost millions of dollars to train and support. As a result of Plame's outing, she could no longer work undercover. Her cover blown, she resigned her position at the CIA. She had been an agent for many years.

The Democrats have tried mightily to get Rove's security clearance lifted, to no avail. In the White House, there is little sign of worry or panic. They still feel that Rove is bulletproof and in charge.

Plame has been sacrificed, as has all the money that went into training her. Her record is that of one who has held highly sensitive posts over the last 20 years. She worked for a CIA front company, which no longer exists. She is beautiful, ambitious, and very intelligent. She was moved back to DC in 1987 in the Alarick Affair, but her marriage to the highly visible Wilson limited her use. She then worked for the CIA's clandestine branch as a manager of others on assignment overseas. Another of Plame's valuable assets as her experience in nuclear proliferation.

Plame was still under protective status when her cover was blown by Rove or Novak, take your pick. Her usefulness has been damaged, and she is now a housemother raising her children. Wilson saying, "I went on a mission for the CIA" hasn't helped hide her visibility.

CIA officials feel the leak is indefensible and many are angered by Plame's claim that she was not a covert agent. Why, I cannot discern. There are lots of CIA agents, who hold their status, and it's not up to Rove or anyone else to end their status.

Plame's blown cover has helped other countries' agents retrace her steps overseas to gain knowledge of other CIA operatives. Being a spy is not a glamorous occupation. You recruit others to do the spying for you. "Information like this travels very quickly around the world," said Jim Marcinkowski, a former agent and now a city attorney in Royal Oak, Michigan.

Joe Wilson feels more or less vindicated by his actions of outing Bush's claims, which demeaned him. He does not feel that he was a whistleblower, who ran afoul of Bush and the White House. He has only tried to right the character assassination perpetrated by the White House. He tried to call attention to a few of the underhanded tactics of the Bush Administration. Nothing more, nothing less.

Rove Uses Iran-Contra Tactics

When Elliott Abrams stood in front of a federal judge in October 1991 and pleaded guilty to two misdemeanor accounts of withholding information from Congress, few imagined he would ever return to government. Surprise!

Fourteen years later, Abrams helped to shape the White House policies for the Middle East. He was not alone. Other key Iran-Contra conspirators included Richard Armitage, Casper Weinberger, and John Poindexter, who resurfaced as key players in the War on Terror.

We all know about second chances, but only after they have paid their debt to society and taken the responsibility for their transgressions. In true neocon fashion, the administration is now returning to Iran-Contra-style tactics in attempting to sweep the Karl Rove incident under the rug and out of the public eye. This, despite breaking news that Rove's testimony in Congress regarding the nature of the leak, contradicts the earlier stories given to the press.

In the end, it looks like a heck of an inside job for an administration that campaigns as a group of Washington insiders.

The New York Times stated that an informant told the CIA that Iraq had abandoned a major element of its nuclear arms program. The CIA did not share this information with other agencies or with senior policy makers.

In a lawsuit filed in federal court in December 2004, the former CIA officer, whose name remains secret, said the informant told him that Iraq's uranium enrichment program ended years earlier and that centrifuge components from the scuttled program were available for examination and even purchase.

The officer, an employee at the CIA for more than 20 years including service in a clandestine unit, which was assigned to gather intelligence related to illicit weapons, had been fired in 2004. In his lawsuit, he said that his dismissal was punishment for his reports questioning the agency's assumptions on a series of weapons-related matters, said Michelle Neff, a CIA spokeswoman. "The agency would not comment," she said.

While the existence of the lawsuit has previously been reported, details of the case have not been made public, because the CIA has heavily censured the documents in the former officer's lawsuit, and his claims are classified.

THE GOP LEADERSHIP

Tom DeLay

AT DELAY'S FORTIFIED BASE IN Texas, a siege mentality rules. Rumblings are being heard. Patricia Haig, a wealthy conservative, spent $2,776 for a full-page ad calling for DeLay's resignation. It urged demonstrators who want 'ethics reform' to rally against his scheduled speech before the NRA. ["It's nice to be with a well-armed group of supporters," he quipped.] It was not a protest against the NRA, she plainly stated.

Her protest is hard to gauge, but there are other signs of restlessness in Sugarland, Texas. It may surprise many to find that DeLay is no hayseed. The former pest exterminator has a degree in biology from the University of Houston and shortly afterward went into the pest control business. [He never snuck into people's homes to "plant rats and roaches", he so often says.]

DeLay is noted for his political conservatism and is very politically aware. In 1978, he was elected to the Texas State House and in 1984 to the House of Representatives from the 22nd District. He became a 'born again' Christian in 1985, but before his conversion he was known as 'Hot Tub Tommy', well known for his drinking, partying, and whoring escapades, and he was one of the girls' favorites.

He has an ardent passion for deregulation. He has three siblings, two brothers and a sister, and two were hired by him in his re-election campaigns. They were paid over $500,000 for their 'expertise.' He has one married daughter, Danielle, and she has counseled several troubled teenagers.

DeLay, as the GOP House Leader, is responsible for developing the issues and policies, which form the GOP agenda and for selecting the bills that the House will consider. He also is responsible for timing the consideration of these bills and coordinating the work of the various House committees.

DeLay's father worked in the oil and gas industry and had several postings to Venezuela's rural interior. For years, the DeLay family made their homes in small towns near the oil fields. DeLay started college at Baylor and later transferred to the University of Houston, graduating in 1970.

At a Ford Bend GOP meeting in 1978, an official suggested that DeLay run for an open Texas House seat. He won and after six years in Austin, he ran and won a seat to the U. S. Congress, becoming the first ever GOP representative elected from Fort Bend County.

The fallout from DeLay's recent lapses is hard to gauge, but the signs of restlessness have culminated in attacks from a GOP editor that runs a weekly county newspaper. His Democratic opponent from 2004 has announced a rematch for 2006. A few other candidates are also considering an entry into the race.

A petition to elect a new House Leader is being circulated to the GOP membership. It needs GOP signatures and has 50 already. On January 8, 2006, DeLay gave up his efforts to regain the House leadership.

Austin is awaiting a judge's ruling on a lawsuit filed by five losing Democratic candidates against the treasurer of a political action committee that they say funneled funds to state races. A criminal investigation is also pending, and recently a GOP member of the Texas House came forward to say he was offered an inducement, barred under state law, to elect an ally of DeLay's, Tom Craddick, as the Texas House Speaker last year.

Other complaints state that DeLay's troubles have affected issues in the waning weeks of the 2005 legislative session. Mrs. Barg, 57, a fellow Republican, signed her ad against DeLay with her maiden name, Paperine. She is "a Texas Republican for Ethical Reform" and posted it at a post office box in a neighboring Missouri city. She said she often used her maiden name and "wasn't trying to hide.

"Tom DeLay is not representing this district. Tom DeLay is taking care of Tom DeLay. He has become an embarrassment to this district. It's time for him to go."

Mr. DeLay's spokesman, Dan Allen, said he was not aware of the ad or the protest, and he questioned the poll's fairness in the Chronicle. "What's clear," he said, "is the Congressman has been elected and re-elected for years because of the work he does for his district." Other politicians, like Eric Thode, blame the Democrats' smears of a good man, duly elected by the people, and it's a Republican district. [Thode is a former public relations man for Enron.]

In Rove mode, Thode also questioned how strong a Republican Barg is. "She hasn't voted in a primary for years, and she hasn't contributed a penny to the party, but had given $750.00 to his opponent, Richard Morrison, last year. She hid her identity until Channel 11 tracked her down." Darlene Hall, the publisher, said she ran the ad "only to make money."

Mr. DeLay's slippage in the district was noted in the 2004 election when he received only 55% of the vote, a drop from the 57% Bush received in the same election.

Mr. Morrison, a lawyer, received 41%. Another possible candidate, some Democrats say, is Nick Lampson of Beaumont, a three-term Congressman.

Defeated by DeLay's redistricting, some moderate Democrat stalwarts have also been looking for a primary candidate to oppose DeLay. Chris Bell, a one-term Democrat from Houston, said, "There is blood in the water, and the sharks are circling."

Thode and others said, "the trips taken by DeLay are commonplace, and many Democrats do the same thing." He was silent concerning the $500,000 salaries DeLay paid his daughter and wife in his political campaign.

Beverly Carter, a GOP precinct chairperson and founder of the other paid circulation paper, The Fort Bend Southwest Star, came out for Morrison in the 2004 election. It earned her a vote of censure by the county organization. She says, "Tom ran a poll eight years ago suggesting that a former Texas Ranger running for the post had no 'local' experience, and we crossed swords on this issue."

Carter says DeLay has shortchanged his district. "There were years when we didn't see him, but now that he's under fire, we have seen a whole heck of a lot more of him."

Major David Wallace of Sugar Land defended DeLay saying, "DeLay has been extremely helpful to the district. He has provided federal grants for transportation improvements, but we had to contribute $3 million to the state to attract a needed highway project."

Mary Denny, chairperson of the Election Commission, has not yet decided on the indirect corporate fund-raising being investigated. She does not know if she will support it or not.

Another bill filed early in the session by Ms. Denny would have stripped District Attorney Ronnie Earle of jurisdiction over campaign law violations in favor of the Texas Ethics Commission. It has been sidelined under a hail of criticism. "The bill was not crafted properly," she said in her defense.

DeLay is named "The Hammer" for his ability to get legislation enacted. He is now entrapped in a Kabuki drama not of his own making. There are two separate investigations looking into his relationship with a bunch of American Indians he hardly knew and cared even less. The other is asking why these same transactions amount to his Indians buying improper influence in a dispute with some even more obscure Indians. One cannot tell who are the good guys or the bad guys – but Tom DeLay, we know, is the good guy, no matter what. Right?

Jack Abramoff (under indictment at present for fraud concerning gambling on the Indian reservations), the elite of elite lobbyists, got $66 million from various Indian tribes trying to protect their gambling interests, and he kicked back $4 million to Ralph Reed. All poor Tom got was a trip or three to Europe, a round or two of golf at St. Andrews, and a meeting with Margaret Thatcher.

DeLay is not paranoid; the press is truly out to get him. It's true, not because he's a screaming S. O. B., but he is the most powerful man in Congress. Remember the media brought down Newt Gingrich and Jim Wright, too. DeLay is down – he is wounded – and so the wolves are circling around their kill. I can't defend their nature, but I know their viewpoint is not a liberal bias.

What a story is hot – hot! The press goes with every morsel uncovered – golf trips sponsored by lobbyists and relatives on the payroll. All roll out effortlessly in The Washington Post. Gingrich has been outspoken in his defense of DeLay, but is he a good character witness?

Gingrich led the charge to impeach Clinton in the Monica affair, even as he carried on his own affair with a young congressional aide while his wife was rolled out of life-threatening cancer surgery. He forced her to sign divorce papers when she was in a drugged state at the time. Gingrich may be a comforting example to DeLay, but only in a 10-year timeframe.

This scandal is real and it's telling is delicious. All its tangents are bogus. Were the tribes trying to influence Congress? Their causes were completely alien to all its members or do the Alabama-Goushatta Indians of Louisiana simply feel strongly that DeLay needs to play more golf? Could Abramoff influence Congress?

Was it illegal to influence one vote? All votes? What in the world difference does it make? (If Abramoff sent money to one of the conservative think tanks for a golf trip for DeLay, the Indians allegedly were paying for the trip before it took place.) Looking for influence in D. C. is like looking for air, after all. You can't point to it exactly, but it's everywhere.

The whole Abramoff/DeLay story is excitingly wonderful. You have a Hollywood plot line – noted lobbyist entangles affluent legislator in tangled mass of lies and deception. The only missing ingredient is a sex angle. DeLay's campaign against gambling on one hand as the other hand helps Indians' gambling on the reservation. Talk about hypocrisy!

Reed is adding the right touch of humor. On one hand, this angelic Reed uses blatant prevarication to cover up blatant prevarication. "I had no idea that his $4 million to stir up anti-gambling sentiment in Louisiana came from gambling interests in Texas," he said. He never wondered where the money came from. This, even after an e-mail from Abramoff refers to "those moronic Tigvas", concluding with, "I'd love us to get our mitts on that moolah. They are all Neanderthals."

After Abramoff gets the casino shut down, he offers his services – for a fee – to get it reopened. It is irony, which cannot be purchased at any price.

Cornered, DeLay is fighting back in the only manner he can. He has intensified his criticism of the federal courts, singling out Supreme Court Anthony Kennedy's work from the bench as "incredibly outrageous", because he has relied on international law and done research on the Internet. This criticism is beneath commenting on; they're the remarks of a desperate man, sewer politics.

DeLay added, "there are a lot of Republican-appointed judges that are judicial activists." Whatever that is supposed to mean, but he pointed to Kennedy as the main example.

Ronald Reagan, the conservative icon, appointed Kennedy to the Court. He has aroused conservatives with his arguments with the more liberal members of the Court. Nevertheless, it is unusual to criticize a Supreme Court justice.

"The time will come," (the Schiavo case included) DeLay continued, "for the men responsible for these abominations to answer for their behavior."

On his trip to the South Pacific, Mariana Islands, he said a territorial government was supposed to pay for travel for two aides to the Pacific Islands. Two Democrats filed forms saying a non-profit group had paid their expenses to the same place.

They were partially wrong. In records obtained by the Associated Press, Jack Abramoff or his former firm paid them, despite rules against such payments by lobbyists! It is not clear if the Commonwealth paid for the trips or if Abramoff was fully reimbursed.

Preston Gates, shown the proof by the AP, said, "We're looking into it. Some things go back to 1996, we are just learning today." Abramoff did bill the Northern Mariana's government for the trips.

Abramoff and Gates represented the Pacific Island government. One project was to prevent and regulate alleged 'sweatshop' garment factories. The rules were never enacted. The Preston Gates billing documents includes a bill for DeLay's Chief of Staff, Ed Buckham (1996) and another DeLay aide at the time.

DeLay was the third ranking GOP member at the time. Abramoff's credit card was used to pay some of the bills. (Another violation of the House rules) DeLay spokesperson, Dan Allen, believes the Mariana's government paid for the two aides, not Abramoff. "I believe the travel was on an invitation basis," Allen added.

DeLay's office did not report the trip in House disclosure records. Allen said it wasn't necessary as the government was paying all the expenses. Andrew Blum, an Abramoff spokesman, said, "Such trips are commonplace, and Mr. Abramoff is being singled out for commonplace actions."

Jan Baron, a Washington lawyer, who specializes in ethics rules and campaign finance, said, "Lawmakers and their aides may demonstrate they had no knowledge of the lobbyist's payments." Questions have been raised about two other DeLay trips, one about his airfare to London and Scotland in 2000, charged to Abramoff's credit card, and the possibility that Buckham's credit card was also used. He had become a lobbyist by 2000.

1. The following payments were made: $2020.00 hotel bill for DeLay and Buckham.

2. A $52.00 travel upgrade for DeLay and Buckham and a $52.00 one for Rudy.
3. Airfare of $5013.00 for Thompson, and a hotel bill of $227.00
4. Airfare totaling $4596.00 for Clyburn and a hotel bill for $227.00

The lawmakers were invited by the non-profit National Security Caucus Foundation, which would be paying the bill. Greg Hilton, who ran the now-defunct foundation, said the group never paid for the trip. They said they were invited, but the foundation never put up the money. Both Clyburn and Thompson filed disclosure reports showing the group had paid for the trip and Clyburn showed the invitation letter.

Hilton, also on the trip, said the foundation was a project of the American Security Council Foundation where he was a director. The foundation promoted a strong national defense: democracy and human rights. Hilton said he was led to believe the territory would pay the expenses and be reimbursed by the private sector. The AP documents were a surprise to him.

The record calls of the Ethics Committee point out a harrowing fact – there are no real guidelines, no clear rules on travel and members. Following the controversy over DeLay's jaunts around the world, news organizations have accused Jack Abramoff of paying travel expenses for DeLay as well as for other members of Congress. They, in turn, say they were not aware Abramoff was paying the bills. Abramoff is now under investigation for his representation of Indian tribes with gambling casinos. He was indicted and has pleaded guilty to the charge.

DeLay has asked Congress to have the Ethics Committee set up a process by "which a member can go to them and submit a proposed invitation on a trip…and have the committee approve or disprove it." DeLay feels then everyone knows what is proper or improper, but he is not pushing it.

Dennis Hastert, the House Majority Leader, says, "I think there needs to be real guidance by the committee about what is acceptable and what is not acceptable. I think we are going to take a look at it." Two Ethics House members recused themselves as they had made contributions to the DeLay legal defense fund (called cronyism by some observers).

Representative Dan Hastings (R-WA) said Representatives Lamar Smith of Texas and Tom Cole of Oklahoma agreed with him that the past contributions "raised doubts" – however unwarranted – about whether these members would be able to judge fairly allegations of impropriety against Mr. DeLay. DeLay, in turn, said he would turn over all his travel records – 10 years' worth – to the committee for perusal, and he asked to appear before the panel.

Hastings, during a now resolved dispute over the rules, previously had offered to begin a formal investigation in May. However, it is expected that any probe by the Committee would begin with a preliminary review before any formal investigation. It has yet to begin.

If Smith and Cole recused themselves, Hastings said he would ask Hastert to designate two House members to serve temporarily on any DeLay investigation. The House will have a pool of 20 members, 10 from each party, to allow the Speaker to choose temporary panel members.

Molly Ivins Column – April 20, 2005

Molly Ivins has made a quotable item out of Delay for her syndicated column. "Mr. D," she said in her April 20, 2005 column, "recently called for good manners on the part of House members. This is as weird as the time he gave us all a lecture on good manners. It's a new role for DeLay "the Emily Post of the House."

"It's not just arguments," DeLay said. "The motives are questionable." It would be the same as if he said, "Screw the Senate", when he learned Bob Dole had cut a deal with Clinton to end the government shutdown caused by Newt Gingrich. "We're in charge. We don't need the Senate," DeLay declared, a grievous breach of civility, I might add.

"We are ideologues. We have an agenda. We have a philosophy. We want to repeal the Clean Air Act," he said in 1995, and ERA.

He told Angela Blankenship, the wife of a business partner who sued him, "You don't want me as an enemy." When the local GOP sheriff hired Ms. Blankenship, DeLay spent $75,000 to defeat him.

"I can't afford you as a brother anymore," he told his lawyer brother, when Randy's lawyering embarrassed DeLay. This was topped only by his spectacular outburst in the Schiavo case. "That's exactly the issue going on in this country against the conservative movement (not re-inserting her feeding tube) against me and against many others. It's the link to the George Soros crowd," he added. "This is a huge concentrated effort to destroy the conservative movement," he declared. "Whew!" said Molly.

According to the Associated Press, DeLay has urged the GOP in Congress, when asked about his ethics problems, to "blame Democrats." He also said it's part of a 'mammoth operation' funded by Democratic supporters designed to destroy him. (It's the eternal victim's presentation of the GOP.)

In the Schiavo case, which he termed 'murder', he criticized the judges in the case, betting them "some day you will have to account for your behaviors" (implying Judgment Day). Later, DeLay admitted he had declared himself 'inartfully.'

A few days later, he keynoted the NRA Convention in Houston, saying, "I feel good. It's nice to know when you are in trouble, your supporters are well armed."

Molly Ivins debunked DeLay's claims about a great conspiracy. "I love conservatives. They are opposed to questionable adventures abroad. It's the right wing nuts I can't stand."

The U. S. is only one of five countries that does not have paid maternity leave, but the welfare debate now hinges on getting the poorest mothers to work longer hours. We are more concerned with a runaway bride or a 13-year-old getting an abortion in Florida or a law in Texas prohibiting suggestive cheerleading maneuvers. Women face motherhood with no real concept of what to expect or what it is or that it may be the first step toward poverty, their first greatest risk.

The Democrats had a program for motherhood but, in another Kerry error, never sold it. Mothers settled for a program of 'security' and 'moral values.' No politician's plan to attend Mother's Day rites, it's no longer an 'apple pie' issue for them. Americans will spend $11 billion May 8 in a sentimental gesture that will last only as long as the roses. When will mothers say that help is not a four-letter word and that motherhood deserves more than a single day?

The private doubts in the GOP over DeLay are spilling into view. A Senate leader called on DeLay to explain his actions and one House GOP member demanded his resignation. Representative Chris Sayers (R-CT) said DeLay "is hurting the GOP majority" and called for him to step down.

DeLay has been dogged for months by new reports on his overseas travel funded by special interests, campaign payments to family members, and connections to a lobbyist, Jack Abramoff, who is under criminal investigation. Sayers is a moderate GOP member who says efforts by the House members to change the rules to protect DeLay only make the Party look bad.

Rick Santorum, #3 GOP in the Senate, said, "DeLay needs to explain his conduct to the public. I think he should come forward and lays out what he did and lets the people judge for themselves." Santorum added that he is up for re-election next year in Pennsylvania and many have noted his adverance of both the president and DeLay.

DeLay's spokesman, Dan Allen, said he "looks forward to the opportunity to sit down with the Ethics Committee chairman to get the facts out and to dispel the innuendo, which has risen around him." Allen also blamed the "George Soros clique for DeLay's problems as an effort to 'slur' the conservatives in Congress."

Nancy Pelosi says DeLay's troubles are distracting him from the more important business facing the House. Santorum defended

DeLay, saying, "DeLay is very effective in leading the House, and he has not been compromised." Christopher Dodd (R-CT) warned GOP members, "be careful how you embrace DeLay during his troubles."

Dodd then cited the new rules recently passed. "These rules require a bi-partisan vote before an investigation can be launched." DeLay's office also began a counterattack in the fall of 2004 against Representative Joel Hefley (R-CO), who was the committee chairman when it came down against DeLay. Dodd warned, "This is not going to go away!"

DeLay upset many Democrats when he took center stage in the Terry Schiavo case, passing legislation to keep her alive. His efforts distanced him from President Bush and many congressional colleagues by his comments after her death about the presiding judges "answering for their actions some day." Later DeLay complained about "an arrogant and out of control judiciary that thumbs its nose at Bush and the Congress."

Bush declined to comment or endorse DeLay's comments, but he added, "I believe in proper checks and balances." Bill Frist defended the judges, saying, "They acted in a fair and independent way." DeLay's comments contained suggested violence against the judges.

DeLay recommended senators respond to questions by saying Democrats have no agenda other than partisanship. They are attacking him to keep the GOP from our legislative program. One supporter said DeLay was referring to a mammoth Democratic effort designed to destroy him as a symbol of the Republican Party. DeLay thanked Santorum for his support.

In an appearance on ABC's "This Week", Santorum said DeLay "has to come forward and lay out what he did and why he did it. From everything that I have heard, everything that he has done has been according to the law."

At a weekly lunch, which was held under terms of secrecy and Don Allen declined any comment; DeLay's case is at the heart of a broader controversy where Democrats accuse the GOP of unilaterally changing Ethics Committee rules. They did this to prevent any further investigation of DeLay. The GOP has denied this, the usual denial. Representative Alan Mollohan (D-WV), the Senior Democrat, said he would renew a push for a bipartisan rewrite of the rules that the GOP put into effect in January on a party line vote.

On January 7, 2006, Tom DeLay ceded his effort to regain the House leadership. The former Leader stepped aside in light of the growing Abramoff scandal in the administration. He will, however, run for re-election in the fall.

One senior GOP member spoke sympathetically of DeLay after the closed-door meeting. "I hope he survives, and I hope he will stay in there and do his job," Trent Lott said, no stranger to criticism himself.

"That's the trouble. GOP members eat their own – Democrats stand by their own till Hell freezes over," Lott added. He was ousted as Senate Majority Leader two years ago, after making race-based comments at a party for former racist Strom Thurmond.

DeLay's private remarks to GOP members followed the script later in the week, hoping to showcase the bankruptcy legislation (which passed). "It was a counterpoint to charges they were 'power hungry.' DeLay's comments were low-key," Lott said.

UPDATE –
January 3, 2006 –

Earmarks

These are the single provisions, which one member may sneak into bills like the budget for his or her favorite project. Earmarks are part of the prevailing corruption, and they have to go. Congress can control federal contracts in this manner, and corporations may direct money in order to get their pork barrel projects passed.

The GOP needs to steal Barney Frank's lobbying reform ideas. (The lone voice crying in the wilderness.) Democrats have been too slow to address problems like Frank's suggestions from their own party and the GOP claims them for their own, as they did in the 2000 and 2004 elections.

All paid travel for and by lobbyists should be banned and whoever is responsible for former members addressing the House should be sent to Siberia. It is an abomination of a high order. All of the lobbyist contacts should be posted on the Internet, where we can all see the manipulation that is taking place. (Newt Gingrich, of all people, has adopted a leading role and after his acts in 1994 is surely the kettle being called black.)

There has to be a call for the enforcement of House rules. There is no way to stop corruption when spending provisions can be slipped into legislation in the dead of night, an act out of Dumas's "Three Musketeers." This is an aberration of the normal House rules. Bills have been passed willy-nilly without any inspection of 800-1,000 word tomes masquerading as legislation for all in the United States.

Let's return to the Ethics Committees, fallen by the wayside since Iran-Contra in the early 1980s. There should be investigations going on most times. The committees should now be composed of former members and former staffers, as Norman Arstein of the American Enterprise Institute has proposed. No current members would be investigating one another, and the committees should be empowered to make recommendations.

Let Congress enforce the 1990 rules passed to curtail spending restraints on new expenditures. Congress must stop the pork barrel projects competing with legitimate legislation.

What has happened to the "ideals" of the GOP? Isn't this the party of fiscal restraint? It stood for reform, and the present administration has made a mockery of these ideals.

Jack Abramoff

Clad in an $800 cashmere topcoat with a Chesterfield collar and a matching $250 black fedora, Jack Abramoff, DC's leading lobbyist, turned himself into the congressional investigating committee conducting the continuing high profile corruption scandal. Abramoff looked more like a Mafia don on the Sopranos than the most powerful lobbyist seen since the days of Boss Tweed in the 1870s.

He and his partner, Michael Scanlon, are now prospective witnesses who know where "all the bodies are buried." Both are charged with multi-million-dollar scams on Texas Indian tribes. The tribes were seeking help with their gambling casinos. For $80 million in bribes, the tribes received NADA.

Under his plea, Abramoff must divulge truthfully the past 10 years of his operation. Under his plea, jail time, which could be 30 years, may be substantially reduced.

Abramoff has close ties to many in Congress and especially to Tom DeLay, who is facing indictments of his own. (Scanlon is a former top aide to DeLay) and has been investigated and has pleaded guilty, also.

DeLay is being investigated for gerrymandering in Texas, plus the distribution of monies to GOP candidates in the 2004 election. This is a major violation of Texas election laws.

Speaking softly, Abramoff answered yes or no to a series of question put to him. He read a prepared text "begging forgiveness from the Almighty and those I have wronged or caused to suffer."

This may become a greater political scandal than Boss Tweed, the Teapot Dome or Watergate. It is said Abramoff had Ohio congressman, Robert Ney (R-Ohio) to introduce legislation to help his clients in the Mariana Islands. It is a charge denied by Ney. There are as many as 30 more congressmen with ties to Abramoff

Ney's former chief of staff has been cited in the documents for violation of the one-year restriction during which he cannot lobby. Abramoff hired him and other staffers to lobby before their one-year restrictions were over. An aide with Ney intervened on behalf of an Abramoff client. Ney also lobbied for FOXCOM, now Mobile-Access, which received a contract with Ney's approval.

Mary Butler, the lead prosecutor in the case, says Abramoff could face a jail term of 30 years. (The knees knocking in the background belong to Tom DeLay, a recipient of copious Abramoff largesse.) Included are all paid expense golf tours to Scotland's St. Andrews. The federal guidelines call for 9- to 11-year jail terms.

All told, DeLay has received 48 free golf trips, 100 hotel and motel stays 400 free meals for himself, his wife, and his staff.

The documents released on January 4, 2006 indicate prosecutors are focusing on benefits provided by Abramoff and his aides to members of Congress, their relatives, and former staffers and their relatives. "This corruption scheme is very extensive, and we will follow it wherever it leads," said Alice Fisher, the head of the Justice Department's criminal division.

"The investigation is ongoing. We are going to expend the resources that are necessary to let people know government is not for sale," Fisher said.

(For the past two weeks, there has been a plethora of money returns by various congressmen, money donated to them in the 2004 election. The latest was a $69,000 donation by House Speaker Dennis Hastert. Sam Baucus (D-MONT) gave back $18,892, including $1892 for a skybox of Abramoff he used; Sam Brownback (R-KS), $43,000, which he will donate to charity; and Conrad Burns (R-MONT), $150,000 (He said earlier he would keep the money.) Ernest Istook (R-OR) returned $6,000.00; Gordon Smith (R-OR), $8,500.00, and Byron Dorgan (D-N.D.), $8,700.00, the vice-chairman of the Senate Indian Affairs Committee. He was among the first to return Abramoff's money. Two hundred twenty current members of Congress have received Abramoff money. Nast received less than $10,000, but 21 received more than $21,500. Twenty were Republicans and five were Democrats.

Stanley Brand, a former counsel to the House, says the investigation is an 8 on the Richter Scale and may reach a 9 or 10 before it's over. They started with the lobbyists, then the outsiders, and then worked up to the public officials. "The members of Congress are the highest on the food chain," Brand reiterated and calls it a "tightly knit set of charges."

Abramoff also admitted to a kickback from Scanlon of $20 million in the Indian casino fraud. "It was a secret scheme we arranged," he said. Scanlon, too, has entered a guilty plea to a parallel conspiracy charge and promised to cooperate in the continuing investigation.

Abramoff has a long list of people he has tried to influence. He gave money, trips, and meals to public officials and their relatives for favorable treatments to his clients. Ney received the most lavish gift – an all-expense paid trip to play golf at St. Andrew's in Scotland. Ney denies he did anything wrong.

The Indian tribes Abramoff and Scanlon fleeced were Mississippi's Choctaw Tribe, the Tigra and the Coushatta Tribes. Others they fleeced were AtoLena Chemicals, Primedia, Inc., and the Commonwealth of the Mariana Islands, the U. S. protectorate in the Pacific Ocean.

Our friend, Grover Norquist, has been friends with Abramoff since the Reagan election in 1980. In fact, he helped get Reagan to carry some states. He has pulled a Bush line, which he used about Kenneth Lay, "Why, I haven't seen Jack in years," he said.

Ralph Reed, executive director of the Christian Coalition, Newt Gingrich, Dick Armey, former House Majority Leader, and Rep. Chris Cox (R-CA) have ties to Abramoff. They are former close friends of Abramoff yet also claim not to have seen him "for years" and hardly know him.

The GOP must blame themselves for the entire fiasco. The day they tried to turn the K-Street lobbying corridor into an arm of the GOP political machine, they opened to door to Abramoff. They let the fox into the hen house. Jack was made for the political climate fostered by Tom DeLay and other GOP leaders.

They, in turn, urged the lobbyists to support the GOP political agenda. They accepted heavy financial support and opened the corridors of power to Jack Abramoff and the lobbyists. Soon, his power reached upward into the echelons of Congress and into the Bush Administration.

"It's all going to be a big black eye for the Republican Party," said Ray LaHood (R-IL), a senior member of Hastert's group and friend of the House Speaker. "Denny will have to speak out against those who will be indicted."

The GOP will have to shake up their leadership after Congress convenes at the end of January. DeLay must be replaced. "We have to get new leadership and begin to move forward," said Sarah Chamberlain Resnick, the executive director of Main Street Partnership, a conservative caucus of GOP moderates.

Although Abramoff admitted to illegal conduct on January 3-4, to some of his dealings to influence Congress, it's really the way these lobbyists always act. "It's business as usual," an aide to Hastert said. He not only plied them with meals, but he opened a restaurant to make it easier to do so. He was the best and biggest of all the lobbyists in DC and as such he garnered the most influence.

The biggest question for the investigators: Did any of the legislators try to use their positions to benefit Abramoff's clients? If true, this would be a violation of federal law.

"Jack Abramoff is a classic example of the pay-to-play system carried out to the extreme," said Fred Wertheimer, head of Democracy 21, a campaign watchdog group. Another survey by the Center for Responsive Politics showed 296 member of Congress received contributions from Abramoff! "Very few lobbyists gave out as much as he did," said member Douglas Webber.

Not only DeLay needs to go; there is a prevailing cancer in Congress, which needs to be exorcised. There is a need to put their entire leadership for review, and this includes Dennis Hastert, the House Leader. "The real problem concerns more than DeLay. A new management is called for, and a new party led by the young bloods in the House. Paul Ryan, Eric Cantor, Mike Pence, and Mark Kirk come to mind," Wertheimer said.

THE RIGHT WING OF THE GOP

Introduction

A conservative government is
An organized hypocrisy.
Benjamin Disraeli
1804-1881

ORGANIZED HYPOCRISY BEGINS AND IS spread by the likes of Rush Limbaugh and others of his ilk. I have never seen the United States as divided as it is today. We have always been a country that has had strong opinions but we have generally treated the other person's point of view with respect. That is, until lately. There have always been demonstrations and divisive rhetoric, but not about mundane things that are being dissed today.

At the forefront of this rancor, Rush Limbaugh still reigns supreme. There are others who would like to suppress him, but they just aren't quite as good at communicating as he is. They find minute molehills and make mountains out of them. Rather than being the voices of reason, they remain the voices of hate.

The rumors and innuendoes they spread about Bill and Hillary were horrendous. The excuses they used to try to impeach this man had no basis. In fact, all politicians whoremonger a time or two. Where is the same rhetoric for the current occupant of the White House who has lied about a war that is killing thousands of our best and brightest? The one who is raping the environment and sending jobs overseas? At the same time he says our economy is improving.

What about a man who praises our troops for the fine job they are doing in the wars in Iraq and Afghanistan and then closes VA hospitals and cuts back veterans' benefits. What about a man who is so worried that two people who love each other might marry or tell the world that they are committed to each other, that he wants to change the Constitution – the document that guarantees our freedoms!

What about the man who brags that he got Medicare drug coverage for our seniors yet did not reign in the corporations which have raised drug prices so that the "savings" seniors were promised are already eaten up by the price hikes? When you hear these people speak – Rush Limbaugh, Ann Coulter, Sean Hannity and any other "newscasters" (read: hate mongers) – listen carefully to what they are saying and whom they are bashing. If we do not speak up in protest, then we deserve what we get from these people. This is hypocrisy at its highest level.

The "Evil" Right-Wing Radio Conspiracy

The media are only as liberal as the
Conservative businesses that own them.
Anonymous

Michael Reagan, son of the former president, said terrorists are not as great a threat as are environmentalists when it comes to the country's security. Sean Hannity referred to actors who oppose the Iraq War as Hollywood leftists. Bill O'Reilly said, after a week of antiwar protests, "these protestors represent a far-left position, a marginal position in this society." Lars Larson called the same protesters "peace idiots". Rush Limbaugh chimed in. He announced that the UN top weapons inspector, Hans Blix, was "an Iraqi toady".

Blix resigned in December 2003, after a year of searching without finding any of the weapons of mass destruction Bush said Iraq developed. Michael Savage adamantly asserted the UN was a proponent of democracy and American values, but its claims were not reflected in its behavior. When callers tried to complain about the war, the hosts merely shouted down those "naïve nutcases".

The long conversations amounted to little more than mutual stroking with hosts and callers gushing over the agreement with each other. The more one listens to these "purveyors of the American way", the more one must agree with Hillary Clinton's assertion about a vast right-wing conspiracy. All these hosts – especially Rush – are so filled with hatred for themselves that they cannot see beyond that, and their tirades are endless.

Ann Coulter

Some fellows get credit for being conservative
When they are only stupid.
Kin Hubbard
American humorist
1868-1930

The Republicans make a great deal about serving their country. War hero, Max Cleland, was defeated in the 2000 election by a vacuous non-entity that cast aspersions on his patriotism. Max had received three purple hearts and lost three limbs in the Vietnam War. The victor, Saxby Chambliss, did not serve. How much more could Max do for his country? He was a patriotic man defeated by a non-entity pol because Rove and the Republicans so violently slurred his character and the voters believed their lies.

If we take a poll of Congress, a surprising fact surfaces. The majority of its members by far had deferments and did not go to Vietnam. John Kerry is the exception. The worst reneger of all was our illustrious president, whose father pulled strings to get him into the Texas Air National Guard ahead of others on the waiting list. Then, when a law passed that said pilots on duty could not drink,

Bush gave himself a furlough for the next year. So much for service to his country!

Now, Ann Coulter, a sweet blonde bitch, is bringing up the issue again (she is 46 years old). She is attractive, looks much younger thanks to Botox, and is well endowed by what men consider to be beauty (no inner qualities have any meaning). Many men in DC seek her as a highly visible token date. One wonders if she isn't just a blonde illusion or arm candy. A good Republican lady couldn't or wouldn't do that, would she?

She has yet to make a substantiated charge that requires intelligence and the ability to understand the issues. She hasn't made a viable charge against the Democrats. It's mostly hearsay and innuendo; illusion and invention are her tools. But she is lovely and has grasped men by their lower body parts. She speaks on a level which 10 or 11 year olds would understand. A 12-year-old would be nonplused by this drivel which she thinks is profundity! There has to be a smarter dumb blonde in the Republican ranks.

Now this intellectually challenged woman has the gall to write a book, an even more unbelievable and reprehensible book called *Treason*. Protesters against her speech of hate pied Coulter in Kansas City and in Texas. (The fee for her speaking engagement – $35,000).

Her book states that anyone who does not support Georgie in Iraq is a traitor. Imagine – just when you felt the Republicans could not sink any lower where lies and deceit are concerned, someone like this dumb blonde bitch comes along to set you on your ear. I wouldn't mind as much if she had any intellectual standing and possessed credentials of any kind. Hers is a faux law degree, and she has yet to try a real case.

Having friends like Georgie, Wolfie, Donald, and Colin is hardly enough to give her credibility. It does not make her a pundit!

But to stun and anger the Democrats she gets an A+. All the while she smirks and assumes the air of one who knows it all when her brain is too small to encompass the most basic facts. She doesn't qualify as any type of seer, and I would like to hear what her dates compare her to when they meet in the back room and discuss their evenings with her.

Where does this blonde bitch get the unmitigated gall to accuse anyone of treason for disagreeing with Bush? Her only reproach is to attack the character of anyone who disagrees with her juvenile assertions. It is a free country the last time I checked, isn't it?

Her social life is so active; one is inclined to feel she was the inspiration for Carrie Bradshaw on "Sex in the City", the popular HBO series. My apologies to Carrie Bradshaw! I feel it is a putdown for Carrie to be so characterized.

Rush Limbaugh – Talk Show Host – Part I

I have become inarticulate
Because of the increased vexation
This man has created in our country.
Paul Dahm
2004

No one in the history of radio has ever so riled an audience to love or to hate him as Rush Limbaugh has done. For years he has acted as chief judge, arbitrator, and executioner of the fate of many Democrats in the news. Unfortunately the spread of this hate doctrine across the airways (which remains unabated to this day) has poisoned the very air we breathe.

But now the chickens have come home to roost. Of all his targets in his role of infamy, none is ranked higher than the drug pushers and users. He said our laws are not stringent enough. He has openly espoused the death penalty for drug violators, and he has ranted against homosexuals and lesbians.

"Whatever goes around, comes around" is now laid for all to see at his doorstep. Limbaugh has been accused of unrestricted drug use for years. In turn, he blamed doctors for prescribing drugs to which he became addicted. On December 15, 2003, he was accused of "doctor shopping". This is a situation where he gets many doctors to prescribe drugs without the knowledge of other doctors doing the same thing for him. It is a most dangerous practice, and has led to overdoses and drug abuse on an enormous scale.

Dan Rather had an unbelievable look when he read the charges against Rush, as if a radio icon was being abused and slandered. I would like to charge Rush with a far greater crime – along with Bill O'Reilly and other FOX network communicators, who have preached the hate doctrine, "which has rent the gentle curtains of our society."

Hillary called it a "right-wing" conspiracy against Bill, but her comments were ignored. Behind it all is Rupert Murdoch. Michael Powell wanted to increase Murdoch's already frightening control of the networks to 45% – (every network is now owned by a conglomerate) an even greater degree than the present 37%.

Murdoch is like the greedy man of yore; the Roman legislator and poet, Seneca, warned us about it in 60 AD. "To the greedy man all nature will not suffice." And this leads us to Rupert Murdoch's sinister political background and presence in our country's affairs.

He is unaware of America's heart. To find this heart, one goes to Iowa or to the hills of southern Indiana, Kentucky or West Virginia. If you have car trouble, you will meet a degree of help you must experience to believe it exists. Everyone wants to help you! It's all part of what makes this country so great. It's like mothers showing up for Little League practice in Iowa.

This is the fabric of which I speak, the rising up to help others. It has long been the silver and gold of U.S. life, the innate quality to care about one another.

So, Mr. Limbaugh, this is the opportunity for you to stand up and be counted. How does it feel when your feet are pressed against the flame? You are no different from those many others whom you have accused of draft dodging, woman chasing, plain dereliction of duty, and unsubstantiated other charges.

It will hurt, Rush, but I'm afraid you have such a core of fellow haters in the GOP and elsewhere. They will all bring pressure to get you off. I hope I am wrong, but Republicans being Republicans, the abuse of justice is their forte.

The rationalization is that Rush's father, a cold, uncaring, vain conservative, victimized him. Addicts have parents like this, and they turn to drugs as their way to rise above the humiliation to which they were subjected. Hired to do football commentary on ESPN, Limbaugh said black quarterbacks were over-rated. But the Philadelphia Eagles went 10-1 for the rest of the season. Imagine! Rush was out of his league on ESPN.

McNabb is the one on the top since Rush's indiscretion and fall from grace. They do have one thing in common. McNabb passed for 2736 yards last season, and Rush has amassed 2680 painkillers from his (and his maid's) doctors.

It took ESPN less than a day to fire Rush for his slurs against blacks. Rush complained on his show in early December, "You people are coming at me from all directions." Now you know how Clinton felt, you bastard!

Rush also complained, "if I had been revealed and had been treated by Dr. Dean, I'll bet they wouldn't be after my medical records." Pretty weak jab, Rush. Not up to your usual hatchet job!

Rush thought he could be a sports commentator because "football is like life, and my life these past months have shown the truth of this." But...maybe he was right. He does know about life as he does football...a big, fat zero!

Rush, every time you open your mouth, you release the grotesque demons hidden in your heart! Grotesque they are: insinuations, distortions of fact, blatant lies and untruths, innuendo, injustice, gossip, questionable rumors. Each is desecration by itself, but altogether they have made America not a nice place anymore.

We are questioning one another's motives like never before, and backbiting has become the rule of the day. Limbaugh has been reduced to desperate measures. He is calling on listeners to keep on listening and taking up Bob Dole's offer to help him. Limbaugh has enlisted one of his biggest fans, The Wall Street Journal, for support.

Rush Limbaugh – Catholic, Addictions, Sex – Part II

Every man has a lurking wish to appear
Considerable in his native place
John Keats

A plague has fallen on the Catholic Church. For years, priests have sexually abused their young altar boys. Bishops have routinely transferred these errant priests to other parishes, and the pastors of the new churches were not advised of the reason for the transfers. The transferred priests found themselves on new, fertile ground to restart their pedophile practices.

For me, a recovering Catholic, it was the most difficult to accept and a far cry from the reverence the priest and nuns taught me in grammar school. I vividly remember the awe we showed toward Father Michael as a living embodiment of Christ's life and teachings.

Suits against the church and the cardinals are now common. In Boston, the worst offender was tried, convicted, and sent to prison. He had abused young boys for 20 or more years. His life sentence was very short. An irate inmate stabbed him to death! In prison, there is no greater crime than that of child abuse and molestation.

The diocese of Boston is selling off church properties to satisfy the lawsuits brought against the church. The cardinal resigned his position and assumed full blame. He realizes the matter should have been dealt with years earlier.

There are many forms of addiction with sexual desire in the fore-front. There is the compulsive eater, whom we derisively used to call "Fatty". Now, overeating has become the biggest threat to our country, as being overweight leads to heart attacks, strokes, and incipient diabetes, the silent killer. [One glance at Rush Limbaugh tells you he has an inordinate love of food. Anyone weighing more than 300 pounds has a problem. He may also be a food addict, along with his drug and sex addictions. Rush's fondness for long fat cigars is taken by psychiatrists as a penchant for latent homosexuality.]

Tons of children have been affected and are overweight (excuse the pun). Cooks, early in life, realize their inordinate love of food and gravitate toward it. They end up working in restaurants as cooks and chefs.

The same drive holds true for the alcoholic who cannot stand being separated from his beloved alcohol, like President Bush. Bush disappeared and later resigned when he could no longer imbibe while on active duty. Often they become bartenders, where nipping on the side is overlooked. I have yet to met a single bartender who does not like to drink or an overweight cook who does not like to eat.

One reads periodically of drugs disappearing from police lockers, where they are stored for evidence. In the latest case in NYC, more than $1 million worth of "coke" turned up missing, by far the largest single stash to "disappear." Policemen, early on, realize they have a desire to steal things and join the force to help overcome these desires.

More rare is the pyromaniac, who loves to see things burn. It is an uncontrollable fascination. One of the largest forest fires in 2003 was set by an arsonist working as a firefighter.

One of the sadder addictions is the one shared by the ministry. Priests, ministers, and rabbis share this common bond. The women parishioners turn to their pastors for help and, in turn, are taken advantage of in their vulnerability. The resulting scandals scar all concerned and rock society. They destroy the lives of all the people involved.

An inordinate sex drive can lead to all types of aberrations. The latest is a sex club frenzy in NYC, a throwback to Studio 54. "One

Leg Up" is a group founded by Palagia. "The aim of this club," she says, "is to help young people come to terms with their sexuality." To qualify for one of the club's parties, one must submit an erotic essay along with one's pictures. Some, proud of their endowments, send nude photos.

If the person qualifies, makes the cut, he or she is invited to the next party. The event begins casually, but at 12:30 AM, a gong sounds and all strip down to their underwear (spin the bottle, sans bottle). "Sex is cool," says partygoer Anna, "and everyone should get a lot of it." Anna is 21 and cool.

The parties have a "Sex in the City" atmosphere. The prevailing attitude of the women attending is like Anna's. "Women should have their own space to explore their sexuality," said one attendee.

The women at most of these parties are in charge and, with STDs to contend with, condoms are required. The women are topless; a dab of paint on their nipples meet obscenity law compliance. Women gyrate together in "group roles". Men find it cool. The young women are comfortable experimenting with many sexual partners and being so totally uninhibited.

The line between public and private has long since been blurred. (Visit any all-male gay club, if you do not believe me.) Young women exhibit no anxiety when they are filmed in sexual acts, but leering is prohibited. A man must ask the permission of the lady.

Rumors are circulating that Rush Limbaugh and some Congressmen and others in the limelight frequent these clubs. Limbaugh is said to have been a regular at the all-men's club, which caters to homosexuality, and he may also belong to "Cake", a heterosexual club.

When questioned about Rush and other members, Grego, Mrs. Gallagher, and Palagia all stated their membership lists were private. If the rumor is true and Rush is a sex addict in addition to being a drug addict, it would not be a surprise.

Once people lose their inhibitions and succumb to an addition, they are easily led into another. Their will to resist further temptation has been diminished to the point of "no resistance."

Rush has sentenced to a drug rehab group for 30 days, but psychiatrists call this a Band-Aid. One cannot overcome an addiction in 30 days, especially one that has lasted a lifetime. If the addict sticks to the program, additional addictions may surface and, if present, may also need to be treated.

AA recovery lasts for the rest of one's life. Progress is referred to in the number of days since the member's last drink. "I've been sober for x-days or x-years."

Any excessive act, which takes over a person's life, may be termed an addiction. Some are small, some large, some easily controlled, and others, like smoking, may be almost impossible to overcome. Gambling, too, with its base of insecurity, is a hard one to kick.

Nude dancing is a form of pornography and an addiction that is censored on many levels of society. Child porn now has a global base and may lead to "acting out." An addiction to prostitution is one in which acting out can destroy one's life.

Consider Rush's life and be charitable, as he has not been with Bill Clinton and thousands of others. He married late in life and is inordinately so successful that he may indulge any proclivities or desires he has. Because he married so late in life, it may have been possible for him to develop many sexual aberrations. Only his counselor at the center can tell us for certain.

Long term, when sex becomes a sport, it can take away the ability to enjoy sex in an intimate situation. Sexual intimacy rarely occurs outside the bounds of a monogamous relationship.

And a solution for Anna was to find a boyfriend who enjoys the parties she enjoys. Anna has attended more than 30 parties and has had more than 100 sexual partners. She quips, "I hope when I am 30, I don't decide to run for public office."

P. S. Limbaugh's third wife sued him for divorce. Rush is now a corporation. He has no heart or soul, and he is dragging us all down with him into the same bottomless pit.

ECONOMY

What Happened to All the Jobs, Mr. Bush?

Economy is for the poor;
The rich may dispense with it.
Christian Nevell Bovee

THE GOP IS WREATHED IN smiles! The economy grew 7.2%, the best since 1984. But how many jobs were created? Economic growth means little without job growth. (Most of the new jobs were low paying in the service sector.)

An impressive rise in exports, consumer spending, and new home starts have built false enthusiasm. Even the rise of business spending has done little to create new jobs. Many of the businesses fled overseas for cheaper employees. Even those that have jobs are concerned. There is little job security, puny raises (or none), and the cost of benefits now being charged to the employee has done much to erode optimism in our economy. Don't forget rising insurance premiums; the third double-digit rise in three years! Pensions are being cut.

No wonder we see and hear Pollyanna-ism. Chicken Little is back to reside in many homes. Since March 2001, the economy has shed 2.7 million jobs overseas and NONE WILL RETURN.

Economists say the unemployment rate must fall below 4.5% before we will feel job growth. It now hovers around 5%. Right now, both businesses and employees are being squeezed. Workers see it in higher payroll deductions, less chance for overtime, and rising hospital costs. Even Boeing employees' pay deductions are rising, in their case, as much as $105 per month.

Wal-Mart has come up with the variable pricing scheme, which allows employees to choose deductibles up to $10,000 yearly. Other companies are following that example. Supermarket employees, out on a long, interminable strike to protect their wages, are all afraid they will be paid like those at Wal-Mart – 50% less than they earn. Wal-Mart has disrupted corporate America, and will continue to do so. This Tyrannosaurus monster has gobbled up hundreds of thousands of businesses and now they are busy lowering our living standards. They pay poverty-based wages. Many employees qualify for food stamps and Medicaid, all charged to states where Wal-Mart employees reside.

In an effort to compete, others are reducing their wages, too. There is no end to Wal-Mart's greedy grasp. Insurance and medical plans compound the problem, and a typical family plan costs a little over $9,000 yearly.

Many other employees are retiring. As whole companies down-size, the costs rise. Tangentially, as fewer employees support the retired, workers bear the burden. A General Motors employee now supports 2.5 retirees, causing a much lower corporate bottom line. Company-sponsored medical care is like the DoDo bird – vanishing – and soon may be gone. Toyota will soon replace GM as the world's largest carmaker.

Companies are being forced to cut costs wherever and if ever they can. Firms cut wages, eliminate Christmas bonuses, and plan to charge workers more for health care. Costs have become an uncontrollable monster for many of our corporations and small businesses.

Wal-Mart

What is Wal-Mart? Why does it concern so many with its expansion plans? [They visualize 2000 or more stores in China alone!]

Environmentalists, lawmakers, academics, and community organizations are uniting to fight this colossus. An organized assault against Wal-Mart is taking shape against the way it does business. (And none too soon. Many feel it's about time, as pristine areas are paved into parking lots and/or more low, rambling, ugly distribution centers rise in 50,000 square foot architectural abominations.)

These groups are uniting to speak in one voice against this megalopolis that pays poverty-like wages and stingy benefits. Former disenchanted Wal-Mart workers are planning an association of protest against a free capitalism idea running amok! How big is too big? When is enough, enough? Will not Wal-Mart be satisfied until they sell in their stores every manufactured item turned out in the world? It seems to be their goal.

Lobbies have formed in 28 states for legislation to embarrass Wal-Mart by divulging the way it does business. Thousands upon thousands of Wal-Mart employees do not have health insurance. "They are independent contractors and responsible for their own health insurance," their executives claim. (So employees turn to taxpayer-financed Medicaid furnished by the Bush administration.) Bush has already bankrupted many of these states with his tax cuts, which cut off much of their finances for social programs.

"We're trying to change their business model, not shut them down," angry protestors state. "We don't just want to challenge them on healthcare or sex discrimination or the environment, where they are equally guilty. We want to pressure them on all three. We're more likely to win if we challenge them on many fronts."

Like Rockefeller's Standard Oil under T. R., Wal-Mart has become a target because of its burgeoning size and economic power. It has 1.2 million workers, more than the population of Utah and Wyoming combined.

With its back to the wall, Wal-Mart is planning a counteroffensive. Recently they took out an ad in The New York Review of Books, in which their chief executive, Lee Scott, defended the company's business practices and accused union organizers of being "selfish".

Wal-Mart is spending millions on TV ads in which blacks, Hispanics, and women say that it is a wonderful place to work, and Wal-Mart in another ploy is donating land for conservation (land abandoned for super centers).

This offensive at Wal-Mart is greater than the past ones that were directed at unions under the AFL-CIO, which tried unsuccessfully to organize the workers. The union is once again in the forefront having added a new coalition that includes student groups, anti-sprawl groups, and anti-sweatshop groups. Senior groups from Common Cause and the National Partnership of Women has also joined in the protest as coordinating members.

The executive director is Andy Grossman, former director of the Democratic Senate campaign. He is one of many tapped for the anti-Wal-Mart movement. Paul Blank, director of the food workers, worked on Howard Dean's political team. "We're focusing on Wal-Mart, because of the huge impact it has on all parts of American life that it touches," Grossman said.

They do provide goods at a lower price, but it comes at a high cost to its suppliers, who are beaten down by Wal-Mart's penny-pinching dictates and to society in general by a plethora of shoddy products. (When you deal in $100 million orders, the clout to conform to their standards is considerable.)

"We're against their low wages, but we do want them to get better," Grossman further stated to his staff of 40, who are backed by several million donated dollars. One million came in the form of seed money from the Service Employees and grants as large as $250,000 from several liberal foundations.

"When you're dealing with a company this big and ruthless, you can't get enough leverage going store to store," said Paul Blank, the union's Wal-Mart director. "Even when you win a draw you lose, because the company will close down that store," he added. "One must realize corporations have no souls."

Even as they gear up for an expanded ad campaign, Wal-Mart and its adversaries seem at times to offer olive branches. Mona Williams said, "We have a lot of common interests, such as affordable health care and ideally we could use our collective clout to partner and make this country a better place." Andy Grossman concluded, "We want to help make them more money, but responsibly."

"We think that many people haven't heard the case from out point of view," said Mona Williams, VP for Corporate Communications. "They have heard only our critics' propaganda. We're convinced that when open-minded people look at the big picture, they will see our critics are way off base."

Lee Scott, the CEO, accused the United Food and Commercial Workers of acting selfishly, and he criticized, in particular, its efforts to block several Wal-Marts planned for California that he said would lower grocery prices there. In the New York Review of Books ad, he wrote, "Thirty-five million other Californians will be asked to pay billions more than they have to for the necessities of life."

Bush Guffaws

Bush is providing Europeans with chuckles. Molly Ivins wrote, "He ridiculed the idea that we were going to attack Iran, and then he added, 'All options are on the table.' We all thought he was joking." They were unaware Bush often contradicts himself even in his next sentence as he did there in Europe. In his mind, he is never wrong and does not make mistakes, even his friendship with Ken Lay in the Enron scandal. ("Why, I only met the man once or twice," he said, forgetting all the dinners and golf games they shared and the fact that Lay was in on Cheney's energy meeting.)

Even the WMDs. It took more than three years for him to admit the intelligence on Iraq given to him was false and flawed. If you disagree with Bush, you are deemed unpatriotic, and you probably support gay marriage and homosexuality, don't you? Or are against the Star Wars program (which, after more than $10-15 billion spent, has shown no signs of working); 63% are against Bush's Social Security plan, according to a recent poll.

All these happenings are blows to the Bush program to which he is still very dedicated. Trent Duffy, a White House spokesman, says, "It's still a number one issue with the President." But there is growing opposition among congressional leaders, the GOP in general, and in the House Ways and Means Committee, where Chairman Bill Thomas (R-CO) has urged generalities rather than a specific plan. They wish more stated support before they will support the Bush plan, and they control the Social Security Trust funds. The issue is dead on the Hill for 2006.

Medicare

I find a medicine worse than the malady.
John Fletcher
1579-1625

In Washington, that sleeping devil, Newt Gingrich, joined the White House in support of the "Hooters and Polluters" $31 billion energy bill, part of the $400 billion prescription drug benefit. Even The Wall Street Journal disapproved of the bill. The energy section was so named for monies in the bill to support and build an energy-efficient Hooters restaurant in Shreveport, LA.

Days later a Gay Rights bill moved toward approval in Massachusetts. Tom Daschle, Nancy Pelosi, and others voted in favor of the bill. Bush can now say he did something about meds for seniors and at the same time passed an energy bill. Sort of like killing two birds with one stone. One Democratic wag calls that "the kind of bill we used to pass."

Bush will also benefit from the agitation coming from the religious right. "The Democrats," Joe Klein says, "are boxed into complicated and unpopular positions because they tend to stand on principle." (Aren't all politicians supposed to?)

When you stop laughing, consider this. The GOP plays everything from the political advantage they may gain. Karl Rove has his tainted presence and fingers in every move they make. The Medicare bill contains large gifts for the pharmaceutical firms and the energy bill gives $23.5 billion to traditional energy producers with billions of additional pork thrown in.

"It's classic machine politics," recalling Richard Daley's manipulation of aldermen in Chicago.

The Wall Street Journal is worried. Bush will have to rescind some tax cuts to pay for all this. As seniors fear being bilked by the confusing new Medicare discount drug card program started June 1, 2004, the Center for American Progress released a new report showing that 20 of the 73 companies that the White House approved to participate in the program have been charged at the federal and/or state level with fraud!

The report, entitled "Paying to Play", shows these 20 companies gave more than $3 million to the president and conservatives in Congress since the 2000 election cycle. That represents more than 60% of the total contributions given to the president and conservatives from all 73 approved card companies. Additionally, seven of the president's "pioneers" (those who have raised $100,000 ore more for him) are Arlington companies approved for the program.

Three of those companies have been accused of fraud. According to Associated Press, Medco president Alan Lotvin recently held a $100,000 fundraiser for the president after the White House overlooked Medco's fraud record and approved the company for the drug card program. (Medco recently was forced to pay $29 million in fines in a probe into "unfair and deceptive acts" in 20 states.)

Similarly, when PacifiCare lobbyist Tom Loeffler raised at least $200,000 for the president, his company was subsequently approved by the White House for the drug card program even though it was recently forced to pay the federal government $87.3 million to settle alleged violations of the federal False Claims Act.

According to the April 13, 2002 Orange County Register, the fine was the "largest civil settlement ever assessed on a company providing health care coverage to federal employees."

And Bush pioneer, Samuel Skinner, is a member of the board of Express Scripts, a company approved by the White House, although its business practices are currently under investigation by the New York attorney general.

Advanced PCS is the company run by Bush's longtime Texas crony and donor, David Halbert. It was approved to participate in the drug card program, even though in 2002 the company "fiercely resisted attempts by the Justice Department to interview some of its employees" for a probe into a prescription drug price-fixing scheme. (During the late 1980s, Bush was an original investor in an early version of Advanced PCS, which netted him up to $1 million.) He rewarded Halbert by allowing Advanced PCS to help draft legislation that created the original drug card program.

The proposed Medicare benefits have created a quandary for the Democrats. Medicare currently is a fee-for-service the way old-fashioned medicine was, getting whatever you needed. That is very expensive.

In 2001, the bill contained a six-city test of managed care, which threw Dick Gephardt into a tizzy. "We're not going to let them herd seniors into HMOs," he proclaimed. Howard Dean said Medicare should not be changed, but the GOP has been trying to do that since 1966. As the real working "benefit" of the drug bill comes to fruition, seniors are beginning to realize how much they were duped!

In the beginning, they were told that the bill would save up to 75% off their bills, but now they have to belong to an HMO with dues to use the "benefit." Seniors have to sign an *unchangeable* contract for a year to be with this HMO, but the costs passed on to the seniors can change daily or even hourly if the HMO wants them to! So much for security for people on a fixed income!

Locked into a bad deal for at least a year minimum, and for what? Studies done by the Heritage Foundation, the GOP's own conservative think tank, says, "out-of-pocket costs for low-income seniors will increase." They continue, "despite the fact that the Senate Medicare bill would cause federal taxpayers almost $400 billion, it might actually hurt more seniors than it would help them". Rather than targeting a prescription drug benefit "to those who really need it, they have chosen to pass the bill that would end up costing millions of seniors significantly more than they pay now."

Bush has outfoxed the Democrats every way they turn. The economy has perked up, but not jobs, the true indicator of recovery. If Bush stabilizes Iraq, look out!

The New Deal
& Its Building Projects

When FDR ascended to the presidency in 1933, the task before him was immense. His first act was to shutter the banks and take us off the Gold Standard. He needed to pass a bank reform bill to protect people's savings. Next, he moved to accomplish three objectives – Relief, Recovery, and Reform. He needed to create millions of jobs and to chill the unrest of the Hooverville protest.

Forests needed to be planted, highways constructed, and the educational system of the country revamped, as many adults and children had to be taught to read. There remained a great need to regulate stocks to prevent another October 1929.

FDR spend six and one half billion dollars to spur the U.S. economy. He changed the face of America with building projects in every state to help provide relief for the 25% of the nation's population who were out of work. The Grand Coulee and Bonneville Dams were two of his largest undertakings. The Los Angeles Aqueduct insured water to a parched Los Angeles. The Pocatello Reservoir, Humbolt

River Aqueduct, Wyoming Drought Canal, and the Nebraska Power projects followed.

In Fargo, North Dakota, the WPA constructed a great sewer system. The Rio Grande Flood Canal and the Denver Water Tunnel came next. In Oklahoma cities, slum clearance was begun and dormitories were constructed at Texas Tech, along with schools in Fort Worth and dormitories at the University of Minnesota.

A civic auditorium in Kansas City, Missouri, the Ozark Power Dam, an erosion mattress along the Mississippi, the great St. Louis/Minnespolis Waterway, and the County Courthouse in St. Louis were completed. The Houston Ship Canal in Texas and over 120 airports linked cities across the nation. The Chicago Sewage Plant was constructed, and in Indianapolis, housing for the poor was built. In Cleveland, slums were cleared and people resettled in West Virginia. Forest conservation started in Pennsylvania and across the country. A great Naval hospital rose in Philadelphia, and the Tri-borough Bridge in New York eased bottlenecks.

In Atlanta, further slum clearance began along with construction of new schools in South Carolina, especially in the rural areas. Bridges were constructed linking Cape Cod in Massachusetts and the Manhattan Midtown tunnels were created. Roanoke Island was restored, and a Lake Okeechobee flood control system begun, but a Florida ship canal was never completed.

Along the Passamaquoddy River in northern Maine, plans for a tidal power project to harness the Bay of Fundy tides (the greatest tides in the world) were never begun. FDR introduced the project in 1934 after Maine created FERA, the Federal Emergency Relief Agency. FERA was the first major relief program to provide assistance, but they felt it was only a temporary, not a permanent, solution. The program raised the hackles of the conservatives in Congress, but they appeased the wishes of FDR.

In 100 days, FDR left an indelible mark on the country. Farming represented 30% of the economy, and farmers rioted, so he paid them to plant less and burn the surplus crops and kill their stock. CCC was created with $1/day jobs – 250,000 enrolled in a matter of days. The National Recovery Act (NRA) passed in 1933 (declared unconstitutional in 1935). The NRA gave government control over business; 541 codes were put in force and a minimum wage of $12.00/week was passed.

Roosevelt staged the greatest peacetime parade in history. In September 1933 Americans marched in favor of NRA. A Blue Eagle was displayed in every story window and signaled a new era of prosperity, which included raised wages and reduced working hours. They also marched for an end to cutthroat competition and to erase chiselers.

The Eagle emblem gave hope to the people, and clubs were set up all over America. Chorus girls wore blue eagles on their panties.

General Hugh Johnson, in a profanity-ridden speech, was the crusading head of this mass movement against unemployment. Second in command of NRA was Frances Robinson, who toured with Johnson across the land. She was his "general secretary", and was sharp-witted and sharp-nosed. "Robbie", as she was affectionately known, called captains of industry by their first names, kept congressmen in their place, and was a power in D. C.

After 100 such parades in a number of cities, the footsore businessmen of the U. S. lay down and slept for the first time beneath a blanket code.

Gabriel, the great Blue Eagle, flew above the White House, but it was over everything – in shop windows, labor troubles, and in the lining of coats.

The Supreme Court vote was 9-0 against NRA and that led to its dissolution, but it was the law of the land for 23 months before its death. Their decision was the first in a series of anti-New Deal decisions. They were photographed in session for the first time as they made the last of the Court's interference and sought to add more members who were more amenable to his point of view.

FDR insisted on fireside chats (27% of them during his office) that folks listened to across America. You could walk down the street to his blaring message and not miss a word. His first fireside chat gave the nation new courage.

Only two photos of him in a wheelchair were ever taken and at one funeral he attended, a platform was constructed up to the door, so he could "walk" out of his car. (He learned to "make do" and had a bottle to pee into.)

In 1934, the election was close to unanimous. They gained 69 seats in the Senate and a like number in the House.

When the 100 days were over and he happily put out to sea in the Amberjack II, he was near to becoming a demigod as any U. S. president had ever been.

Roosevelt, upon his return, appointed his Cabinet:

- Treasury, William Woodin, president of the American Car & Foundry Corporation
- Justice, Homer Cummings
- Navy, Claude A. Swanson, an ailing senator from Virginia
- Agriculture, Henry Wallace, a farm editor from Iowa
- Labor, Frances Perkins, a NY social worker and the first woman in a Cabinet
- Secretary of State Cordell Hull, a survivalist
- Secretary of War, George Dern, a Utah mining man (not a Morman) who rose to the governorship
- Patronage and Mails, Jim Farley, a simple politician
- Secretary of the Interior, Bull Mooser, an irascible reformer/lawyer from Chicago, and
- Commerce, Daniel Roper, an old-time politician from South Carolina.

William Woodin and George Dern died but the others officered the New Deal during its first four tumultuous years.

The major relief program was the CWA, the Civil Works Administration. The CWA was created to study and make recommendations on the problems of economic security. Headed by Perkins, the CES included Henry Morgenthau, Jr., the treasury secretary, and Henry A. Wallace, the agriculture secretary, as well as Hopkins. The committee concentrated on unemployment, old-age security, and national health insurance, which was discarded over raised protests by the AMA, the American Medical Association.

Their report was sent to Congress on January 17, 1935 as The Economic Security Bill. The bill was aimed at the continuing problems of unemployment and economic need. It was an omnibus measure also aimed at those considered unemployable, meaning the elderly, children, and the blind. It included establishing a longer-term program for those temporarily in need when they got laid off from their jobs. The other side of the bill was assistance for those who could work but could not find a suitable job. Another bill passed in 1935 – the ERAA – Emergency Relief Appropriation Act. It provided an unprecedented sum of $5 billion to fund Public Works projects, the famed WPA, which put food on the table for millions of families.

Out of the ERAA came programs such as the National Youth Administration and the CCC, the Civilian Conservation Corps, which employed teenagers and other unemployed young people. The CCC started many young men on their way to becoming men. These programs were based on a stagnant economy and guided by the theory that it might remain so, and that the government had the duty to provide jobs.

While working on ERAA, Congress also debated The Economic Security Bill, which passed 372-33 in the House and 77-6 in the Senate. In the final version of the bill, which Congress renamed the Social Security Act, Congress made some changes, many of which would have a significant impact on the course of social welfare.

The old-age public assistance was placed first and support came most loudly from the followers of Dr. Frances Townsend, who supported a flat grant pension, but it was voted down. (A version of his bill was discussed during the Civil Rights debates in the Johnson Administration during the 1960s.) The Townsend proposal was replaced in favor of including the self-supporting old-age insurance program of the Social Security Act. This was a victory for FDR and the supporters of the CES bill.

Other significant changes were made including a provision allowing the federal government to determine if each state's assistance programs gave recipients "a reasonable subsistence compatible with decency and health." It was defeated in a move by southern conservatives to eliminate or curtail benefits for Negroes and made it impossible for effective control of state welfare programs.

In committee, Congress reorganized by creating the Social Security Board (Title VII), a three-member agency, which gave authority over all the programs except the Public Health Service and maternal and child welfare grants. These were given to the Labor Department.

The Social Security Act passed the House by a voice vote on August 8, 1935 and the next day passed in the Senate. It was signed into law by FDR on August 14, 1935.

The first four titles set up the care of the Social Security system. Title I: Old-age assistance. OAA was public assistance for the needy elderly. Title II: Old-age benefits were the centerpiece of the Act. Title III: Unemployment compensation (UC) set up a federal-state employment insurance program funded through payroll deductions and employer contributions. Title IV: Aid to Dependent Children (ADC) provided public assistance to children deprived of parental support to allow their mothers to raise them at home. The act also contained a maternal health, crippled children, and child welfare grant (Title V), which was a federal grant-in-aid to states that resurrected the defunct Sheppard-Towner Act to provide money for education and public health care for pregnant woman and young children. Title VI established the Public Health Service and aid to the blind. Title VI was a public assistance program to support disabled individuals in the one group everyone agreed was unable to find gainful employment.

Taken together, the programs were aimed at two groups. First, the temporarily unemployed, the large group of working age that could not find available and suitable work in the current (or future)

Depression, and second, the unemployable, those who, due to age or disability, should be taken out of the work force and given public support.

But just as the work-relief programs had shortcomings, they did fulfill FDR's protection "from cradle to grave". The programs had areas of limited coverage. The most glaring errors were the old-sage insurance and unemployment, which excluded many worker categories, most notably agricultural and domestic workers. Also, public assistance was left to the states to determine and establish eligibility criteria and benefits.

The result was that programs varied greatly and they were vulnerable to the efforts of some states to exclude groups of Americans. Thus, African Americans, other minorities, and women, disproportionately employed in non-covered employment categories and subjected to state efforts to exclude them, received little immediate assistance from the programs. On the positive side, proponents of the expanded social welfare system saw the Act as the first step, with gaps and limitations, to be addressed over the years.

The early Social Security Act rode rough waters. The conservatives rallied against it and called it socialism, getting something for nothing, giving up your independence, etc. Others were against the payroll deduction tax, saying it took needed money out of the economy and tended to favor a larger old-age pension program. Supporters of the Act also feared that the Supreme Court would overturn the Act because of the payroll tax feature (one of the bases for FDR to try and "pack" the Supreme Court with those who would favor his programs).

But the Court in Steward v. Davis (1937) and Helvering et al. v. Davis (1937) upheld the Social Security Act. Another potential threat was the popularity of the flat grant pensions for the elderly. The idea of providing income maintenance for the elderly had been growing in popularity during the '30s and the Townsend plan was the most visible of all the plans that were discussed. It was introduced into Congress several times to replace Social Security, but because of the immense cost of providing this much money from the general revenues, it never had much of a chance.

The Act was revised in 1939 to strengthen the old-age insurance programs and thwart the old-age pension movement. Benefit payments were set to rise in 1940 and the amount increased. In addition, a survivor's provision was added, making widows with children eligible if their husbands died before retirement. Changes in the assistance program elevated aid to dependent children to the same level as old-age benefits. No comprehensive insurance program ever made it to the House floor.

The next revision occurred in 1950. Disability insurance was added and a caretaker grant into the ADC program greatly increased its cost. The OASDI coverage was expanded to include most workers. The public assistance programs underwent major changes, beginning with their separation from Social Security in 1963. In 1965, Medicare and Medicaid addressed the last major gap in coverage, providing health insurance for the retied and the poor respectively. Old age and disability programs were folded together in 1972 to create Supplemental Security Income (SSI) while AFDC was changed to Temporary Aid to Needy Families (TANF) in 1996. Despite its flaws, Social Security was a major step in the federal government providing economic security and a major source of retirement security for working Americans.

THE BUILDING PROJECTS

Senator Norris of Nebraska always wanted to redeem the good-for-nothing $150 million war baby called Muscle Shoals. The New Deal set out to salvage not only the waterpower but also the fertility and humanity of the whole underprivileged Tennessee Valley. The dam was named Norris Dam in his honor.

The $896 million structure of the TVA was thrown across the Clinch River to make cheap electricity. The only complaints received over the project came from private power companies. The two biggest builders of the New Deal were the TVA and the Public Works Administration. The entire cost of the TVA was less than one-month's cost of PWA.

The Fort Pech Dam in Montana was built to control the Missouri floods, which devastated the area every spring. A dirt dam, it is a giant mud pie four miles long.

The New Deal and FDR borrowed billions of dollars to work on thousands of projects. Mountains were tunneled, rivers dammed, aqueducts laid, canals dug, battleships built, landmarks restored, slums cleared, and 6201 schoolhouses built or repaired. The level of unemployment remained fairly much the same at 25%.

The Florida Ship Canal began with $5 million of WPA money in the wake of the 1935 hurricane. Its merit was rather dubious as it endangered South Florida's water supply. After studies were made, Congress refused to supply the $576 million needed to complete the project.

The re-election of FDR in 1936 was a testament to his popularity. Poor Alf Landon, lugubriously crisscrossed America in the Landon Special. Few turned out to listen. In Boston, crowds for FDR roared themselves hoarse and women fainted in the milling mobs of acclaimers.

By day and night, under sun, thunderclouds and rain, from Denver to Boston, FDR spoke triumphantly. He had a smile of silver and a voice of gold. When the election ended, had FDR reported the State of the Union to Congress, he might have summed it up in the electoral vote: FDR – 523, Landon – 8.

On a soggy inauguration day, FDR spoke for two hours. As the rain poured on the assembled 40,000 spectators, the president said, "If they can take it, I can, too." When finished, he ordered an open touring car and at the end of a 15-minute ride to the White House, everyone in the car was drenched. A cape was put over FDR, but his soggy hat was continually raised in response to cheers from the crowd.

The spectators stood in puddles of water, trying to keep dry under umbrellas purchased for $2. From above the plaza, it was a sea of umbrellas greeted FDR, but beneath each one was an intensely interested person anxious to hear what the president would say.

Seven of the Supreme Court Justices attended hoping to be mentioned by the president. They were disappointed. The two absentees were Stone and Brandeis.

Negro Democrats, led by J. A. Morris, assistant attorney general of Pennsylvania, held the only inaugural ball. West Point cadets were in demand for cocktail parties as FDR viewed the inaugural parade. His tush and toes were warmed by an electric radiator. The tribune where FDR stood had bulletproof glass sides. When he learned this fact, he ordered them removed. That parade lasted for one-and-a-half hours, which is short for an inaugural parade.

Mrs. Roosevelt's inauguration dress and hat were ruined, and her fur coat sopping wet. They were the wettest First Family to enter the White House for four more years.

FDR's popularity was shown in a June 1938 poll by Fortune magazine. He had 70%+ poll numbers among factory laborers, farm workers, and he ranked very high with other labor groups. He had a 59+% rating with the unemployed, 63% with housekeepers, and 61% with farmers. Fifty-nine percent came from white-collar workers, 57% from business owners, but only 46% from professional workers. His numbers fell among the retired to 43%. Students came in at 39%, and the executive support for FDR was lukewarm. The business curbs –many of which were termed unlawful – that Congress placed on them by Congress explains these percentages.

In general, the lower classes were in favor of FDR, and the upper middle class was against him and disliked his New Deal, which lessened their power.

As war loomed on the horizon, FDR instituted "Lend Lease" in order to supply England with food, arms, ammunition, ships, and planes. America, led by Charles Lindberg's isolationist outbursts, was not in favor of Lend Lease. If the truth were known, Lindberg secretly supported Germany at the same time plans were laid for more battleships and new plane designs to keep abreast of the Luftwaffe. FDR angered Japan by cutting off their supply of raw materials and aid. He may have had a premonition about Japan as early as 1937.

Cordell Hull, secretary of state, supported FDR's beefing up of the military. Overall, 63% of Americans supported these efforts on rearmament and 54% on FDR's foreign policies. The only dissent came from Congress, which grew less enchanted with the New Deal. In 1936-37, they declared some of its acts to be unconstitutional but the voters stood behind FDR 523-8. Only Maine and Vermont voted for Landon in 1936.

Overall, FDR's approval ratings far outweighed his disapproval ratings. This was just as true in the southwest as in the southeast or the Pacific Coast, mountain states, and the Midwest. FDR was easily the most popular president we have ever had.

The only dissent in general was against his reorganization bill and his general attitude toward helping the poor. "It takes away from our Puritan heritage," said one, "of work, thrift, and foresight. We are drifting away from ability and the will to do."

What Happened to the Missing $3 Trillion ...Or Is It $4 or $5 Trillion?

Endless money forms the sinews of war.
Marcus Tillius Cicero
106-43 BC

Bill Moyer had a guest the likes of whom I have never had a chance to see. His name? Franklin C. Spinney, the recently retired accounting department head. He oversaw the now $400+ billion defense budget. He said that too much of the Pentagon's budget is being wasted on

Cold War weapons systems and that the budget-making process is fundamentally flawed.

The folks at truemajority.org propose trimming the fat at the Pentagon and using the money to fix some of the domestic problems this country faces. Even though these issues are extremely important and vital, they are also controversial.

Spinney could not agree more. He was the only man to stand and fight against the pillage on an extraordinary degree. So great, in fact, the military-industrial complex cannot account for $3 trillion spent. How, you ask? By dividing the various units of the Pentagon into more than 65 divisions, so that they cannot keep track of what the others are doing. They may all be working on the same defense project, so who gets shortchanged?

Ask the M-16 rifleman in Vietnam, whose weapon jammed when he tried to reload. The Vietcong overran his position and he was killed. He was not alone. He was only one of hundreds more. The situation was so out of hand that our troops picked up the AK-47s left by dead Vietcong, as they were much more reliable than the M-16s.

How many soldiers died in this manner? When a torrent of letters reached Congress, an investigation showed it was not Colt, the manufacturer of the M-16, but the ammunition suppliers that were totally separate from the M-16 division. The damn ammunition had never been tested and Colt was right. It would not always work in their M-16s.

Inscribe that on the tombstones of all the men who died as a result! The Defense Department cannot be changed by any one complaint. The Pentagon is required by law to do an audit every year, but every year the answer is the same, "We can't balance where the money goes." Wolfowitz and others tried to do away with even this non-working audit; they didn't want any controls.

The result: a $3 trillion shortfall. (And over the years, it may be $14 or $15 trillion of our tax dollars). And who was in charge of the Defense funds? None other than ordained rabbi, Dov Zakheim. With his departure from the Bush Administration in 2004, the mystery of the missing funds was left wide open to speculation.

Bush still presses for more Star Wars money, when a successful result is not assured. Billions of dollars poured into a system doomed to failure. But it was the pet project of the Gipper, so it operates anyway. They even tried to promote Star Wars as an antidote to 9-11 even when a working program would have been useless. Result? More billions for Star Wars and Homeland Security, the farce perpetrated on the taxpayers.

I'm afraid the Gipper is the one to blame. When Reagan began to pour billions into defense in the 1980s, costs began to rise so quickly that today the CEO's compensation has gone from $5 million/year to $25.8 million annually. The same is true of all defense contractors; those endless voracious pets that consume tax dollars. Conversely, when less money is appropriated, as under the Clinton budgets, costs went down. You figure it out. It's much too deep for me.

IRAQ

The Army's logicians can see what's needed on the battlefield. Troops have been plagued by lack of ammo, spare parts, and fuel, a logistics mess of epic proportions. Vehicles had to be cannibalized for spare parts, and replacements took three weeks. Humvees were easily destroyed because they had no armor.

Even now, it takes the Army 34-38 days to move the requested spare parts from a depot in the U.S. to Iraq where they are needed. The Pentagon needs an overhaul in the worst way. They just are doing the job, which is required of them. Consider this fact: 27,000 contractors, who owe the government money, are still getting contracts with the government.

SOCIAL SECURITY

Poor Bush is in way over his head, and the country
Is in bad shape because of his stupid economic policies.
If that makes me a Bush-hater, then sign me up.
Molly Ivins

THE ONUS AGAINST SOCIAL SECURITY by the conservatives is longstanding. The Bush plan to derail Social Security had its origins in 1935, and their conservative stand on the Act has never changed. In 1959, Barry Goldwater spoke against the Act and made this a part of his 1964 goal for the presidency.

When Ronald Reagan was president, he too began an effort to dismantle the Social Security Act. He had long been a foe of the Act and was a supporter of the Goldwater agenda.

When the GOP lost 18 seats in the House in the 1982 mid-term election, the Republicans abandoned their outspoken resistance. It has been revived under the George Bush II presidency of 2005. Like the tactics leading up to the scare about WMDs, Bush and his chief lieutenant, Karl Rove, are stating Social Security is in crisis and needs to be replaced by his plan of individual retirement accounts, which promise a greater return than the present Social Security plan. The conservatives support the Bush plan, but stands for and against it have risen.

The "Bushies" put for the same reasoning against Social Security as Goldwater did early in 1960. They have united under the Bush plan for individual retirement accounts based on the assumption the stock market's rise will provide a better income for retirees than the present plan. They feel Social Security has led people to support the plan as an answer to their salvation. They disagree with FDR's intonation of "from cradle to grave" security and feel these ideas have destroyed our "puritan ethic" of work, thrift, and foresight. Bush is just as certain his plan will create greater voter participation, as they will be a part of the government in this new investment program.

Let's take a look at the health of the Social Security plan, which Bush terms as being in crisis as he once also believed his warnings about Iraq's WMDs. Peter DeFazio (D-OR) disagrees. "What crisis?" he asked. He offered his own plan of lifting the wage ban subject of the Social Security tax. Today it is $90,000 and millionaires of the country pay no Social Security tax. A portion of each worker's tax could be set aside in diversified stocks to insure the solvency of Social Security.

Nickolas Erhausen spent 30 years as a claim representative in Eugene, Oregon. He speaks as a citizen not as a representative for Social Security. He stated we have a false idea of the program developed in the midst of the Great Depression of the 1930s. It was a forced marriage between socialism and capitalism, so there were impurities in both ends of the program. It is not a tested welfare program or a compulsory insurance program with coverage and rates determined by Congress, not by executive whim. Some who never marry or never have children and die young never will receive a benefit. Others with children will receive their benefits if they die or are killed.

Historically, Social Security is one of the best programs ever designed on such a large scale. The costs of running this program run less than 1% a year!

Let us compare this cost to the new pension program in Great Britain. In the 1980s, with the guidance of her friend Ronald Reagan, Margaret Thatcher junked her nation's pension program in favor of one Bush is now proposing for the United States. Great Britain's program was working very well and was backed by extensive gold reserves. (It was not broken, so why did Thatcher set out to fix it?)

Today, Britain's retirement program has run upon the shoals. Costs of running the program have skyrocketed. Twenty to 30% commission fees on each retirement account are paid to stockbrokers (as would Bush's program do). Initial charges have resulted in payments of hundreds of millions of pounds to cover false claims made by these brokers. They sold programs to the workers, which promised pie in the sky, but gave out only cornbread.

Britain's program is doing so poorly; the country is casting about for a new and better program and has cast covetous eyes upon our program of Social Security. Ironic, isn't it?

Conservatives, who cautioned about "the distant future", insisting privatization was the only answer, caused Britain's problems. But they did not have to indulge in the $2 trillion borrowing program, which would be necessary under the Bush privatization plan. Their gold reserves were extensive enough to cover this cost, so Thatcher did not have to drive Britain more deeply into debt but it simply is not working.

Norma Cohen, a reporter for The Financial Times, writes, "It's a bloody mess!" Her report matches the report issued by Britain's Pension Commission that warned, "Seventy-five percent of those with private investment accounts will not have enough savings to provide adequate pensions." Guaranteed pensions have been cut and workers who believed they would get high returns have gone for naught.

What went wrong? The costs and risks of running private investment accounts outweighed the returns on these accounts, and many of the sold programs were badly planned and based on false premises. The issuers of these plans were forced to pay $20 billion in reparations.

Bush extols the virtues of his personal choice plan and often accuses skeptics as being elitists who believe the government makes better choices. Fraud aside, the fees paid to a financial manager have become a major problem. "Reductions in yield resulting from providers' charges absorb 20 to 30% of an individual's savings," said Britain's pension manager.

When Bush was confronted by the shortcomings of Thatcher's "walk in the wilderness", his story suddenly changed. He proposed to hold costs down by tightly restricting the choices made by invest-ment people by carefully regulating the money managers. (There go people's choices.) These promises made by Bush are simply not credible!

Even if the initial legislation were tightly regulated investments by private accounts, it would be followed by a hoard of lobbyists. They would use any manner to loosen their regulations and all the rules. The usual ideologies and financial firms would take a voice over the administration eager for fees. It has already started. The Finan-cial Services industry contributed lavishly to the Bush inauguration (2004), to the tune of more than $20 million.

The chairman, Jon McCrery (R-LA) of the House Security Com-mittee was accused of accepting $200,000 in contributions over the past four years, a clear violation of the ethics rule. The contributions came from securities funds and commercial banks that would all be beneficiaries under the Bush plan, which uses them to set up these accounts. In its defense, the Bush team is running ads against McCrery in his hometown of Shreveport, LA. The team is using the Internet to collect the necessary funds and hope to show they were not involved.

As far back as a 1978 run for representative from Texas, which he lost, Bush aligned himself with Reagan's stand against Social Secu-rity. The Bush platform was less regulation, lower taxes, similar to Barry Goldwater's stand on these issues. Both he and Reagan were dead set against Social Security.

Bush's stand at the time was, "Social Security is always short on money and nearly unable to pay benefits. This was a blatant false-hood, as Social Security was in salient good health in 1978. Bush has a deep belief in private ownership and the wealth-building power of the stock market.

Early in the 1980s, Bush became familiar with a laboratory for Social Security in Galveston County, TX, and two others. All three had opted out of Social Security to join a private program with con-tributors roughly equal to the Social Security tax.

This is the one now used in Chile (in the same trouble as Great Britain, by the way) and is wrongly cited by the conservatives as evidence that private accounts could work. But are they better is a matter of some debate. (Argentina's private account system is experiencing similar deep troubles as those in Chile and Great Britain.) Bush predicted Social Security would be a "bust" as early as 1982.

Bush has a great affinity for the stock market. His great grandfather founded an investment bank, and his grandfather ran Brown Brothers Harriman, one of the most prominent firms on the street. What was once an idea that appealed to the young Bush as he sat at their feet and drank at the Goldwater font of knowledge has now become the greatest gamble of his political career.

Greenspan, Bush's economic advisor, raised payroll taxes in 1983 to meet a crisis in Social Security, and it worked. It is the beginning of the Bush political logic that Social Security was failing or it would fail at some time in the future. In 2001, Bush appointed a commission to come up with a plan for private investments in Social Security, which has directly led to the stand of what we are experiencing today. It is the apple of Bush's eye, and he's staking his presidency on putting it over. This is no spur of the moment decision on his part.

One of Bush's most steadfast opponents in this issue is Molly Ivins, the political columnist. She has declared in print – George Bush is a liar, and Bush has made no moves to counter her accusation. She has been at his side for and against bush all the days of his political life. She recently criticized his $200 million effort, at the taxpayer's expense, to convince all the red states that Social Security is in peril, which it isn't, according to Molly. She has proposed that his investor accounts will cost between 20 and 30% per account.

This, along with the less than 1% to operate Social Security, has made many think twice about private accounts. Social Security is in no danger of going broke before 2042 or beyond. This figure varies from day to day, but "the sky is not falling" as Bush opportunes.

"Bush is trying to profit, using his own figures," Molly writes. "He projects them to infinity, well into the year 2080. How can we be concerned about a crisis that far into the future? No one can. We're not dealing with people who argue in good faith, so let's get it straight. Bush does not want to fix Social Security – he wants to kill it! Just as Reagan and Goldwater wanted to do in the past.

"They wanted to end it, not just to partially privatize the system. They wanted one like the pointy-headed heroes at the University of Chicago made up for Chile, which is the poster child for why we shouldn't do this."

Molly points out (1) Bush's plan does not fix Social Security. It does nothing to shore up the program, no fix, nada. (2) Bush employs a gloom and doom scenario to make his case. This is not true despite his words "The crisis is now." There is no crisis.

There are changes to be made. Ron Wyden (D-OR) has proposed raising the limits of the tax from $90,000 to $200,000 a year. This act alone would cure the 2042 shortfall and make Social Security solvent for many years beyond. "Bush's infinity figure of $11 trillion is just that, a figure. It's pure horse poop and he knows it."

Bush has predicted in his gloom and doom scenario that the accounts will be so bad because the economy is so bad they won't make any money. His figures are too rosy. "We will have more money," he has said, and there really is a free lunch. Tell that to a senior who survived the Great Depression!

Bush has maintained he will not entertain a cop-out and he wants Congress to make his tax cuts permanent. What most people do not realize are these facts:

- 54% of the tax cut goes to 2/10s of 1% of Americans who make at least $1 million a year.
- 97% of the original tax cuts go to the 4% who made $200,000 a year.

They will be fully effective by the year 2010. The cost alone will total $8-16 trillion in 2015, not including relief for the alternative minimum tax as a measure popular this year on the hill. If these two were cancelled, it would help to avert cuts in healthcare, childcare, housing assistance and food stamp assistance for low-income workers.

What about the legalized bribery of campaign finance by corporate lobbyists? $200 million will be spent to convince us to privatize Social Security and change the laws on class-action lawsuits. Are all laws in Congress passed to benefit the rich and the corporations? They want us to support the thieving of these special interests – no one has ever seen this much money spent on a single bill – the previous high was $10 million by the insurance companies to defeat Clinton's health plan.

Tort reform, another Bush goal, Molly says, means simply, "Americans give up their right to sue these bastards!" It's a big right to lose say those who agree with Molly's stand. This is just as phony as the Social Security ads. In reality, it's a fight between big business and the lawyers.

Bush is striking out at AARP for attacking his plan. Senator John McCain (is he really a Republican or a stooge for Bush's programs?) and AARP run ads wherever the two speak in favor of the plans. McCain said, "Some people tell me we don't have to worry until 2042." I asked him rhetorically, "Have we not an obligation not only to the present, but also to the future."

Bush insists, "It's not a political issue, one party trying to get ahead of the other, so nothing gets done." Social Security, bar none, is the most divisive issue around. McCain also urged Jeff Bingamon (R-NM) to support private accounts. Bingamon told McCain that Bush's plan would do nothing to strengthen the solvency of Social Security and will lead to a reduction in benefits for seniors. "It's true," he continued.

"In 50 years, Social Security will have to pay out more than it takes in, but there are steps we can take right now to strengthen Social Security (Bingamon is a member of the Senate Finance Committee, which has jurisdiction over Social Security). Privatizing Social Security is just not the right answer." He said.

Bush has taken to misleading blacks on their benefits. Since their life expectancy is lower, their chance of collecting benefits under Social Security is less. This is another falsehood put forth by Bush to intimidate blacks.

Younger blacks die disproportionately early in gang warfare, accidents, from AIDS, and are subject to HBP and diabetes more so than whites. These figures lower the life expectancy rate significantly and care caused by lifestyle differences and poor access to healthcare.

A new healthcare program instituted in Harlem seeks to address the day-to-day insult of racism blacks face, a greater access to doctors and nurses in schools and clinics set up to address AIDS, HBP, and other aspects of healthcare that blacks do not get. This program has cut 75% of the visits to emergency rooms at the hospital.

This is a first step in addressing a growing health problem that leads to a lower life expectancy in blacks. If these factors are omitted, black life expectancy factors out at 67.3 years vs. 68.6 years for whites. So what Bush tells blacks is false and misleading, another cheap effort to get their vote.

One factor Bingamon and others are addressing is raising the cap on the Social Security tax to $200,000 from $90,000. This one act alone would cover the shortfall in 2042, pushing it back a decade or more. Many people who draw Social Security do not need its help. They are the independently wealthy, about 9% of the population. If their benefits were cut off, the Social Security shortfall would disappear significantly.

Double dippers are another case to be evaluated. Should a person who gets on government pension be entitled to another? Billions alone are at stake in this one category. It would be too much to expect they would give up one or the other.

USA Today, early in March 2004, ran an editorial on Social Security outlining the facts as they saw them?

"2018 – takes in less than it pays out
"2042 (or 2052) – the Trust fund runs out of money

"2009 – the first wave of Baby Boomers will begin to draw benefits. When they do it will expose the gimmicks the Bush campaign is using to sell their 'crisis' to the people. Decades of irresponsible budgeting will then threaten the future retirees."

The excess monies collected over the years have been credited to the Trust Fund and Treasury IOUs deposited (The GOP contends the money is already spent). In 2009, the shell game begins to end. By 2018, Social Security will begin to draw on these IOUs – unless corrections are made ('tinkering', Bush calls it) the deficit will skyrocket. All this could have been avoided, and it still can be reduced.

Five years ago, we were on the way to paying on the deficit (national debt). The lawmakers simply began to borrow the excess money for Social Security benefits. This is no longer an option due to our dire budgetary situation, and Social Security will soon be a drain on the Treasury, already under a tremendous financial burden. It's a maxed-out credit card, where you lose the flexibility to take on new debt to finance the old.

A question is then raised. If Social Security will soon make the debt worse, wouldn't it be better to address the underlying deficit? To put it another way, when Bush embarked on a 60-day, 60-stop tour to promote Social Security overhaul to private accounts, are we really addressing the right problem? The bottom line shows the government, through profligate borrowing and policies that create red ink for decades to come, is simply passing the burden onto future generations – my grandchildren and theirs?

[USA Today stated if deficits are left unchecked, these chronic increases will more than offset any good, which comes out of Social Security reform. They will make the government more beholden to its creditors. (What would happen tomorrow if they wanted to collect? The mere mention of South Korea considering other investments for their surplus monies sent the Dow Jones down over 100 points.)

As the deficit surges like an uncontrollable Bay of Fundy tide, so does the interest on the national debt. Continued borrowing ($2-3 trillion, estimated cost of privatization) will only force the low interest rates up, and they spur the economy. They have been less than 6%, but these rates cannot last. "We do not hold."

USA Today said, "reform of Social Security is not worthwhile. It is only one of a number of stops that should be implemented, such as urging Americans to save more. Our balance of payments – imports to exports – is threatening to reach $600 billion this year. It is a recipe for financial disaster."

Bush's tour of the Midwest became heated. The battle over 'strengthening Social Security', as the White House calls it, has renewed the conflict between the same people and organizations that clashed in November. The liberal move-on.org, labor unions, the U. S. Chamber of Commerce, and several umbrella organizations argue for or against with equal tones of ferocity against the personal investment accounts proposed by Bush.

They use many of the same campaign ruses and tactics. One GOP ad compares Social Security to the Titanic in boisterous town hall meetings. Mass mailings are sent to reporters. Some of these groups were in on the Swift Boat ads against John Kerry and the top officials who worked to unseat Bush.

Brian McCabe of Progress For America and a leading supporter of Bush said, "I think a lot of people thought we wouldn't see much on this issue after the election, but Social Security came out of the box quickly and a lot of the groups engaged last year are engaged once more."

The Democrats are making their case against Bush's program in the heavily GOP districts where the incumbent congressmen are already wary of the coming 2006 elections. Many of them are fearful of embracing Bush's idea of private accounts and some have spoken out against privatizing, citing problems in Chile, Argentina, and Great Britain, whose programs are in deep trouble.

Representative Earl Pomeroy (D-Neb) went to see the District of Minnesota Representative Gil Gutnecht. Paying for the trip was Americans United to Protect Social Security, an umbrella group headed by the AFL-CIO and the American Federation of State, County, and Municipal Employees (AFSCME).

"If the president takes privatization off the table, our organization could cease to exist," says Brad Woodhous, the spokesman for American United. He denied a fall-out over the election when he was the communications director for the Democratic Senatorial campaign committee.

The battle over Social Security has caused a rift between the AARP and USA Next, a more conservative group whose members include former TV host, Art Linkletter. "AARP is actually to blame for the predicament we find ourselves in today," said Charlie Jarvis, chairman of USA Next.

A continuing USA Today article on Social Security shows the other side of personal accounts. Put another way, it's like going on vacation and borrowing to buy a home. When you borrow to go on vacation, there's nothing left to show when it's over, but when you buy a home, it becomes an asset. With personal accounts, workers get an asset they own and control.

By enacting comprehensive reform, we would eliminate the long-term threat of Social Security's unfunded obligation while the government's near-term borrowing might rise as we bring forward some Social Security costs. Its long-term borrowing needs would decline dramatically – assuring today's younger workers that their children will be able to enjoy the benefits of a strengthened Social Security system.

Bush also desires to eliminate the Estate Tax, but on the other side Robert Ball, seconded by David Obey (D-WI) wants to use this tax to fix the shortfall. Ball figures that by raising the wage cap on Social Security above $90,000 and by refiguring the cost-of-living adjustments, we could eliminate the shortfall. The heart of the matter is to designate the tax on estates over $3.5 million to Social Security. It would target the inheritance tax of America's richest sector of society of the coming generations.

Bush is after the AARP, which is largely noted for promoting afternoon naps for the elderly. But AARP supported Bush's Medicare Prescription Bill with its $800 billion cost and the anti-regulation bill of 1996. This is an abomination, which has cost everyone with cable television a rising monthly bill, up 20% since 1996. Bush is irritated they do not lend their support to everything he proposes.

When he was the governor of Texas, he tried to pass a law, which would make it a crime to criticize the governor. It failed.

In a late March 2005 AARP meeting, an overflowing crowd at Eugene, Oregon (a larger hall had to be secured) assembled to protest Bush's "Tear down Social Security Tour" in favor of privatizing. "He is trying to dismantle Social Security," said one of the speakers.

Barbara Meese of the legislative committee said, "Social Security is our #1 priority, and let's leave it alone. If it isn't broke, don't fix it. Just repair the cracks." Many agreed with her, and her speech was loudly applauded.

"The stock market goes up and down too much," one person said. "My parents lost everything they had in 1929," said another. And a younger man noted, "I'm still trying to recover from the downturns of 1996 and 2000. [when it fell 500 points in a single day.] It's this privatization stuff that is too risky. I wouldn't put a dime of my Social Security tax into this program. Two men next to him agreed, patting him on the back.

Another retiree quoted a Molly Ivins column. "Bush has lied to us since he was governor of Texas, 'By the time most of us retire, the system will be broke.' This is just not true. He says that unless Congress acts today, it will be too late. This isn't true either; it won't be bankrupt, as he says. All the system needs is a little tinkering and it will be fine up to 2080." She received loud cheers.

Surprise! The Fox Network supports the Bush plan. Brit Hume and William Bennett (the recovering gambler) took FDR's words out of context in their spiel on the Social Security issue. When FDR said, 'the old age pension plan' should eventually be supplanted by 'self-supporting annuity plans', he was referring to a pension plan that was created as a temporary support plan for those who were too old to pay into Social Security at the time of its creation.

These pension plans were, in fact, replaced by 'self-supporting annuity plans' – the funds are now supported by Social Security taxes. FDR did, in fact, suggest 'voluntary annuities by which individuals' initiative can increase the amount received in old age.' But he meant these merely as a supplement to, rather than a replacement of, current Social Security benefits.

Bush also calls on FDR as he debates food stamp cuts to save farm subsidies (80% of which are paid to corporate farms, pig- and chicken-raising corporate boondoggles). Even as Bush plans to dismantle Social Security, he speaks glowingly of FDR. "He did a good thing and it worked." The discussion today is to build on what he 'put in place' but the issue has changed radically since 1935.

FDR's grandson, James Roosevelt, a former senior official of the Social Security Administration, has vociferously opposed the Bush plan and many polls support his opposition and skepticism. They have shown a 56-37% disapproval rate against the Bush plan! Other polls show a decline since he began his barnstorming trip across the red states in early March. [Bush never challenges anyone who may challenge him. All his appearances are carefully choreographed and those who ask questions are "plants".] Bush's words cannot be trusted.

He spends his time trying to soothe seniors' fears at his staged conversations and before the young people toward whom he is now directing his latest pitches. He is all about soothing fears. (The ones he has created.) He has repeatedly told audiences he understands about the 'safety net' and that he was committed to preserving this net.

He is also trying to relate to the Democrats (who are non-committal in their sworn opposition to privatizing). For his Memphis, Tennessee event not long ago, he invited Representative Harold Ford (D-TN) on the platform in a failed attempt to win him over to his side. He seated Ford in the third row. Ford, who is running for the

Senate in 2006, has stated he opposes Bush's plan but he does favor private accounts, which is a fence-sitting position that pols assume so well. But Ford favors accounts like IRAs in addition to, rather than displacing, benefits from Social Security.

Ford remained unimpressed by Bush's staged event. "It wasn't a conversation," Ford said. "More like an echo." The conservatives are counting on Ford as a potential backer of private accounts.

In Bush's State of the Union address, he said his goal was to "build a better world for children and their retirement security is more important than partisan politics." If Ellen Goodman were a younger woman, her concerns would be centered on the "train wreck that is fast approaching". The Bush tax cuts are the tax burdens of tomorrow, which concerns the children of today.

Columnist Leonard Pitts worries about the Bush propaganda mill on Social Security and his religious policies, which are affecting the field of science. There are Bush 'pundits' who pressure scientists to actually alter science when it conflicts with their political goals. Stem cells, the hope of the future, is one, and possibly more frightening is the affect of the religious right, who have 20% of our population now discouraging the teaching of evolution. In its place, they substitute creationism, a fanciful tale of the Genesis creation of the earth and its people, another Bible myth. 99.9% of all scientists believe in evolution.

"There is absolutely no scientific evidence to back up their claims, save for the Bible, which 'says so, so it must be true. It was okay to believe this in 10,000 BC, but today it is a grievous error, an insult to any thinking person. It comes from Bush's claim "I am a messenger of God." What a frightening authority that is to contemplate.

(The program also provides disability benefits to those too sick or injured to work. In reality, blacks that make up 13% of the recipients receive 17% of the benefits. This runs counter to the Bush statements.)

On balance, Social Security benefits more blacks than whites, notes the Social Security Administration's Liebman and AARP. Only the conservative Heritage Foundation says otherwise. Social Security can be the difference between poverty and a decent standard of living for lower income people. Of all the reasons for personal retirement programs, racial returns from Social Security are not among them.

The disparity in the cities is too great. In Los Angeles, Chicago or New York, life expectancy for males living in poverty was 59 at age 16. The death rate of blacks at birth was 2 to 1. They have less access to healthcare and die of asthma at a rate three times that of whites. Fifteen- to 19-year-old blacks die violently more than whites and this fact alone takes seven months off black life expectancy.

The conservative Cato Institute is locked in battle with liberal groups who are against privatization. They have, for 60 years, been against the entire Social Security program. They lashed out at the USA Today article. Cato said, "These are not very bright politics, especially the ad which linked AARP to same-sex marriage and also the introduction of other non-relevant issues remotely related to Social Security." USA Today stated they would not back down. "They can run but they can't hide," said Charlie Jarvis, a spokesman.

Let's take the measurement back to Reagan in 1981. His platform aimed to shrink government spending and many Republicans believe that is when it began, and the Democrats have a better record. The GOP has added spending every year in office – $36 billion vs. $25 billion. The national debt has gone up more than $131 billion and over $400 billion under Bush. (He will have no choice about rescinding many of his tax cuts.)

As I said early on, Molly Ivins has termed "Bush a wholly owned subsidiary of Corporate America". One more group, the NRA! Anything the NRA wants from Congress, it gets! Anything it doesn't want is shoved under the rug. Despite a rising vocal support against assault weapons, Bush stood meekly by and allowed his leaders in Congress to allow the 10-year-old ban to expire! Now anyone in the United States can stroll into a gun shop and purchase an AK47, an UZI, Tec 9 or a Kalashnikov or any other military weapon of mass murder!

The NRA is sponsoring legislation supporting the gun manufacturers and dealers, giving them broad immunity from liability in civil lawsuits. Hefty campaign contributions by the NRA gave these bills a good chance of passing and are on the fast track. This is an umbrella not given to any other U. S. industry.

Bush conservatives are concerned that liberal professors run universities' classrooms. A University of Oregon spokesman says liberal professors are not able to present an articulate description of the conservative position, but they often try. The University of Oregon requires a student to take two courses in multicultural studies in which ideological subjects cannot be ignored and in the humanities, it is a 'given.'

Conservative students routinely have the opportunity to engage in a vigorous debate and a clash of ideals. Overzealous liberal professors sometimes shout them down, but they shout right back. It makes for spirited debate and intellectually honest discussions. And that's why students are here in the first place.

Today we have a whole army of young conservatives assaulting the walls and halls of knowledge. They purport to know more than their professors know. These teachers have spent a lifetime of study to become proficient in their disciplines. These spoiled young men and women, mainly from well-to-do families, and are relating the views of their staunchly conservative fathers, who, for the most part, have not read a scientific journal in 20 years, the day they graduated. These men support the complaints of their children, whose backgrounds stressed the accumulation of wealth (rather than ideas) and the accumulation of status in their upper-class groups.

These same young men and women, who are protesting liberal ideas, should get down on their knees and thank their teachers for the ideas they inculcate into their brains. If they disagree with them, it is more to the better – their teachers are challenging them to think. God forbid they wish to do that. What is this teacher saying? What does he believe? What do I believe or what have I been taught at home? Who is right? What is the truth? Is there any one truth? Those should be their concerns and are the thoughts engendered in their young minds.

Starting academic careers are notoriously underpaid. Ask anyone who was ever a T. A. (Teaching Assistant). The career itself appeals to those who are anti-materialistic and idealistic by nature. The college campus itself is a refuge from the conservatives of the business and military worlds.

Bush questions the Trust Fund, from which Social Security benefits are owed. On April 5, 2005, he called into question the value of government bonds when he visited the Public Debt Department in Parkersburg, West Virginia. He used a filing cabinet containing $1.7 trillion in bonds as a prop for his campaign for private Social Security accounts. The bonds represent money owed to the Social Security system by the Federal government. They are due to be redeemed in 2017 when benefits paid and obligations begin to exceed its income.

"There is NO trust fund," Bush said. "Just IOUs I saw firsthand." He said at a subsequent rally [which echoes what my doctor told me three weeks ago], "There is no Trust Fund left. It's all been spent!" Can this be true?

Americans rely on these Trust Fund monies to pay benefits coming due in 2017. Is Bush trying to renege on the government's obligations? The GOP has spent $1.7 trillion to pay for the $2-3 trillions in lost tax revenues caused by the tax cuts. Is Bush trying to tell the American people the government does not have to honor this obligation to them? And what about that smug comment my doctor made to me?

"What's more," Bush asked "if the Trust Fund is a black hole, everyone who pays Social Security taxes and every employee who pays matching amounts ought to stop!" This year alone, Americans will pay $160 billion into the Trust Fund, and this year, as they have done for the past five years, the government will borrow this $160 billion, spend it, and issue bonds as a promise of repayment.

We are the richest but the greatest in debt nation in the history of the world. This must end! Americans cannot afford to buy every item which China and the Far East produces. We need to stop this internal bleeding, which will reach an additional $600 billion in our owed balance of payments, just this year, 2005.

We must stop the Wal-Mart mentality, which states that more and more stores are the answer and more lower-cost items are necessary to life. It is a creeping economic disease, and it may overwhelm our economy some day (if it has not already done so and we are too unenlightened to see it).

Bush's Social Security, forecasts are in grave doubt and need to be addressed. On April 7, Bush was angered when he heard Senate GOP leaders discussing getting Democrats' support without the personal accounts Bush wants. Such a move would mark a tactical shift on the part of the GOP. Their discussion comes at a time when the Bush agenda appears to be stalled in Congress. The Democrats adamantly oppose any inclusion of privatization to shore up Social Security.

In the Senate, officials say leaders are far less interested in the alternative under which Senator Charles Grassey (R-IA) of the finance committee says he would draft. It is a bipartisan bill without personal accounts. Grassey held meeting during April 2005 and plans to present legislation this summer. He told supporters from his home state of Iowa that while Democrats are united against personal accounts, he believes there are several who are willing to discuss the outlines of his bill.

Grassey said a proposal by Senator Robert Bennett (R-UT has been the topic of much conversation. It involves reducing guaranteed benefit levels for future retirees based on their earned incomes. There would be no reduction for future retirees in the lower 30% of wage earners and the current beneficiaries would be unaffected.

Judging from the march of the Bush plan, Paul Krugman calls it a hoax. "In 50 to 60 years from now, it might work, but in the next 25 years, when the real budget deficit occurs, it does absolutely nothing!" Reporters are adding to the public's confusion. They echo Democrats' complaints but do not acknowledge the difficult choices, which the baby-boomers will have to make. The reporter's failure may be termed "math phobia".

The CBO estimates seniors will spend $1.8 trillion on drugs alone in the years 2004-2013, but reporters ignore these long-term costs, much to Bill O'Reilly's glee. Costs rise dramatically every day. We - the Congress, that is - should be debating these costs, yet they too remain silent like the proverbial ostrich. If reporters were doing their job, we would all be aware of what is going on. They are guilty, Samuelson says, of 'journalistic malpractice'.

The new Bush budget envisions deficits forever in the future. The sky is really falling, Chicken Little. Bush's budget cuts, 150 social programs, Grover Norquist, and the neocons are in ecstasy! It is a step in their stated in the direction - to cast off all the socialistic programs of the FDR New Deal.

Norquist is head of one of Bush's most effective issues management programs. He has been an outspoken foe of Social Security since his Harvard days, and he has many congressmen pledged to his creed of 'opposing all tax increases'. Former Speaker of the House Newt Gingrich, who failed in 1995 to derail all social welfare programs, calls Norquist, "the person who I regard as the most innovative, creative, courageous, and entrepreneurial leader of the anti-tax efforts and of grassroots activism in America."

Together Gingrich and Norquist would dismantle every social program ever created to help the indigent population of our country. They alone may take the shame for our homeless populations and 100 million children going to bed hungry every night. Their greatest target has always been Social Security, and they advocate the Bush plan. They oppose food stamps and aid programs for the poor with equal determination. "What this country needs is another Great Depression" Norquist is rumored to have said. He also said, "Then people would have to do for themselves without any government help."

Norquist will never get an award as a great humanitarian. He, not John Kerry, is a true elitist, one totally absorbed in himself. If he were capable of true feelings, of any empathy, he might be able to realize we live in an incredibly complex world, which has left these people behind, like so much flotsam and jetsam.*

There are millions who are incapable of dealing with the world around them. The GOP is incapable of empathy for people who do not have the required intelligence or education to confront an increasingly complex electronic world.

I know it would be hard for Grover to admit these people need our help. How can the richest country in the world have ever knowingly let children starve and grown men and women left to wander aimlessly down the corridors of our cities to die unnoticed and untended? Do you really care, Grover G. Norquist? I think you have never thought of them for one minute.

Kathleen Pender, another columnist, tries a different spin. "Bush's plan," she says, "has less flexibility than a 401K. If you decided to invest a part of your tax, you could never take it out or get loans on it. Investment options would be limited."

If one made $50,000 a year, one could contribute only 2%, but it would be mandatory as a tax. Investments in a life-cycle fund are patterned after a thrift savings plan similar to 401Ks invested in government bonds and corporate funds. At age 47, the funds automatically go into life cycle funds.

Bush has said he is willing to raise the $90,000 cap. Rick Santorini, the Senate appeaser extraordinaire, says he "doesn't know many GOPs in favor of this." Others say the GOP would be accused of raising taxes. "We're not falling for that," they said. Bush called for proposals "without retaliation on his part."

Dennis Hastert said, "It's not something I would do, but the soup's not done yet." Eliminating the cap system would mean Social Security would be solvent to 2025 and beyond all the way to 2080!

Other matters to be addressed are the glaring inequities in the Social Security tax. If you made more than $87,970, no taxes were collected. If you work as a barber, you pay on 100% of your income. If you are an MD, you pay on 33% of your income. And a CEO pays on only 2%. Apply the tax to the cap plus 10% of earned income in

* See Appendix A.

excess of the cap for the next 10 years until 100% is paid. One half of these monies could be applied to the shortfall. It would make the tax more acceptable and benefit the economy.

Bush's plan would not kick in for years when many of the Baby Boomers will be dead. For the next 45 years, his plan would cost more than it would save. Bush says all we would have to do is 'borrow' the money needed to make it self-sustaining. The Werner memo talks about borrowing $1 or $2 trillion (added to the $437 billion deficit for 2004 – now $637 billion as a result of Katrina and Rita, and possibly more) and use this money to cover the transition costs. Similar numbers are found in the media.

Privatization would cost an additional $3 trillion in its second year and $5 trillion more in the decade after that. In 2015, we will have added $15 trillion to the debt!

Bush's plan should encourage people to save more and create more capital for our future greatness. It's time to think big. Social Security and tax reform will go a long way toward getting one into the ownership society. [Note: It says nothing of the right to sue or criticize that, which is being taught. There is no 'addiction' to study in a student that feels he is infinitely wiser than his professor is. Suing a professor as Baxley claims as a right for students is too far fetched for one to contemplate.]

Recently, a new group www.ProtestYourCheck.org announced plans to spend $1 million on an ad criticizing Bush's plan. It shows an iceberg, and announcer says, 'Look below the surface and you'll find…benefit checks cut almost in half and $5 trillion in new debt.'

Robert Samuelson, the eminent economist has put his own spin on Bush's plans. He warns us about the Social Security cuts, which are coming. Reporters are failing to do the math of plan Bush. His recent bill for the Medicare Drug Plan will cost double what Bush said. "Reporters are missing an obvious fault. His plan does not address the baby boomers' retirement costs. In 2004, Social Security, Medicare, and Medicaid cost $965 billion, 8.4% of the GNP. By 2030, the cost will rise to 14% of the GNP or $1.6 trillion", he warns.

"Is Social Security reform in the public's interest?" people ask. President Lyndon Johnson had to ram his Great Society program through Congress in 1964, so there is precedence. America became a better place for it, but Grover Norquist and his conservatives want to dismantle the Johnson program, too.

Bush is defying the rules of history and the advice of his own counselors. When Johnson signed the civil rights bill, he said, "I have just turned the South over to the GOP." Bush may do the same in reverse if he continues to pursue privatization and make the South Democratic once more.

[Aside: We are all deeply indebted to *Doonesbury* for its explanation of Social Security benefits a la Bush in Tampa, Florida on February 4, 2005. Bush said, "Because all which is on the table begins to address the big cost-drivers for example, how benefits are calculated, for example, is on the table. Whether or not benefits are raised or not, benefits rise, based on wage increases or price increases." That sure makes it easy to understand Mr. President.]

"What about the price tag of the Bush plan?" asked Krugman. The press is shying away from this huge obstacle as they are doing regarding the growth of the deficit. Krugman has stated that health-care costs are the real problem, not Social Security. It's true when we spend far more on health per person than any other country.

Karl Rove reiterated the positive chance the GOP has to privatize Social Security. "For the first time in years," a memo read, "it is an issue we can win." The public has to be convinced of two contradictory things Krugman wrote. "1) Drastic change is needed right away and 2) the looming cost of the baby boomers' benefit payments. The GOP has admitted Bush's plan does nothing to reduce the cost even with the best of circumstances. "It's just an excuse to slash social insurance programs," say many detractors.

"The Bush strategy is not washing," Krugman says. As soon as the voters heard that privatization would involve benefit cuts, support for 'reform' was greatly lessened. Another bad sign: Across the nation,

GOP governors, finding their constituents really wanted social services, are now talking "tax increase."

The best bet is that Bush will make the poor suffer (by cutting down on food stamps and other social programs), but he will fail to make a dent in the middle class entitlement programs. The best theory is "to starve the least programs", not the whole beast. The cry is that there is a looming fiscal crisis on the horizon. Bush's most trusted advisor, Alan Greenspan, isn't wrong about that. It could bring down the whole GOP administration like a desk of cards when someone shakes the table.

Americans who enter the workforce after the Bush plan goes into effect and choose to open private accounts as guaranteed income received after retirement should know that if anything goes wrong, if they invest in the wrong stocks, for instance – these benefits would be nearly eliminated. Samuelson and Krugman have presented a scenario for financial disaster.

Workers with private accounts would open to CLAWBACK, a nice euphemism for having to mortgage their future in order to finance their accounts. Secondly, these private accounts do nothing to improve the finances of Social Security (not for many years in the future). Bush admits this fact – there would be large benefit cuts in addition to the CLAWBACK.

Jason Furman of the Center on Budget and Policy Priorities, estimates that the guaranteed life of a worker born in 1990 and after additional benefit cuts would be only 8% of the worker's prior earnings, compared with the 35% benefits under Social Security today! This really means that under Bush's plan, workers with private accounts whose stock fared poorly would be *destitute*. (They would time travel back to 1937.)

Why should the working class of America be exposed to this much risk? [It's easy for Bush to promote. He bought a ranch and a mansion with the inside money he made in the Texas Ranger sale – estimated at a little over $14.6 million. Yes, Gloria, there truly is a Santa Claus, if you are a Bonesman.]

There are two questionable and vexing points for seniors. If you choose a personal account, you give up a certain amount of your Social Security benefits. You come out ahead if your personal account exceeds 3%. It is possible but not without risks, according to Samuelson. Today's t-bonds pay only 1% over inflation. It used to be 3%.

To earn more than 3%, one would have to put money into stocks and bonds. There is more risk involved if one's income was not above the poverty line. One would need an annuity to make up the difference. Today, a couple earning $12,490 is below this line. The more one invests affects the amount of benefits and more likely the need for an annuity. The amount received is to appease the critics who feel the accounts may leave some people penniless. It makes it very difficult for Bush to strike a balance between ownership and benefits to be received.

Two trillion dollars has been set aside in a reserve fund backed up by Certificates of Deposit payable by the U. S. government. The GOP says these funds have already been spent by the rising budget debt, but this is not true. There is enough money in these CDs to fund Social Security well up to 75 years from today. At that point, money would have to be borrowed from the General Fund to cover the shortfall.

"What about the price tag on Bush's plan?" asked Krugman. "The press is shying away from this huge obstacle as they are doing regarding the growth of the deficit." Krugman has stated healthcare costs are the real problem, not Social Security. "It's true we spend far more on health per person than any other country, yet rank near the bottom among industrial nations in indicators from life expectancy to infant mortality. Our healthcare has the highest costs and the worst results!"

The GOP has admitted Bush's plan does nothing to reduce the cost even with the best of circumstances. Americans are in debt up to their eyeballs, and the new bankruptcy law has cut out their only avenue to a new start in life and as the ad stated, "I can't pay the interest on my bills. Won't someone out there please help me?"

THE DEMOCRATIC PARTY

Let's Bring God Back into the Democratic Party

We do not walk alone.
Great Spirit walks beside us.
Know this and be grateful.
Elizabeth White
Hopi pastor, educator, and mystic

I KNOW FEW PEOPLE WHO do not believe in a higher being. The American Indian saw the One Above all around him, in the trees, in the animals, and in the waters. They did not walk alone; the Great Spirit walked beside them. No one could reproach the Indian for not believing and caring for his Mother Earth.

The GOP has made a great deal about their faith-based initiative that has turned out to be more symbolic than substantive. They proclaim, "Let no child be left behind" and then do not pass funding that will make this a reality.

An Indian would say, "Great White Father, him speak with forked tongue as he did when he took our lands from us."

One Democratic candidate left his church because they could not agree on where a bike path should go. The religious issues of this campaign are far greater – prayer in schools and same-sex marriage – and the GOP leads the field in these issues. Democrats, too. Let's take a stand and discuss these issues openly.

There are many religious issues that Democrats can grasp and make themselves heard. Bush is trashing our environment; the Tongass Forest in Alaska is now slated for clear-cutting. Smokestacks spew CO2 and arsenic into the air, and the GOP turns their heads. **THIS IS A RELIGIOUS ISSUE!** No president or corporation can poison our air with impunity when there are measures like SCRUB-BERS, which may be employed and these pollutants erased. Let's make this a religious issue.

What has Bush done about poverty in this country? How many children go to school each day with no food in their stomachs? Funds for free lunches have been cut or eliminated altogether. In a rich country like ours, no one should go to bed hungry as these children are allowed to become malnourished. **THIS IS A RELIGIOUS ISSUE!**

Did not Jesus say, "Blessed are the peacemakers"? Is this a part of the GOP's religion – to wage war on an inferior country like Iraq? The GOP has created false reasons for their new war – there were no WMDs, no hidden missiles, Saddam was not part of 9-11. He has no ties to Osama bin Laden; in fact, they are mortal enemies. **THIS SHOULD BE A RELIGIOUS ISSUE FOR ALL OF US, NOT JUST THE DEMOCRATS OR THE GOP.**

God is a personal issue, but He is not a private issue. It is wrong for the Democrats to restrict religion to the private sphere. The GOP has made this an issue solely on terms of individual moral choices and sexual ethics. Allowing the GOP to determine religious issues is suicide for Democrats.

Who has the right to determine the moral issues? Karl Rove? George Bush? The GOP? Not all of us adhere to the same values, and moral issues are open to interpretation.

I do not know anyone who does not believe in a higher power. Not to do so makes you God!

Democrats must unite and take the moral ground back to the people to decide. This should be debated at every political gathering.

I wish Bush had read Keats on truth. "Beauty is truth, truth beauty. All ye know on earth and all ye need to know."

Bush believes he is the whole enchilada. Some even claim he's been appointed by God to lead us. And he "modestly" agrees, head bowed, but smiling. There is no end to his obfuscation. One day this, another day that. Who knows what he will say tomorrow? Whatever works, he believes, and when thwarted, he puts his goals in a different dress. And he chided Kerry for changing sides! "He seems to believe," as one columnist said, "win some, lose some"!

Under Clinton, the U. S. enjoyed worldwide acclaim, friendship, and good relations. All that has vanished in the face of George's cantankerous behavior. In Europe, they call him the "Boy Emperor".

"You're either with me or against me." What the hell kind of foreign policy is that? Can a man, wholly owned by corporate America lock, stock, and barrel be president of all the American people? The recently passed Medicare Act to give a drug benefit to seniors favors only the pharmaceutical companies and HMOs.

Bush's HUD Secretary resigned to run for the Senate in Florida to replace Sen. Bob Graham. Karl Rove urged Mel Martinez to run for the seat to be a candidate for the U. S. Senate, Martinez's looks and demeanor could easily get him an acting spot on the Sopranos. All this cheating, the half-truths, the innuendoes, and the outright lies; this is George Bush's real religion. Don't be fooled! Don't let him set the religious agenda!

Need for Religion – Part II

I am a millionaire. That is my religion!
George Bernard Shaw
1856-1950

Surveys have shown that people who go to church regularly vote for the GOP. Dr. Dean buried himself in the primaries when he denied his religiosity. He lost a great part of his base.

Bush, on the other hand, has chosen the divisive issue of gay marriage to forge an even stronger base among fundamentalist Christians. Bush and Rove know there is no chance of passing an amendment to the Constitution banning gay marriage. Such issues take years and often fail. They are appealing to his "compassionate conservative", of which there is no such thing. It's a Rove catchphrase, which has an appeal to two separate political groups and which created a gentle issue for Bush. Worse, it's an oxymoron!

In Bush's latest attempt to downplay the power on the real issues – the war, the growing deficit and the loss of jobs – he is reaching back to the tactics of his father in 1988. If a scurrilous approach worked in the past, why not run it by the peasants and the great unwashed again and see if they salute as they did so many years ago?

Bush's conservative base has grown restless watching his non-action on the real issues, and he needs an issue to re-ignite their loyalty and charge up their votes. They're also upset about increased government spending and his plan to liberalize immigration in an era when so many have lost their livelihoods.

Part of Bush's and Rove's policy is to take the public's mind off the important issues. Gary Bauer and Pat Robertson have applauded his attack on gay marriages, as have many Christians.

In 1988, George '41 manufactured a number of issues to divert the people. The Pledge of Allegiance was raised, Dukasis's paroling of the criminal, Willie Horton, who killed again, then the desecration of the flag in his insistence of non-tolerance of the American system. All these smokescreens worked in the elder Bush's campaign. Bush II hoped the gay marriage issue would work for him.

Bush has mobilized a strong base of protest against abortion, prayer, and patriotism (the last refuge of scoundrels). Homosexuality and the popular culture are all working to his advantage.

We need to cast the loss of jobs as a religious issue. Corporations are embracing China and India for their new capitalism, which says its okay to desert towns and cities that have built their prosperity around a particular industry. If they can save you pennies on the finished product, it's okay to invest in these two countries and in any other that can save them money. The bottom line rules!

To destroy the economy of even one American community is a true non-Christian act; not whether two people who love one another may unite and profess their love to the world. It is a very loving thing to do and does not need the criticism of a George Bush. Besides, it's for us or the state to decide, not the federal government. George, it's time for you to re-evaluate your philosophies - if you have any outside allegiance to the corporations that are slowly destroying America by obliterating its economic base and rationalizing it as "good business practice", and opting out on pensions owed to the workers.

One should not stand by and watch the desecration of the American capitalistic system and still be a Christian conservative. Take away all the tax incentives these corporations have been given over the years. They dodge millions – billions in taxes, using loopholes, which have been granted to them.

Our trade deficit with China is nearly $1.25 trillion and growing. Is this not an aberration of the highest order, a non-Christian thing to tolerate when you are destroying the livelihood of millions of people? Roll back NAFTA. It has only been an excuse for countries to violate environmental concerns.

The Mexicans are not gaining a greater economic base – their average rate for a 54-hour week is less than $5.00 a day. In turn, their landscape is becoming an even greater sewer, and law enforcement is becoming a serious problem. It's so bad the subway has to run two trains, one for men and one for women. If they didn't, women would be "groped" endlessly, even assaulted, as other men cheered the perps on! Is this progress?

In an effort to blunt the loss of factory jobs, working at McDonald's has been classified as industrial work. Each hamburger assembled is now an individual work. The people creating them are the same as workers on an assembly line at Ford or General Motors. Imagine?

The jobs created out there, George, are figments of your imagination. George, rein in your minions, who are attempting to promote such nonsensical ideas.

I know the "Peter Principle" is winning when I hear such things contained in an economic report. The jobs being created over there, George, are like the weapons of mass destruction. They are there, but you haven't found them yet.

Laura Bush is the consummate Stepford wife. She's on the stump advocating Bush doctrines: a quality teacher in every classroom by 2005 and no child left behind and no money to implement those goals. She is out there to show George is "compassionate" and that's it. She's become a bully-pulpit prop to encourage young people to get into teaching. She's defending a sham, just like any good Stepford wife should do. It's only a pseudo-serious effort, but poor Laura doesn't realize this. She is angry because people are criticizing her husband. It's very sad Laura is more compassionate than George could ever be. She is only performing her wifely duty.

AFTERWARD

KATRINA POINTED OUT THE GOP philosophy – look after the well being of America's wealthiest citizens. Katrina made clear their cruel treatment of the poor, yet the GOP continued to insist that non-defense budgets must be slashed to pay for reconstruction.

Bush contends there is no reason to rescind his tax cuts that benefit the wealthy. He suggests cutting social programs and delaying the Medicare prescription drug plan would provide a measure of assistance for the poorest Americans but these cuts would hurt the poor the most. The reprehensible Bankruptcy Reform bill not only takes away these protections from people in dire straits but also makes no exceptions for those caused by natural disasters.

The difference is clear. The GOP turned aside an amendment to exempt natural disasters from the new bill but it was defeated in a straight party line vote. John Conyers (D-MI) attempted to reintroduce an exemption for Katrina's victims, but the GOP refused to bring it up for a vote. It's time for the government to open up its heart as people have done all over this country and at least do the same.

Bush on Katrina

Bush is talking up a Gulf recovery, but don't be too surprised if he doesn't follow through. He has said no amount of money, no effort, would be spared. $200 billion, no problem! This will be bigger than the Marshall Plan.

The country has placed its faith in Bush before and has come up empty. In March 2003, in another nationalized TV appearance, he told us we had no choice but to go to war with Iraq. He was sitting on the most lethal weapons ever devised. So, we went to war although Saddam had not fired the first shot.

Since then, we have lost almost 2500 men and women in our military ranks and have spent $200 billion and counting. The weapons Bush claimed Saddam had have never been found. Bush and the neocons boldly lied to us.

Now he is making the same promise to rebuild the Gulf coast and the city of New Orleans. The cost – no problem. We'll just cut down on all the unnecessary expenses of government (i.e., all the social programs of FDR and President Johnson).

In Iraq, on the same day Bush reassured us about New Orleans, a report was issued that the continued violence in Iraq has frightened away any prospective investors, which has slowed down reconstruction and, worse, disrupted oil production.

Even in Jaf, The Times stated, an Iraqi city often cited as a U. S. success story, our officials acknowledged that reconstruction has been slowed by very poor planning, corrupt contractors, and a lack of any continuity among coalition officers. Polls have turned against Bush in the past few weeks, and he has the lowest approval rating of his administration, less than 32%. He promises, but he really doesn't know how to deliver, and we are losing faith in him.

Bush disputes his early days of BACCHANALIA and drug taking (he was not alone in the Baby Boomer culture). He refuses to say he did drugs – yes, he inhaled – bedded whores and young, naïve women, was drunk, and a true reprobate. "When I was young, I did foolish things" is his only defense for his misdeeds. He was a stiff shirt and straight arrow following Clinton's prolonged adolescence.

Bush's election in 2000 was a reaction vote for someone who promised to restore dignity to the White House. No more little office parties, no more Hollywood stars jumping on the Lincoln bed.

In this time, Bill Clinton was just a warm-blooded good ol' boy from Arkansas, who could feel everyone's pain – he was a reaction to the cold New England, out-of-touch George H. W. Bush, himself a reaction to tough-guy Ronald Reagan, who was a reaction to the peanut farmer with a preacher streak, who was a reaction to the corrupt era of Watergate.

Bush's post-Katrina-Rita persona defies belief. He, who was so slow in responding to Katrina, has suddenly emerged from his dormant state to present the new Bush – nothing short of having a new enlightenment from God Almighty. Every time you look up, he is in the way of FEMA workers trying to repair the storm damage. (21 trips so far)

Bush has astounded his fellow conservatives by declaring that poverty in the U. S. has "roots in the history of racial discrimination, which cut off generations from the glorious rewards of the capitalistic system". One might think the Johnson program for poverty had been reborn. "We have a duty to confront this poverty with bold action."

People are amazed at this over-simplification of longstanding failures (since Julius Caesar's day and the earliest hunter-gatherer society).

Heretofore Bush has had zero interest in attacking poverty. Zilch! Nada! He has done just the opposite. All the programs, which have been cut by the tax cuts, were programs that constituted a safety net for the poor!

You may believe in his present rhetoric if you wish, but many others and I feel it's just one more Rove speech to cover up the failures of the Bush Administration. Bob Herbert compared it to the truth where Sally pulls up the football before Charlie Brown can kick it. How often can he be fooled? Pretty often, right?

Bush Appointments

Molly Ivins continues her 100% disgust with the Bush appointments, the latest appointing a veterinarian to head the Woman's Health section of the FDA. "The only reason he was chosen," says Molly, "was because Michael Brown was busy running FEMA in Homeland Security." He too was exhausted by his handling of the Katrina disaster and had to get home to his wife and walk his dog.

The last head of Woman's Health, Susan Wood, had quit in disgust over the failure of the passage of Emergency Plan B, the availability of the morning-after contraceptive pill to be sold over the counter against the FDA's own scientific advisory board. Lester Crawford refused to okay its sale. (On September 23, Crawford resigned. Like Brown, a political appointee, because he was a good friend of Bush, he couldn't take the heat in the kitchen.)

The Bush appointments may be traced back to his mother Barbara not laying down the law in his childhood which has resulted in the Iraq War and other acts of petulant pique. There is no other way to explain these childish appointments. "My way or the highway", that's George's mantra.

There is Erwin Faulke's appointment to Assistant Secretary in charge of the health and safety of workers. Who is Erwin Faulke? He is a partner from the most notorious union-busting law firm in the United States. It was an act, Molly says of "a certain arch, flippant malice on Bush's part."

Another pick placed a timber industry lobbyist at the head of the Forest Service. He has also appointed a lobbyist who represented the worst air polluters in the country as head of the Clean Air Division at EPA. At Superfund cleanup we find a woman whose last job was teaching corporations the best ways to avoid and evade the regulations put forth by the Superfund.

The recent rise in gas prices has the whole country in an uproar. The FTC has been so embarrassed by governors' demands for an investigation that they have capitulated and will investigate if there was price gouging. Unfortunately, a former lawyer who worked for Chevron/Texaco will head the probe.

As a result, the public is not being well served by this plethora of obscene appointments. These men and women are incompetents of the first order far beyond the limits that the Peter Principle envisioned. Many are anti-competent in positions of responsibility.

Another bastion of femininity, The Violence Against Women expires October 1, 2005 and must be re-authorized by then. An Office of Violence Against Women exists in the Department of Justice. After Bush entertained the misogynist Musharraf from Pakistan only days ago, this act too is in jeopardy. Every year more than 300,000 women in this country are raped and more than four million are assaulted. Funding for family violence has been cut by $48 million this year. Not a good sign.

The Bush Legacy

Is it too late for him to rescue his legacy for posterity? Is he really a good guy or warmonger, who led us into a war, which has cost almost 2500 American lives and untold thousands of Iraqi lives? Many are so appalled by the Bush policies, his arrogance, and attitude that they are incapable of seeing how he could have been re-elected in 2004. But, then again, was he?

James Robison, a Dallas, Texas TV person, said he recalls saying when Bush was governor, "I want to be remembered the rest of my life, when I walk into a Wal-Mart to buy bass lures," as "This used to be our governor. His father was the president, that is."

Bush once said, "I can't explain it. I feel I'm supposed to run for president. My country needs me at this time." The president, a "born-again" evangelical, is also a former pilot. "If Jehovah is his co-pilot, navigator, and bombardier, Bush may regard talk of legacy as super-fluous, if not sacrilegious."

Legacy is no more than lame-duck talk, journalistic jargon. The coffee clutch meetings are more West Wing scenes than reality. It would be insane to govern in terms of a future legacy.

The Bush antics in the White House were easily foretold when he was the governor of Texas. As president, he has pushed Demo-crats aside, pushed his tax cuts, gotten the U. S. into a controversial war, ignored international treaties, nominated right-wing judges, expanded police powers, boosted military spending, and – worst of all – rolled back environmental protections. These are all marks of a self-centered juvenile personality, which has little regard for anyone but himself.

There can be little argument he did not change the tone of DC and only made it more contentious. He was not a uniter as he promised us but a worse divider than Nixon. Partisans will blame the Democrats, and they in turn blame Bush's stubbornness but no reasonable assess-ment of Bush has to acknowledge the venomous partisan divisions he created.

Bush seemed to grasp and revel in the insidiousness of the divi-sions he created all through his eight years of what many see as the most calculating political presidency in history (led by the Machia-vellian Karl Rove). The American public now longs for a reliable politician, who speaks without endless strategic considerations. It is often so bad, his spokespeople are reviled when they answer ques-tions asked by the media.

Bush campaigned as a man from the center, one tolerant and respectful of his opponents' views. He was to be a man beyond poli-tics, was broadminded enough to be a compassionate conservative, yet he has become an oxymoron.

As a candidate and as governor, Bush seemed at ease with ideological diversity. He opposed the issues of the far right and this became evident early in the days before 9-11. He opposed gay marriage and abortion, even in cases of incest and rape. He believed he, like Billy Graham and other religious zealots, had a direct line to God, who had chosen him to lead the country.

After the controversial choice of him to be president in 2001, he promised to heal the great divide it caused, but he made little effort to do so. He never made a run at a constructive consensus, and he made a mockery of his promise "not to serve one party but to serve on nation." As soon as he walked into the White House, he was transformed into a conservative demigod and purist, who felt he had won a mandate to govern as he wished.

In his first day in office, he issued an order to cut the family planning programs, which counseled on abortion, a move, which inflamed the Left and delighted the Right. In the next weeks, he reneged on his promise to cut CO_2 emissions and abruptly withdrew the US from international treaties. He named only a single Democrat to his Cabinet and pushed through the controversial appointment of John Ashcroft, further alienating the Left.

The Right became the center of his governing! When an opponent created controversy, he denigrated Democrats, who were accused of "playing politics" when they fought his tax plans. The Democrats also opposed his education bills, resisted his trade policies, rallied against his Social Security plans, blocked his judicial appointments, and stood in the way of John Bolton's appointment to the United Nations. Very little that Bush proposed was agreed to by the Democrats, who banded together as never before.

Bush believes in the 51% - never mind the 49% who disagree with him. They don't count, as long as you win. That's all that matters.

He is Vince Lombardi – there is no second place, but 50% is hardly a point to rally the nation around. His changes for Social Security, tax reform, the Iraq War, and Supreme Court nominations are hard tasks for a 50% majority to control with. Custer thought he had a 50% chance at the Little Big Horn, and look what happened to him.

Bush's appointment of John Bolton to the UN as Congress was on recess – Bush loves his contentiousness – it reminds him of his youthful days when he, too, was a maverick and a whoremonger.

If Bush were truly concerned about leaving a legacy for his girls, I would like to take the temerity of suggesting a few changes in his rough approach to politics. Here are 10 ways, Mr. President, you can shelter your legacy:

1. Rove's getting into deep doo-doo is a break for Bush in disguise. It presents a chance for him to once again become his own man. Rove should be shunted off to a deep dark room in the back of the White House. He is failing you, George. It's true he "won" two elections for you, but he has not managed to get a majority on your side. His manner is too abrasive and does not create trust in your pronouncements. People feel there is a hidden agenda in whatever he says and does. People do not respect Karl Rove, and you need this respect.

2. Quit blaming the opposition on politics on all these issues – the war, John Bolton, Social Security – they are all no more political than you make them with your disapproval. You need to elevate the debate on these issues by being more respectful of the Democrats' motives.

3. Quit blaming The Washington Post, New York Times, and Washington in general in an attempt to score political points. It's not a basketball game; it's much more serious.

4. Hold more press conferences. You have been setting a record for the least number since "Silent" Cal.

5. Have you thought about a visit to the embattled governor of California? It's not a foreign land and many of your constituents live there. He needs your help, and a visit would be beneficial to you both.

6. Make a stronger effort to befriend conservative members of Congress. Invite them to the White House for lunch and a beer or two. (I have faith in your non-al pledge.)

7. Stop acting like someone on "So you want to be a super millionaire", who has won the $10 million prize. The Lord knows – we all know – you don't know it all. Practice more true humility, not accidental humility.

8. Don't join the radical Republicans, like DeLay, Frist, and Gingrich, who live only to demonize the Democrats. They need the exposure; you don't.

9. For God's sake, stop your promotion of creationism! You are courting the converted when you do so, and you irritate the large number of intelligent people who do not believe dinosaurs came over on Noah's Ark. (If this were true, they would have gobbled up all the other creatures.) This makes people laugh at you.

10. Personally, I hope you do not follow any of my suggestions. If you do, it would make you a much stronger leader, and I have fallen in love with all those weaknesses that I have cited.

You could also cut down the stage managing of your every appearance in public. The people are tired of you speaking only to informed crowds, which have been carefully screened for dissenters. You are doing more harm than good for yourself. Remember South Carolina in 2004 and John McCain. That one act could have cost you the election if McCain had "seized the moment."

People scoff at the mention of Richard Nixon's name, but he left many great legacies to the American people – the Environmental Protection Agency (which your minions are chipping away piece by piece), the volunteer Army, the 18-year-old vote, desegregation of Southern schools, and the Occupational Safety and Health Administration (OSHA). These are all positives, Mr. President. Where are yours? If you end Detente with the Soviet Union and opening up China to the world, it's an outstanding legacy.

We Democrats mourn that Gore and Kerry could not offer more in their campaigns, which were listless and misdirected. The only image they presented was a macho one. George Bush was a reality, the prodigal son come back home. He was an admitted screw-up while his foes pleased their elders. Raymond Chandler would have characterized Gore and Kerry as "Tarzan on a big red scooter."

The fact that FDR and Lincoln suspended civil liberties during wartime (FDR regretted what he did to loyal Japanese citizens), it does not excuse Bush's actions at Abu Ghraib and Guantanamo Bay.

"There is no such thing as the past", said historian David McCullough. "Adams and Jefferson did not go around saying 'Isn't this fascinating, living in the past? Aren't we quaint in our funny clothes?'"

They lived in the present, but it was different from ours, and they perceived reality in a different way. The most positive move Bush could make to preserve his legacy would be to approve the stem cell bill. His legacy would be extended into the far future, and millions would be beneficiaries.

Bush Crossed the Line

As if it were yesterday, I remember walking into John Prince's freshman literature course. John held up two books for us. One was *Animal Farm* and the other was *Brave New World* by George Orwell. In Orwell's book, he imagined a world in which everyone was watched by Big Brother, a symbol of a brutal totalitarian regime. Mr. Prince told us these two books were avenues into the future for us, and he told us to read them carefully and to remember the lessons they taught.

It has been years and years since I heard John's words, but today – December 15, 2005 – the Bush presidency introduced us to Big Brother. Bush admitted he gave the NIA (National Intelligence Agency) permission to tap phone lines and emails here at home and overseas. He did not require them to get a warrant to do so and in essence became a real life Big Brother. The whole program was covert, not overt. Therefore, it did not require a warrant. And this made it a crime of the first magnitude. Bush then had the effrontery to accuse The New York Times of committing treason for its divulgence of the spying program in a time of war.

George Will, the conservatives' mouthpiece, defended the president's program. Will claimed the liberals have a program of "extended supervision of life." He was parroting the words of Ronald Reagan from 1982. It was not the Democrats who brought the Terry Schiavo case before the world, telling a woman what she could do with her body. It is conservatives like Will who claim the right to tell us with whom we may fall in love.

Conservatives also claim tax reform (used to gross inequities) as an attack on free speech. Tax reform is an issue sorely needed since the days of Richard Nixon. Bush, for years now, has implied those who disagree with his words and works are "un-American", for their disagreements on the Iraq War.

Bush will not discuss any issue before a general crowd. His speeches take place only before carefully selected conservative groups, and even these are carefully monitored to keep out anyone who may dissent. Will agrees with Bush's stands on the issues.

With the spying program, Bush has pointed a finger at us as being Big Brother. It would have made Orwell laugh at the Bush antics. Bush claims the authority was his under the Patriot Act, which has been criticized from Day One when it was passed.

Now our lives will be an open book. We will be forced to divulge the most intimate details of our lives. (Isn't privacy an inherent right of the citizens of a democratic society?)

Bush has used sophisticated computers and all the new advances in software to monitor our citizens. The information gleaned is passed on to private and public agencies. Each of us will soon have his or her own data sheet, which will begin at the date of our births (as if credit agencies do not already have most of the pertinent data).

This, unfortunately, is only the tip of a Titanic-like iceberg. Other organizations are carefully tracking our income (except the super-rich who have it stashed in secret accounts overseas, possibly $10-15 trillion) and our spending habits, and what books we read (they are trying to get librarians to divulge which books we check out; thankfully they are refusing to do so). It you get a speeding ticket or even a parking ticket, it will be recorded and all our cell phone calls will be monitored. Many of our freedoms have been stolen and are being taken from us every day the GOP continues to run our country.

If you indulge yourself through the use of credit cards and fall behind paying, it will be recorded and your credit rating red-flagged. This means a higher interest rate on your car insurance. Woe be to those who fall deeply into debt. It will be cash upfront for them.

Looking for a job? You will have to substantiate every detail of your life, your grades in college, and the status of your marriage. Do you discipline your children to be good, upstanding citizens unlike Jeb Bush's kids and George's twins?

What do you do when they mix up your credit card report or when you become a victim of credit identity theft? It could take months or years to regain your rightful standing. Computer theft of one's records is a growing problem, which grows larger every month and year.

If all this hasn't frightened you enough, I hope at least you will stop taking lightly all of Bush's and the Neocons' acts. Remember mostly Molly Ivins' warning, "They do not only wish to govern, they wish to rule." The dissolution of the Bankruptcy Act was the first of many acts in their plans.

Privacy is the greatest of man's gifts. Shakespeare said, "What infinite heart's ease must kings neglect, that private men enjoy! And what have kings that privates have not, too, save ceremony, save general ceremony?"

EPILOGUE

IF WE GO BACK TO the time of Eve, Cro-Magnon, and Neanderthal Man, we will find the residing place of Grover Norquist's and the Neocons' mentality. In those days, the reptilian brain guided men, kept them safe in their primitive existence. Trust, caring and concern were words not found in the lexicon of their speech.

These words came later on when man learned to work in some kind of harmony with his fellow beings. Wars were fought as the reptilian brainstem still ruled. Thousands, millions were killed as men sought the one true answer to their existence. (They did not find it. It does not exist. We each must find our own.)

Religion seemed to provide an answer and soon there were 1,000 of them and serious wars began to be fought over their creeds. The reptilian brain still ruled many groups that thought they were better.

All was not lost. Gentle, loving, caring people arose. Man created music and poetry.

Left out was Grover Norquist and the Neocons. They were content to languish in the reptilian stems of their brains. It still rules many. World War I and World War II testified to this. (Since 10,000 B. C., there have been only 64 years when a war was not being fought somewhere in the world.

Iraq is our today war fun by these unfeeling, uncaring reptilian brainstem men. It is still a driving force, not a recessive one.

When will these men learn the wisdom of e. e. cummings: "Giving, and giving only, is the reason for living."

In each of us there is a semblance of a reptilian brain Freud called it the ID. It is a remnant from the first reptile like salamander like amphibian who shed its fins and developed feet which he used to crawl up on the land in 300 BP. It was the first of thousands of evolutionary steps which led up to the humanoids three million five hundred thousand years ago. These higher beings would rule the earth and all its creatures.

Within the ID we find the lower powers of the human brain. There is little spirituality and no care and concern for fellow humanoids. Their wish and goals are of no concern. As humanoids because Homo Sapiens is a branch of the evolutionary tree weakened and broke off. The lifes of humanoid developed ID like qualities unlike those we accept as being human like.

These ID like brains retained all the reptilian like features of the earlier creatures. They were hostile and warlike. They lacked little concern for other beings. Some from this tree ruled over the land. Their names are legion: Caesar, Alexander, Mohammed, Hulagu Kahn, Kaiser Wilhelm, Hitler and Mussolini, to name but a few.

In our time Abraham Lincoln joined a new party, the GOP. He was elected but his party was one who followed their own inclinations. BossTweed is an example. These grew like a modern day Wal-Mart and in the early 20th century, President Theodore Roosevelt had to pass anti-trust laws to reign them in.

With the election of Ronald Regan in 1980 the GOP became once more a powerful entity. Iran Contra was the result but the reptilian like brains which were behind these schemes. With the election of George W. Bush, we soon found ourselves in another unprovoked war based on phony information once again led by the war like reptilian minds of his cabinet and administration. We were not greeted as liberators in Baghdad as Cheney and Wolfowitz had promised.

Grover G. Norquist was in ecstasy as the Bush tax cuts forced cuts in spending for the poor and only benefiting the top 10 percent. He danced as the poor suffered loss of the benefits which enabled them to barely stay alive. (If a poll were held, Norquist would easily be elected "Meanest Man in the United States".

Norquist and the others supporting the tax cuts are ignoring the thundering economic train wreck which Samuelson, Paul Krugman and others promises just likes ahead. Our debt in 2005 reached $400 billion not counting additional monies for the Iraq war .

Norquist and others are calling for more tax cuts to "strangle and starve the beast." We stand precariously on the edge of bankruptcy and Bush adamantly claims there will be no tax increases, the only solution to stop the approaching cataclysm.

FINAL THOUGHTS

Once fully enslaved, no nation,
State, city of this earth ever
Afterward resumes its liberty.

DICK CHENEY STANDS FOURSQUARE BEHIND Bush. He, too, believes in unlimited spying. It has been his guideline since he apprenticed under Nixon and Kissinger. No acts or expressed thoughts are too far beneath his ken. You can scramble your house on Google, but we all know where you live, Mr. Cheney, in the deep dark gloom of the Forest of Weir. Blurring his residents' image is right in line with his ability to turn things upside down.

And let us not forget Rummy, Cheney's sidekick in the Ford Administration. It was Rummy who recommended Cheney to Ford and the one who succeeded him as chief of staff when he was elevated to the defense secretary post in the Ford Cabinet. (Ford – another outstanding example of the Bush mentality. A good linebacker, but a poor man playing chess and bridge, those games which require intellect or choosing men of good character to lead us.

Maureen Dowd tells us that these two were exponents of wiretapping in the Nixon Administration. They believed in the unlimited power of the presidency.

Cheney went on record in expressing his distaste of the erosion of power of the president. It is easy to see Cheney is weak in history, for he never read Churchill, who said, "Dictators ride to and fro on the backs of tigers." The tigers are getting hungry.

Cheney said the president "needs to have his constitutional powers unimpaired (which would make him a dictator) in the pursuit and conduct of national security."

"What about checks and balances," Dowd asks. "Warrants, civil liberties, they are all so 20th Century" Mr. Cheney said. When Nelson Rockefeller pushed a plan to help develop alternative sources of energy, which helped to table the motion? Dick Cheney, of course. He is, Dowd says, "a menace." I admire her clear thinking.

It is difficult to say when this corruption of our political system will end. Abramoff is just one of over 14,000 registered lobbyists in DC. Most are honest, and their work is not a crime. They follow the 1st Amendment guideline, "the right to petition for a redress of grievances". That's what they do. They do not, as Abramoff has done, commit conspiracy, mail fraud, bribery, tax evasion, and attempt to corrupt members of Congress.

Abramoff is a modern day Icarus – he flew too high that he has been burned and has crashed to the earth. Only the greediest and dumbest get into trouble with the law. The K Street program of Tom DeLay in 2004, where he let it be known that GOP representatives would get a warmer reception on the Hill than Democrats would get. Those using the lobbyists of Tom DeLay, in other words. This can be labeled extortion on DeLay's part and is just one of many abuses which must be stopped.

Representatives and senators must raise $10,000 a day in order to finance their election campaigns. Lobbyists can and are a source of money, which may be tapped for some of this money. What are needed are stronger rules like those promoted by Senator John McCain (R-AZ). If more stringent laws are not passed, there are more Jack Abramoffs waiting in the wings for their opportunities.

Duke Cunningham in California is a perfect example of the greed that lobbyists are capable of creating. Not satisfied with just money, he took cars, a yacht, and a mansion to satisfy his growing greed. After 10 years, he stands crying and repentant for his misdeeds before the bar of justice.

The Mantra of the Democratic Party
For the 2006 and 2008 Elections

The neocons, led by penny-pinching Grover G. Norquist, have emphasized more tax cuts and paring away of social programs. The last one, the cruelest of all, as it diminishes student loans and makes college out of the question for many due to elimination of Pell grants. In Europe, if a student passes the test, he or she receives a college education from the state.

Food programs, aid to dependent women and children, and food stamps all have been cut. The homeless continue to walk the streets of our cities, and children continue to go to bed hungry, yet Bush and his cronies have the temerity to ask for $80 billion more for the War in Iraq.

We must all fight the GOP emphasis on the material rather than the spiritual. Remember the mantra I have proposed for the Democratic Party for the 2006 and 2008 elections:

> Giving and giving only
> Is the reason for living.
> *e. e. cummings*

ABOUT THE AUTHOR

The author holds a Masters Degree in History and Education from Miami University in Oxford, Ohio. He has done additional graduate work at De Paul University and Ohio State. He has written six additional works, the most successful of which was *The Rainbow Bridge,* his grief therapy work, based upon his well known poem. He has prominently taken a part in every Civil Rights Protest and worked in all elections since the days of JFK.

He has been a tireless advocate for women's rights and was an early member of NOW in the early 60s. In 1976 he led the fight to pass ERA in Maine to make it the law of the land. The law failed as Phyllis Schafly came to Maine and spoke out from the capital steps against it.